'A welcome addition to literature on the case method in business education, this book provides an original insight into how business students can approach case analysis projects with confidence. The benefits of using this book on case work will be felt by students before, during and long after the completion of their analytical work.'

Professor Julie Hodges, *Professor in Management,*
Durham University Business School

'This book provides a timely and highly useful companion for executive students grappling with the challenge of analysing complex case data on their postgraduate programmes. Chris Williams has extensive experience in lecturing our students at all levels of business education, and he clearly stands out in case-based teaching. Great that his experience and method are now available to everyone by this publication. I would highly recommend engaging with this book before and during a significant case analysis module.'

Professor Mark van der Veen, *Director of the Amsterdam Graduate School of Business,*
Faculty of Economics and Business, University of Amsterdam

'This book fills a massive gap in the business and management literature, providing excellent guidance on how to analyse cases that will benefit students, academics and consultants. Cases form a key part of education in business and management; yet there has not been, until now, a book that clearly sets out the various ways that exist to analyse and then create career impact from them. Readers of this book will benefit greatly, improving their abilities to strategize and analyse complex situations with uncertain outcomes.'

Professor Matthew Allen, *Head of the EPIB Department, Professor of International*
Business, Manchester Metropolitan University Business School

'In this lucid, insight-packed work, Williams uses decades of hard-won experience to show readers how to develop an analysis of strategic case studies. Well-designed case analysis is a foundation of how we understand the role of business in our social world, making this book an absolutely essential guide for every business and management scholar and student today.'

Professor Jason Miklian, *Professor in Business and Peacebuilding,*
Centre for Development and the Environment, University of Oslo

T0313085

Strategic Business Case Analysis

This textbook provides students with the skills and techniques necessary to analyse business case studies from a strategic perspective. With career development and impact in mind, the book goes beyond simply listing tools, instead teaching students how to prepare for a major strategic business case analysis project, how to position their analysis on a spectrum from reductionist to holistic approaches, how to critically engage with theory and case data, as well as how to leverage their work after completion.

A logical approach is offered, taking the reader through the analysis journey, from preparing to analyse a case study to conducting the analysis and maximising the impact going forwards. A comprehensive analysis task is incorporated, which asks the reader to reflect on a range of case data, understand the choices of analytical positioning and tool selection, and develop an analysis based on this positioning. Further pedagogical features include:

- Reflective practice exercises at the end of chapters, allowing the student to self-identify areas of strength and weakness as they develop through the process.
- Worked examples based on cases reproduced in the book, allowing the student to follow the analytical process that the author went through in different analysis modes.
- Quotes and analysis insights from former students who have previously conducted a strategic business case analysis, aiding reflective practice.

As case study analysis continues as a core component of teaching across business schools, this unique text will help to build key skills in advanced undergraduate, postgraduate, MBA, and executive education students conducting strategic business case analysis. Support material includes PowerPoint slides as well as video content.

Christopher Williams is a Professor in the Strategy, Entrepreneurship and International Business Department at ESSCA School of Management in Paris. He previously worked in other business schools in the UK, Canada, France, and the Netherlands. His research interests include international strategy, innovation in international firms and contexts, health R&D and organisational resilience. Before entering academia in 2007, Dr Williams spent two decades in industry, mostly in innovative and international environments, including 10 years with IMS Health. His research appears in journals such as *Research Policy, Journal of World Business, Journal of Management, Journal of Management Studies, Asia Pacific*

Journal of Management, International Business Review, Journal of Business Research, and *Journal of International Management*. He has also published a range of teaching cases on strategy and innovative issues in international contexts and is author of *Venturing in International Firms: Contexts and Cases in a High-Tech World* (2018), *Management Consultancy for Innovation* (2019), and *Organizing for Resilience* (with J. You) (2021).

Strategic Business Case Analysis

Christopher Williams

Routledge
Taylor & Francis Group

LONDON AND NEW YORK

Designed cover image: © a-r-t-i-s-t

First published 2024
by Routledge
4 Park Square, Milton Park, Abingdon, Oxon OX14 4RN

and by Routledge
605 Third Avenue, New York, NY 10158

Routledge is an imprint of the Taylor & Francis Group, an informa business

© 2024 Christopher Williams

The right of Christopher Williams to be identified as author of this work has been asserted in accordance with sections 77 and 78 of the Copyright, Designs and Patents Act 1988.

British Library Cataloguing-in-Publication Data
A catalogue record for this book is available from the British Library

Library of Congress Cataloging-in-Publication Data
Names: Williams, Christopher, author.
Title: Strategic business case analysis / Christopher Williams.
Description: First Edition. | New York, NY : Routledge, 2024. |
Includes bibliographical references and index.
Identifiers: LCCN 2023026191 (print) | LCCN 2023026192 (ebook) |
ISBN 9781032265698 (paperback) | ISBN 9781032265728 (hardback) |
ISBN 9781003288916 (ebook)
Subjects: LCSH: Business education. | Case-based reasoning.
Classification: LCC HF1106 .W625 2024 (print) | LCC HF1106 (ebook) |
DDC 650.07/1—dc23/eng/20230623
LC record available at https://lccn.loc.gov/2023026191
LC ebook record available at https://lccn.loc.gov/2023026192

ISBN: 9781032265728 (hbk)
ISBN: 9781032265698 (pbk)
ISBN: 9781003288916 (ebk)

DOI: 10.4324/9781003288916

Typeset in Berling
by codeMantra

Access the Support Material: www.routledge.com/9781032265698

Contents

Figures

Tables

Preface

Conducting a strategic business case analysis as part of your management or executive education is a significant investment. It is an investment of your time, your brainpower, and your networks. There may also be some upfront financial costs. And it may be a big cause of stress and anxiety for you and those around you. If you want to complete your studies successfully, the investment clearly must be worth it.

The aim of this book is to help you make the investment worth it. A strategic business case analysis should be more than a tick-box exercise as part of a wider qualification. It can be a lot more than just something you need to complete to graduate. It can be a highly profound exercise with implications for your longer-term career, for the organisations you serve or wish to serve in, and for the world around us. If you are minded to approach your strategic business case analysis as a tick-box exercise, please read no further – this book is *not* for you! But if you want to approach your strategic business case analysis with the 'bigger picture' in mind, please read on. The book seeks to capture the essence of how careful forethought and planning, vigilant execution, and developing a plan for impact will make the investment pay back manyfold.

My view is that conducting a strategic business case analysis as part of your management or executive education is a lot more than just an academic exercise. I came to this view because of three sets of experiences working with the case method in business schools and in different countries.

Firstly, I reached this opinion as the result of *teaching with cases* at business schools in The Netherlands, Canada, France, and the UK in the fields of strategy, international business, and management consultancy. I found that only teaching with cases in specific classes – while highly useful for learning objectives of programmes – does not do the power of case knowledge justice. Students prepare for and learn from cases written by others in their classes before moving on to the next class and the next case. But case knowledge can be more – it can also be developed by students themselves and customised by students for their own career needs.

Secondly, my view has been informed by working in educational *situations in which students are given the opportunity to undertake case writing and analysis*. Often these projects carry significant weight towards the final grade, they can be months long, they require the writing of many thousands of words, have an intricate analytical component and they involve a supervisory aspect and engagement with members of academic staff. My experience of helping to set up a Strategic Case Analysis module on the MBA programme of a leading business school has also guided my view that student-centric case knowledge development is more than just an academic exercise.

Finally, my view has been informed by *being a case writer*. I have been lucky enough to write and publish over 30 teaching cases in collaboration with many other authors, mainly with Ivey Publishing. Again, it has become clear how the knowledge around specific cases does not stop with the case research and publishing activity for a specific deliverable. Certain cases become entrenched in the mind. You find yourself checking the annual reports and announcements of the case companies many months and years following the publishing of the case itself. You end up following the career paths of individuals involved in the case, paying attention to news reports and events related to the case organisation. My experiences of teaching with cases, helping students develop and analyse their own cases, and publishing my own cases has taught me that strategic business case analysis is more than just a tick-box exercise!

Strategic business cases are typically a description of a critical situation facing a leader (e.g., CEO) or senior management team within an organisation. A strategic decision needs to be made. Our emphasis in this book is on situations and decisions that are strategic in nature. These strategic situations are complex and non-trivial, and they have significant implications for the organisation. The decisions that lie at the heart of a strategic business case are typically ones that do not have a clear or obvious answer. They are essentially problems that challenge even the most experienced managerial minds and strategy talents. They are decisions that can be looked at from many different viewpoints, can be disagreed upon by managers and analysts, and can have dire consequences for the organisation involved if made in haste, bias, or because of misdiagnosis. This book is about strategic cases. It is about helping you as a management or executive student turn the challenge of conducting a strategic business case analysis into an opportunity to develop and enhance your own career and have real impact.

The primary objectives of the book are threefold.

1. Firstly, the book will give you knowledge and skills on how to conduct a business case analysis from a strategic perspective. This is the core part of the book. I have found that management and executive students are asked to conduct case analysis on strategic issues involving organisations with little guidance from their institutions on how to do this. One cannot accomplish a strategic business case analysis based on a traditional methods course emphasising qualitative methods or quantitative methods alone or working with supervisors with little knowledge of cases. These methods courses are very useful in preparing students for traditional research dissertations, but not necessarily for case analysis. And supervisors also have their limitations. This book helps by showing you how a *Case Analysis Spectrum* – which ranges from reductionist approaches on the one hand to holistic and systems approaches on the other – can help you make sense of complex strategic choices. You need to understand this spectrum when deciding how to tackle your case.

2. Secondly, the book will give you insights into how to benefit from the 'bigger picture'. The process of conducting a strategic business case analysis needs to go beyond a rather narrow focus on tools and techniques for case diagnosis to also include how to prepare for the analysis in the first place and then how to leverage the analysis in the

years afterwards. This is the aspect of the book that will help you with the payback you deserve from your investment in the project. This 'bigger picture' theme is a prominent part of this book, and indeed is reflected in the structure of the book.

3. Thirdly, the book will help you to develop the ability to critically engage with real world case data and academic theory during the practice of strategising. As you develop your career in more senior positions, in leadership, and perhaps in consultancy or entrepreneurship, you will gain more knowledge about how to make strategic decisions amidst uncertainty and risk. The practice of strategising is something you will be continually engaged in. Your cognitive abilities and heuristics will develop as you challenge yourself repeatedly in complex situations. Having a critical approach to strategy is crucial. Challenging assumptions – including those long-standing beliefs within organisations about the 'correct' or 'right' ways of doing things – will matter as you adopt more strategic roles. Taking a critical view of what people around you are telling you, what you are reading, what the numbers may mean – having the confidence to do this will matter. The book will help provide that confidence as you go through the process of a strategic business case analysis in an educational setting. This critical view starts at the point of carefully selecting a case to work on, and it includes the aftermath and how to leverage benefit from your experience of conducting a strategic business case analysis.

For supervisors within the academic system, the book can also help academic faculty and instructors assuming the role of supervisor for strategic business case projects. While many will have experience of the case method in teaching, and some may have researched and published their own cases, many will not have taught a module or part of a module on how to conduct a strategic business case analysis. Many have not made the connection between the process of analysing a case strategically and the progress of a student's own career. While this may vary from institution to institution, the high ratio of students to supervisors means supervisors' time is limited. Some institutions even provide guidance on how much time a supervisor should spend with each supervisee during the supervision. This may be as low as 5 or 6 hours over a 6- or 9-month period. The problem is that once you get into conversations with your supervisor about the 'bigger picture' of strategic business case analysis, you find yourself burning these 5 or 6 hours very quickly. Supervisors are encouraged to refer strategic business case analysis students to the material in this book. This will allow the supervisor to guide the student through some of the key milestones in the project (e.g., choice of case and questions for analysis, overall stance and approach, choice of specific tools and approaches) and to be more efficient in this respect. Supervisory meetings are often short, and the use of this book will allow the supervisor to make effective use of their time, by referring to certain segments or examples in the book.

To the consultants out there … the book can also be useful in strategy consultancy. The consultancy industry often publicises its impact with organisations, describing them as 'cases'. The book gives advice about how to approach the analysis part of a case assignment (normally associated with a specific client) to have the greatest impact for the client. Some consultants in the strategy consulting industry do not have experience studying in a business school or management education environment. Some may have transferred into strategy consultancy from neighbouring sectors such as financial consulting and accountancy, or from legal or even engineering disciplines. If you are one of these types of consultants or are in a junior role just setting out in consultancy, this book could be useful because it provides a framework for approaching complex cases (client issues) as well as ideas on how to leverage case analysis (client projects) for future benefits.

The book would not have been possible without the assistance and support of some key institutions and people. I remain eternally grateful to Ivey Publishing for permission to reproduce in full three cases within the book. These are *Time Out: A New Global Strategy to Bring Back Profit*, used to illustrate a reductionist approach to case analysis, *Brightwater: Clean Water from Broken Wells*, used to illustrate a holistic approach to case analysis, and *Olympus and the Whistleblower President*, used to illustrate a hybrid approach. I am also extremely thankful to Nick Waters and Katherine Neufield for sharing their experiences of their own strategic business case analysis on their respective MBA programmes and their reflections on the 'bigger picture' throughout the book. You will find their personal reflections both in the earlier part on preparation, as well as in the later part on maximising impact from your work. The many conversations I have had with former MBA students and academics involved in post-experience education have been highly valuable and too many to mention here.

I really hope you enjoy reading and using this book in your own strategic business case analysis journey. As mentioned above, I firmly believe that the time, energy, and stress expended on a project like this as part of your management or executive education should be seen as an investment. And like any investment – buying a house, buying a car, buying some shares, setting up a business, investing in education – it is necessary to carefully think about the payback equation both before *and* after. The book encourages you to do this and I hope you can realise impactful outcomes for yourself, your current and future organisations, and the world we live in because of the ideas and suggestions throughout the book. Good luck!

Christopher Williams
Rouen and York, Spring 2023

CHAPTER 1

Introduction

CASE STUDIES AND STORYTELLING IN BUSINESS EDUCATION

It is safe to say that in business education the real world matters! That is where business cases come in. Business cases are detailed descriptions of what has happened in past business situations, in the *real world* of organisational life. They tell stories, showing what happened over a period of time for a focal organisation, its leaders, and its key stakeholders. They tell the story of the successes and growth of organisations, as well as decline and loss. Indeed, the challenges and problems facing the leaders of organisations as they strive to cope with unexpected changes in the environment are a core component of business cases. Storytelling through cases in business education matters – it allows people to learn from other people, managers to learn from other managers, for business history to be transmitted from the past into the present and the future. Learning through the storytelling of cases is not new. As McDade (1995) notes: it is "as old as the ancient storytellers who told a narrative (case) to promote children's individual discovery of wisdom, knowledge of the surrounding world, and development of the thought processes of survival" (p. 9). At the core of the telling of stories of business cases lies the reality of organisational life: the desire for businesses and organisations to form, grow, compete, make a difference, and survive.

Benjamin (2006) also noted how: "Storytelling is particularly valuable for ensuring one's survival in today's continually changing global environment" (p. 159). Storytelling through case studies became commonly used within organisations in the industrial age as a way of transferring cultural norms and behavioural expectations within the organisation from the past to the present and future. Stories became a means of communicating to employees what is expected of them (Benjamin, 2006). But storytelling through cases also became extremely common in business schools as a means for learning about decision-making in difficult business situations. Sometimes the decisions made by organisations are effective, sometimes they are ineffective and counterproductive. Telling the real world stories of these situations through cases allows management and executive students to learn beyond the abstract theory of academics, resonating with them and their own experiences in a way that theory is less adept at doing. Business cases came to embody a 'rhetoric of reality' (Augier & March, 2011).

Like most fictional stories and novels, business cases are very rich stories. They have a qualitative (textual) component that one reads and follows. Most also have a quantitative

DOI: 10.4324/9781003288916-1

(numeric) side, a means of comparing and benchmarking performance, or understanding the environment in which a focal organisation exists, using numeric indictors. They are also rich because they typically have multiple dimensions and can be seen through different lenses. For instance, they may have a leadership component, a marketing component, and a technological component … in addition to an accounting and financial component. Increasingly they have had an ethical component (Falkenberg & Woiceshyn, 2008), and have shown an awareness of sustainability and environmental concerns as well (Edwards, Benn & Starik, 2017). Cases reflect the reality of organisational life. They are rich, and they can often be highly revelatory – coming with an element of surprise and being the first to uncover a phenomenon, issue, or storyline (Bengtsson, 1999; Trigger, Forsey & Meurk, 2012).

But unlike fictional stories, business cases are not imagined. At least not entirely. Some are disguised to preserve the identity of the organisation or individuals in the organisation. Having taught with some excellent disguised cases I can vouch for their usefulness in class – they do allow management and executive students to discuss key issues and learn from each other. And some business cases might be published as scenarios. They help to educate and test students' abilities in defined technical areas, such as accounting and finance, and for appraising different futures. But most published business cases are not anonymised. Indeed, one of the virtues of case research is to be able to analyse a phenomenon in its natural setting (Yin, 2011). It is the reality of the situation that matters for effective education. It creates relevance, it allows group and class discussion, and it is issue oriented (Schaupp & Lane, 1992).

You (2022) describes a 'sensitising' approach for understanding business students' experiences of cases before-, during-, and after-class. Her study looks at case use in a traditional class teaching environment and underscores the relevance of storytelling in management and executive education. She develops four themes related to students' sensitising to business case studies: (1) learning agency (prior experience and motivation of students for learning with cases); (2) learning success (developing students' skillsets through class participation); (3) learning well-being (building social, cultural, and political capital while learning with cases); and (4) learning social justice (being respectful and tolerating others' views during the case method). These four dimensions highlight how one needs to think differently when learning through storytelling in business cases. For instance, the traditional view of what we mean by 'success' is less applicable; what is more important here are the soft skills students develop for the long term.

THE IMPORTANCE OF *STRATEGIC* BUSINESS CASE ANALYSIS

In this book we are concerned with the analysis of business cases that have a strategic element. These are cases that describe business situations of strategic importance to the organisation(s) involved. The use of the word 'strategic' is an essential term of reference for our journey. We are less concerned with business cases that deal with smaller, operational problems and matters that are not fundamental to the long-term survival and effectiveness of an organisation's overall strategy. Solving problems that are strategic in nature will matter more for your leadership and impact aspirations; it can help you transition towards leadership if you are not already in that position (Nguyen & Hansen, 2016), or becoming a better leader (Toegel & Barsoux, 2012). It will have a stronger relevance to the 'bigger picture' for you as you seek to influence decisions with ever-greater strategic importance.

So, what do we mean by *strategic*? Firstly, the use and interpretation of this adjective may vary widely. It can be highly subjective. What one person sees as a strategic issue, another may not. Secondly, organisations and businesses change as they innovate and adapt to survive and grow. What may be strategic in one era may not be strategic in the next. Thirdly, what is seen as a strategic issue or challenge for one organisation in one context may not be seen in the same way by another organisation in a different context. Organisations differ enormously in terms of their fundamental purpose, ownership structures, performance, and ways of seeing the world.

Given these caveats, we will proceed on the basis that *strategic* business case analysis is analysis of business issues and situations in a natural setting and that requires strategic thinking to be solved. These problems tend to have a lot at stake. They will require large investments or change programmes for the organisations involved. They require thinking for the longer term, not the short term. They require an appreciation of the whole organisation in context, rather than just a small part of it. According to Graetz (2002), strategic thinking differs from strategic planning in that it is not concerned with planning as a rational, step-by-step process of preparation and positioning the organisation; it is more concerned with the creative, dynamic, and responsive capability that is needed when assumptions about the environment change.

Liedtka (1998, cited in Graetz, 2002) notes five characteristics of strategic thinking: (1) taking a holistic view of an organisation within context; (2) a focus on intent and addressing the misfit between internal resources and capabilities and the environment; (3) connecting the past, present, and future; (4) involving the generation and testing of hypotheses; (5) intellectual opportunism and exploiting new opportunities. The large investments and thinking over the long term to solve strategic business issues and challenges will require many, if not all, of these attributes of strategic thinking. I would also add an additional point: there is no single right or wrong answer in strategic thinking. If we are trying to solve a strategic problem for an organisation, how do we know if we are right or wrong? Different leaders approach strategy in different ways. The same applies to consultants, commentators, and analysts whose views are often at odds with one another. Even the owners of firms – whether they are dispersed public shareholders or a small, concentrated group of family owners – will have different cognitive biases and experiences that will lead to different views. Does this mean that one strategic thinker is wrong, and another is right? The answer to this is: no. Given the passage of time, we will find out for sure which was the better strategy, assuming we can agree on the measurement of effective strategy. One firm may have a higher profit margin, but a worse environmental record. Another may have a lower profit margin, but a better environmental record. What is important is that there is a CEO or leadership team in place to build consensus for the strategic thinking that is required and to be able to justify their choices to the relevant stakeholders of the organisation.

TABLE 1.1 Examples of less strategic versus more strategic cases

Sector	Less strategic case		More strategic case	
Education	Brown, Rich & Holtham (2014)	A new module for undergraduates at a specific business school	Gioia & Chittipeddi (1991)	Strategic change in a large public university
Hospitals	Chao & Terry (2012)	Operational challenge reducing wait times in a hospital emergency medical department	Denis, Langley, & Cazale (1996)	Process of strategic change in a large public hospital
High-tech	Workman (1993)	Impediments to a marketing department's influence on product development at a computer firm	Hacklin & Wallnöfer (2012)	The business model as a strategising device in an international high-tech multimedia firm

Table 1.1 provides examples from different sectors of cases that are 'less strategic' versus 'more strategic' in nature.

If we accept that strategic business case analysis concerns business cases where strategic thinking is required, strategic business case analysis constitutes a valuable capability for strategic leaders. It will guide them in their mission to build strategic consensus around the perceived 'best' way forward at a given point in time. It will enhance the chances of successful outcomes, although as mentioned above, we will never know if an alternative strategic decision would have been better. For these reasons strategic business case analysis is a valuable capability to develop as part of your management or executive education. It will help develop you for subsequent career progression and impact.

In addition to this, strategic business case analysis can be used to document, analyse, and learn from organisations seeking to provide solutions to some of the biggest challenges facing society. These include addressing grand challenges and helping to meet the United Nations' Sustainable Development Goals (UN SDGs). Cases have a rich history in this domain and increasingly show the strategic thinking by firms as they address grand challenges (e.g., Grodal & O'Mahony, 2017; Hamann, Makaula, Ziervogel, Shearing & Zhang, 2020). By developing skills in strategic business case analysis during your business education, you will be in a stronger position to guide the organisations you serve towards alignment of their strategy with UN SDGs. As Pedersen (2018) notes:

> With the SDGs in place, business now [has] a much clearer set of long-term global priorities with political tail wind, and the alignment between policy makers, civil society and the private sector is much stronger. The SDGs are a great gift to business!
>
> (p. 21)

The UN SDGs are a gift to strategic thinking and the process of strategic case analysis too.

Likewise, the role that strategic business case analysis has in preparing organisations to deal with digital transformation is a vital theme to consider. The role of cases in understanding the challenges of digital transformation in the modern era has been highlighted by academics (e.g., Vukšić, Ivančić & Vugec, 2018). Cases provide substantive insight into the organisational systems and environment surrounding the technological aspects of any digital transformation project. As stated by Tabrizi, Lam, Girard and Irvin (2019): "70% of all [digital transformation] initiatives do not reach their goals" (p. 1). They put an emphasis on the broader strategic picture, not on any specific technology. Indeed, their first lesson reads as follows: "Lesson 1: Figure out your business strategy before you invest in anything" (p. 2). Tabrizi et al. (2019) also place an emphasis on having an appropriate organisational culture for digital transformation and having policies that take into account the perspectives of customers and employees. This point about digital transformation not being about technology, but about strategy, is underscored elsewhere in the literature (e.g., Kane, Palmer, Phillips, Kiron & Buckley, 2015).

Strategic business case analysis is about solving strategic problems for organisations that are grappling with challenges, including the grand challenges and the possibilities (and risks) of digital transformation. When conducted in an educational environment as part of a management or executive programme, strategic business case analysis can help you develop capabilities in strategic thinking that you can draw on for many years to come. However, experience has shown that, just like the organisations they study, students face challenges when developing and analysing strategic business cases.

THE CHALLENGES FACING STUDENTS OF STRATEGIC BUSINESS CASES

If you are assigned a strategic business case analysis or choose to undertake one as part of your studies, it can be daunting. It is entirely probable that you have had little by way of training in how to prepare for and execute the writing and analysis required for an in-depth strategic business case project. If you are anything like a 'typical' management or executive student, you are more likely to have undertaken many individual analytical tasks and exercises in specific modules and courses. Many of these involve case material. And it is likely that you have already participated in case discussions and presentations (including in groups) in class situations. It is reasonable to expect that you have had some experience in report writing, either in a professional context or as part of your academic career.

Strategic business case analysis is different. Students often do not know how to translate these experiences into a coherent written development and subsequent analysis of a complex strategic problem facing an organisation and how to deliver this within a tight timeframe and word limit as a major piece of individual work for their degree.

Let us consider three main areas of challenge:

1. *Lacking capabilities in case writing*: In some instances, you are required to research and develop the case material itself, rather than working from an already published case. Putting aside the challenge of identifying and selecting a case organisation to research

in the first place, how does one go about documenting the backdrop and details of the strategic problem? How does one tell the complex story within the constraints of a limited word count? One needs to decide which aspects of the case story are imperative to convey, identify sources of information to use (primary and/or secondary), access and understand those sources of information, and produce the qualitative and quantitative content of the case in a way that best reflects the true storyline (Leenders, Mauffette-Leenders & Erskine, 2001). One needs to decide if the case will be explicitly decision-oriented or adopting a wider purpose such as encouraging discussion about the changing situations facing managers to enhance thinking (Lundberg, Rainsford, Shay & Young, 2001).[1] These capabilities may sound straightforward, but they take time to develop and execute, and there is scope for errors and mistakes at all stages. One needs to become familiar with the context of the case being researched, and show a humility towards the phenomenon (Gill, 2016). More practical challenges may include trading-off space limitations with the richness in case data, getting the balance right between qualitative narrative and quantitative data, and making sure that the complexity of the story does not overwhelm the reader and make it difficult for them to follow. There are further challenges for non-English speakers writing in the English language and how key passages of text communicate the content the authors intend them to communicate (Nathan, 2013). Taken collectively, the challenges here are clearly not trivial.

2. *Lacking capabilities in case analysis*: It is also common that students have little prior experience of in-depth case analysis beyond the group work and class discussions on more regular courses. Writing a 10,000-word analysis of a single case over many months is not the same as discussing a case in class in a 1-hour session or presenting a case as a group after a few hours work. This higher order of magnitude for case analysis matters and many students will not have done this previously or had training in how to do this. What are the capabilities needed for strategic business case analysis? There are lots of aspects to this: the ability to look at case situations holistically as well as breaking them down into manageable research units and analytical chunks (Verschuren, 2003); whether the case should be analysed around explicit decisions or rather to promote a broader discussion and developing thinking about changing situations (Lundberg et al., 2001); the ability to select and utilise the most appropriate analytical tools; the ability to write up a report and present your arguments in a compelling way; the ability to take a critical tone and reflect on a case critically in light of an academic theory or lens (McDade, 1995). These are all challenges that students often must confront.

3. *Stress and anxiety*: Given the weight placed on conducting a strategic business case analysis on a management or executive programme, the challenges as noted above, the time pressures that students face (many of whom balance family- and work-life with their studies), and the uncertainty about investment payback, it is not surprising that students may become stressed and anxious by the prospect of the project. Evidence suggests that help from more experienced peers on management and executive programmes can help reduce levels of stress in students (Allen, McManus & Russell, 1999). Such mentoring may play a role in reducing the stress facing students conducting a strategic business case analysis. However, overall well-being during the process remains a challenge. Not all institutions may offer an effective mentoring opportunity. And other

sources of stress are likely to interact with the specific pressures of a strategic business case analysis. Other pressures may include financial ones (Andrews & Wilding, 2004) and those related to work–family conflict (Carlson, Derr & Wadsworth, 2003). Carlson et al. (2003) describe the career triangle as consisting of work, relationships, and self-development. If one assumes a strategic business case analysis to be at the self-development edge of the triangle, it can potentially come into conflict with work and other relationships, such as family relationships. Carlson et al. (2003) examine this through the lens of internal career orientations. These are orientations that each student will have and can include: (1) a getting ahead orientation, (2) a getting secure orientation, (3) a getting free orientation, (4) a getting high orientation, and (5) a getting balanced orientation. Not all internal career orientations are directly related to stress, but they can create conflict between work and family life to varying degrees (Carlson et al., 2003). Stress and anxiety during the process of conducting a strategic business case analysis as part of a management or executive education programme clearly is a challenge.

DIFFERENT PERSPECTIVES ON STRATEGIC BUSINESS CASE ANALYSIS

The approach taken in this book aims to help you overcome these challenges and is centred on appreciating and respecting a 'bigger picture'. This relates to careful forethought and planning, taking an appropriate stance for the analysis, and then leveraging the project for impact afterwards. Appreciating the 'bigger picture' also means understanding the broader system of actors that are involved in the case research, writing, and analysis process. Let us look at four of the main types of actors involved and their perspectives.

The practitioner perspective. Firstly, we have the managers and leaders of the focal organisation in the case. The key consideration for these practitioners is the strategic issue that needs to be resolved. As Shrivastava (1987) notes: "The usefulness of strategic management research ... lies in its ability to provide decision-makers with a rationale for making decisions and thereby prompting actions in organizations" (p. 79). This perspective matters because it will be these practitioners that ultimately define the issue, who will be feeling (or would have felt) the heat because of the issue, and who would be (or had already been) grappling with ways to resolve the issue. This perspective also matters because these same practitioners will be providers of information to use in the case writing process, either because they agree to be interviewed and/or observed (primary data collection), or because they provide company reports and other documents (secondary data collection), for use by the case writer. They are also likely to act in a gatekeeper role, connecting the case writer with others to elicit information for the case writing process. They will be potentially very interested in the outcome of the strategic business case analysis, should the work be produced in a format they can access, and even better, if the case analyst can present the work to the practitioners involved in the case. The practitioner(s) involved in providing data to the case writer may be the main protagonist(s) in the case ('this is my predicament ... what can we do to resolve it?'), but they need not be ('this is our company's predicament ... what can our board do to resolve it?').

The case writer perspective. Secondly, we have the writer(s) involved in researching and writing the case itself. This could be a seasoned academic, a professional case writer, or a mix of authors from different disciplines. The main interest is to produce case material, often in the form of a structured document with qualitative text and quantitative and qualitative exhibits, which tells the story and identifies the strategic issue(s) at the heart of the case.[2] It is important to consider the case writer's perspective for two reasons. The first is that the case writer has made decisions about what to include and what to omit from the case. This is critical because it says something about what others believe to be the critical information relevant to the strategic issue in the case. When you come to assess the case, you may decide that more information is required to conduct a thorough analysis and that you may need to collect additional information. The second reason that the case writer's perspective is important is because the case writer may be you! If you are conducting your strategic business case analysis on a programme where you are also requested to research and write the case itself, you will adopt the roles of both case writer and case analyst. So, you will have to think carefully about the choice of case, the focus in terms of strategic issues, decisions, and time frame of your story to be told. This will have a large bearing on what you then end up analysing.

The student perspective. Thirdly, we have you, the student. You are the one assuming the role of case analyst and seeking to make sense of the complexity of the case in a meaningful way. You will be required to develop and apply your capabilities in strategic thinking to accomplish the task. You clearly have an interest in completing your studies to graduate. But your broader career goals and aspirations can be directly linked to how you approach your strategic business case analysis with the 'bigger picture' in mind. This book is aimed principally with you in mind. The 'bigger picture' involves the careful forethought and planning, the justification of analytical stance, and then leveraging the project for impact. Your career matters, and you have invested in management or executive education because you want to stretch your knowledge and skills, achieving a payback on the investment.

The supervisor perspective. Finally, we have the supervisor perspective. This is normally an academic individual at the institution in which you are studying. It could also be an external or adjunct brought in by the institution to supervise business student projects. Supervisors may or may not be active researchers. They are normally involved in class teaching in addition to supervising capstone research projects such as a strategic business case analysis. They are rooted in the academic system surrounding the case, applying the rules of the academic and institutional systems in the supervisory and grading process. You will have the opportunity to interact with your supervisor during the study and gain feedback on your progress and work. While these interactions are critical, they represent a very low fraction of the overall time you will spend on your project. So, making the most from these interactions is vital. Supervisors will likely have many other students to supervise, alongside other academic duties. They may not know your case as well as you do. In many respects, it is up to you to teach your supervisor about your case.

Figure 1.1 provides a schematic of these four types of actors.[3]

These roles often overlap. Students may be asked to act as case writer for their own case, which they will then analyse. Supervisors may also write cases that are used by students in capstone projects or class teaching. Practitioners may be involved as co-authors

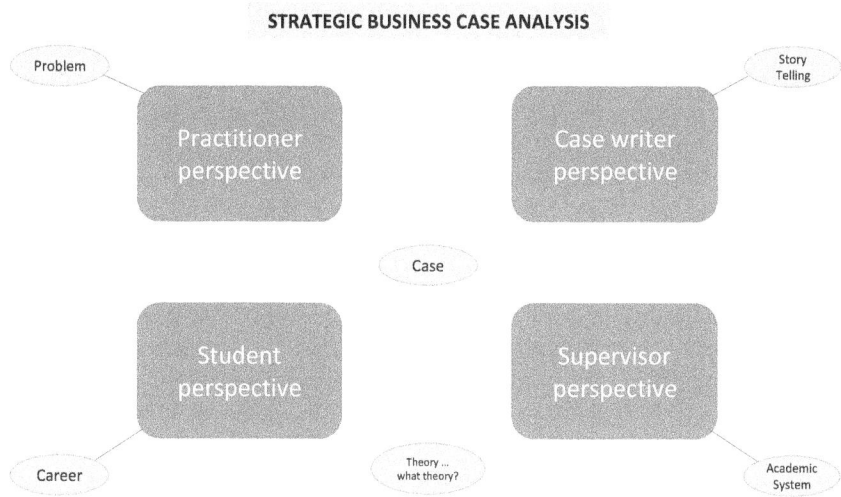

FIGURE 1.1 Different perspectives in strategic business case analysis

in cases and have some input into the case writing process. You may be a part-time executive student adopting both a practitioner role (the case is about your employer), the case writer role (the academic institution requires you to research and develop the case story), *and* the student analyst role. So, these four roles are not necessarily mutually exclusive. What is important is they all share one central focal point: the case itself.

STRATEGIC BUSINESS CASE ANALYSIS, CASE KNOWLEDGE, AND IMPACT

Let us now turn our attention to the centre of Figure 1.1, the case itself. As noted above, the case itself describes an actual business or organisational situation, a strategic issue (or related issues), and normally a strategic decision that needs to be made (Leenders et al., 2001). The case itself is not the same as the analysis of the case. While the case contains the storyline and the key information related to the strategic issue, the analysis is where we develop answers. The analysis consists of the choice of techniques to analyse the case data, the application of those techniques, the presentation of the results of applying those techniques, and the discussion of what those results mean.

In the same way that case data can consist of both qualitative and quantitative aspects, techniques for analysing cases can be with qualitative data analysis techniques or quantitative ones. It would be tempting to think that most business case analyses are qualitative in nature. After all, the top business and management journals published up to 11% of their publications based on qualitative case studies between 2002 and 2011 (Runfola, Perna, Baraldi & Gregori, 2017). However, consistent with historic trends in business and management academic publishing, this is a relatively low amount. The same authors show how the number of qualitative case studies published in top business and management journals has oscillated over that period – it certainly did not increase (Runfola et al., 2017). Quantitative case analysis does remain popular, particularly in fields such as production economics, supply chain analysis, operations, and finance (Dubey, Kothari & Awari, 2016).

An example of a qualitative analysis on case data is that conducted by Dieleman and Boddewyn (2012) on the Salim Group in Indonesia. Through extensive use of interviews with insiders, the authors provide insights into how the business group was able to manage political ties. In emerging economies these political ties are strategically significant – allowing firms to access critical resources and perform over the long term. The qualitative approach in Dieleman and Boddewyn's (2012) study was suited to the nature of the problem which, as the authors state, involves analysis of "less visible processes" (p. 77). An example of a more quantitative analysis on case data is that conducted by Validi, Bhattacharya, and Byrne (2014). Their analysis of distribution routes for milk in Ireland aimed to reduce carbon output and costs for the dairy supply chain. The dairy sector was a strategically important one in Ireland, with the country being positioned third globally in terms of milk consumption on a per capita basis. It also exported more dairy products than it consumed. Given European Union regulation changes, pressures on production expansion and the need to reduce carbon footprints all at the same time, their analysis identified realistic distribution routes to underpin the design of a new domestic distribution network.

These examples – and many others – raise the question of case knowledge surrounding any given case. What is case knowledge? Who owns and controls it? How do we access and analyse it? These are crucial questions to consider. Case knowledge is more than the information documented in a written or published storyline of a case. Case writers deliberately leave information out when formulating the storyline – this is a necessity, given the word count limits on published cases and the limits on lengths of student deliverables. By analysing a case you are creating new knowledge about the case. But the notion of case knowledge goes beyond the case writer and the case analyst. The main protagonist(s) in the case will have a lot more knowledge about the organisation, its internal and external environments, and its financial and non-financial performance than will be captured by a case writer. Going even further, every single employee or person connected with the strategic issue in the case will embody knowledge and experience related to the case. Clearly, no single person or entity will be able to own and control all case knowledge. Intellectual property (IP) and company secrets will be protected by law and institutional enforcement. But much tacit knowledge residing in individuals, along with explicit knowledge in the public domain, extend the boundary of what we can call 'case knowledge'.

In terms of accessing and analysing case knowledge, this is where the scientific method comes in. As a case writer you will typically access diverse sources of information (both secondary, pre-published sources, including Internet sources, as well as primary first-hand sources, typically interviews and focus groups) to construct your case storyline. As a case analyst, you will need to choose and apply the most appropriate tools and techniques to your case data. Case knowledge is a dynamic body of explicit and tacit information and intelligence linked to a strategic issue facing an organisation. It evolves over time and through interactions between the main actors involved in case analysis. No single person or entity owns it, and you will need to become deeply embedded in knowledge of the case, both to understand it and also contribute to the development of case knowledge through your project.

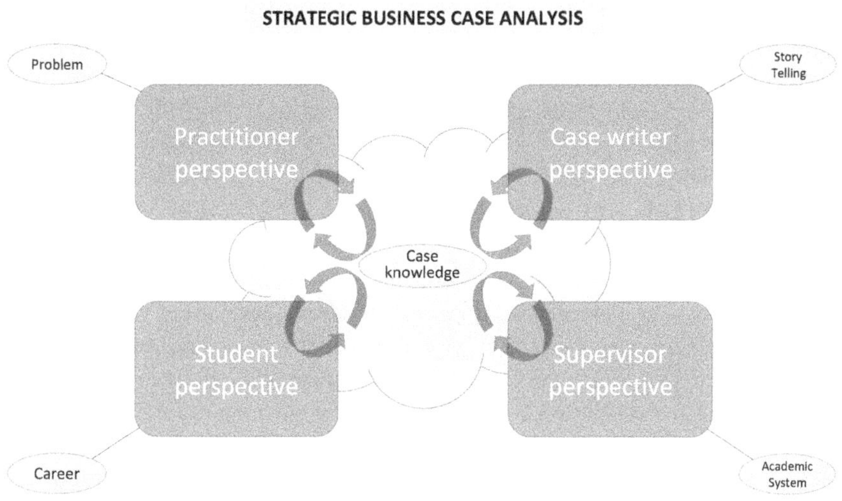

STRATEGIC BUSINESS CASE ANALYSIS

FIGURE 1.2 A schematic of case knowledge in a strategic business case analysis

Figure 1.2 provides a schematic of this situation.

Your contribution to case knowledge through a strategic business case analysis provides the foundation for impact based on your project. There are various ways in which impact can be viewed. Firstly, there is the impact you might be able to achieve within the practitioner community, and with the strategic issue at hand. In this book we will refer to this as externalising the impact of your work. Secondly, there is the impact you can achieve for yourself, for your own personal development and career. We will refer to this as internalising the impact.

From an externalising perspective one should consider how the analysis can contribute to addressing the strategic issue(s) identified in the case. Your work can count towards addressing the specific issue in the specific organisation within the case. Arguably, this is easier to do if you are conducting a strategic business case analysis on your own organisation and have a level of seniority or influence within your organisation to direct actions to be taken in line with your analysis. This might be more difficult to achieve if you are an 'outsider'. In this situation you would need to yield considerable influence, perhaps in your role as a consultant, investor, or lobbyist. Externalising impact can also be about providing new knowledge on how the general class of strategic issue identified in the case can be addressed. You may be able to share your analysis and insights with a broader array of interest groups and stakeholders that want to solve the type of issue you address. Externalising impact can be achieved in different ways depending on the level of your integration within the focal organisation, and what you want to achieve. At one end of the spectrum, you can simply try and disseminate your findings. This can be done through publishing your work or seeking to present your findings to appropriate management and policy audiences. At the other end of the spectrum, you yourself are involved in carrying out the specific actions derived in your case analysis. In this instance you can obtain additional learning and insight and continually develop your case knowledge as you seek to enact change. In addition to the practitioner and policy audiences, you might also seek to externalise impact within the academic system. This might entail working with your supervisor or another academic on publishing your analysis, helping to develop theory, and/or using your case and case analysis in class discussions. Your work might also resonate with the case writing world, especially if you researched and wrote the case that was used as a basis for your analysis. An obvious way you can achieve impact here is by publishing your case as a teaching case and including some of your analysis in the teaching note. These activities can help you maximise the value of your work with specific stakeholder groups. There is nothing stopping you being more adventurous and attempting to have impact across as many of these groups as possible.

From an internalising perspective, impact is all about developing yourself personally and professionally. The project can help underpin growth and advancement in your career. This may happen in various ways, including developing your skills in leadership based on your insights into strategic problem solving amidst uncertainty and a changing environment. It may help you challenge your own assumptions about what it means to be an effective leader. The project may also develop your consultancy skills. Here we refer to both hard skills (e.g., collecting and analysing secondary data, report writing) and soft skills (e.g., networking and building relationships to access primary data for subsequent analysis). When you execute consultancy assignments in the future, you may draw on your experiences of conducting a strategic case analysis for the benefit of your client. The project may help you in your entrepreneurial endeavours, such as developing a small business that you have, or launching a new enterprise. The process of conducting a strategic business case analysis will give you insights into the nature of risk facing entrepreneurs in a given setting, and also provide a basis for addressing those risks if you later assume an entrepreneurial role. Being able to critically self-reflect before, during, and after a strategic case analysis will help you internalise the impact from your work.

STRUCTURE AND APPROACH OF THIS BOOK

The structure of the book is based around the three main phases mentioned so far, namely pre-, during-, and post-analysis.

Part 1 will consist of three chapters that offer guidance in the critical period of preparation before the core case analysis work would begin. Part 1 is about *Preparing for a Strategic Business Case Analysis*. The three chapters deal with the following topics: choosing a case to analyse (Chapter 2), placing the case in strategic context (Chapter 3), and deciding on the questions for analysis (Chapter 4).

Part 2 will consist of three chapters that will guide you through the technicalities of *Conducting a Strategic Business Case Analysis*. The approach taken is to develop the notion of a Case Analysis Spectrum (Chapter 5) and discussing why it is important to position your case analysis appropriately on this spectrum. There will then be examples of approaches and tools along the Case Analysis Spectrum (Chapter 6), before worked examples are given based on three different cases reproduced in full (Chapter 7).

Part 3 will consist of two chapters that will provide guidance, suggestions, and ideas about how you can *Maximise Impact from a Strategic Business Case Analysis* over the long term. It is here we will discuss the question of externalising and internalising the impact from a strategic business case analysis (Chapters 8 and 9).

You are encouraged to use the reflective practice exercises at the end of each of the chapters to self-identify areas of strength and weakness as you progress through the book. These will be an opportunity to reflect on experiences, capabilities, and preferences in connection to the various topics covered in each of the chapters, encouraging you to identify strengths, weaknesses, and areas for further learning and action.

NOTES

1   Lundberg et al. (2001) classify case objectives into three: (1) acquiring, differentiating, and using ideas and information; (2) issue identification and differentiation; (3) action formulation and implementation.

2   Case writers often must produce teaching notes to accompany cases that are intended to be used in class settings. Teaching notes provide guidance and additional information for the facilitator of the case discussion in class. Not all cases have accompanying teaching notes and you will not usually have to produce one for your strategic business case analysis unless you get to a point where you would like to submit your work for publication as a teaching case to a case publishing house.

3   Other actors not mentioned but associated with these four domains include: other stakeholder groups linked to the practitioner and the strategic problem, actors such as journalists and commentators who also have an interest in the case and have written or broadcast about the case, your family and friends who give you support and encouragement throughout your studies, and people within the academic system (such as administration and support staff within a business school) who are available to guide and enforce the institutional rules of the process.

PART I

Preparing for a strategic business case analysis

CHAPTER 2

Choosing a case to analyse

WHERE ON EARTH SHOULD I START?

To conduct a strategic business case analysis, you need to have a case to analyse. The question of case choice is crucial: it sets the agenda for your work ahead (Seawright & Gerring, 2008). A suitable case needs to be provided, chosen, or developed. When they are provided (normally by the supervisor, module leader, or institution), students have little influence. But sometimes students have a say and can choose an already existing case or develop a new one. It is important to understand and appreciate who decides the case you will be analysing. This is influenced by the academic requirements of the program at the institution where you are studying.

There are pros and cons for the student having a say over the choice of case. There are different implications for the project work when the student has been involved in prior research and writing of the case. If you can do this, your case knowledge arguably will be more in-depth, with a greater tacit component, than if you are simply handed a case to analyse. In this book we make no requirement for – or assumptions about – whether the case to be analysed is an already published case or is a new one developed by the student. However, a good start point is to reflect on whether the case is provided, chosen, or developed. Table 2.1 outlines the pros and cons, along with key considerations, for these three paths for case selection.

If the case is provided to you, you will need to find ways in which the process of analysis (rather than the process of case writing) will benefit you career-wise, as well as the impact it may have for external stakeholders in the future. The emphasis for you will be on the analysis, what new skills you will develop in doing this, and how you link the outcomes of the analysis to ways of maximising impact for yourself and others.

If the case choice is something you have some say over, for instance choosing one from a case library, there is a higher chance of closer alignment to career needs. This may be on the basis of a specific organisation, its industry or location, or the type of strategic issue at hand in the case. The point is you can choose the case deliberately keeping in mind links to your own career development and impact. You are still somewhat restricted in that the case is something written by a different case writer, and the choice of material to include in the case has effectively been decided by someone else. However, this path does allow you to focus more time on the analysis, and it potentially opens up the world's complete library of published cases for your use!

DOI: 10.4324/9781003288916-3

If the case is developed by you, you have a high level of freedom to pick an organisation and strategic issue that are closely aligned to your career needs and interests. This will take more time of course, and you will have to play the part of the case writer as well as the case analyst. It will be important to check the grading regime for the assignment at your institution and make sure that the amount of time and effort you spend on the case writing part versus the case analysis part are in proportion to the expectations of the institution. Case writing can be fun! But too much time spent on the case writing part can mean the case analysis part is rushed against a strict deadline. So, balance is the key word here.

After you have clarified the selection path for your case and appreciated the key considerations for the mechanism facing you, a good next step is to think carefully about the nature of the strategic issue that, when analysed comprehensively, will give you a basis for career growth and impact.

You can do this by identifying and creating a small list of strategic issues and problems that matter in your view. Let us consider some classic definitions of what a strategic issue is. Ansoff (1980, p. 133) defines it as a:

> development, either inside or outside of the organization, which is likely to have an important impact on the ability of the enterprise to meet its objectives. An issue may be a welcome issue, an opportunity to be grasped in the environment, or an internal strength which can be exploited to advantage. Or it can be an unwelcome external threat, or an internal weakness, which imperils continuing success, even the survival of the enterprise.

According to Camillus and Datta (1991, p. 68):

> Most strategic issues are triggered by threats or opportunities which originate outside the organization; they can be defined as developments which in the judgement of strategic decision makers are likely to have significant impacts on the organization's present and/or future strategies.

In terms of identifying strategic issues, Murphy (1989: 103) suggests asking the question:

> what are likely to be the positive or negative impacts of macro and micro environmental forces on the business? This suggests defining issues as opportunities or threats and assessing the potential impact of such opportunities and threats on the key success factors of the business.

Strategic issues, then, are about developments or events that have not become decision events; the organisation affected by the strategic issue has yet to resolve it (Dutton & Duncan, 1987). They can take many different forms. While many pose financial threats to a focal organisation, writers have increasingly emphasised the social nature of strategic issues (Bonini et al., 2006). Bonini, Mendonca and Oppenheim (2006) describe the changing nature of the social contract that companies have with society. A broader set of stakeholders becomes important, including the society and community in which the company is embedded, academics, the media, and not-for-profit organisations. Issues here

TABLE 2.1 Case selection paths

Path	Who decides?	Pros	Cons	To consider
1 – Provided	Your institution: the programme you are on tells you which case to analyse	• You do not have to write the case; you can focus all your time and effort on the analysis	• The case writer (and publisher) has already decided what information is relevant • You may need to search for new information about the case that is not included in the document(s) you are given • The case was chosen by your institution – it may not necessarily suit your career needs	Finding ways to connect the analysis to your career needs; identifying how the analysis – rather than the case – will be impactful for you and other stakeholders
2 – Chosen	You: you are given some flexibility by your institution to select a previously published case	• There is an opportunity to pick a case that is better suited to your interests and career needs • You do not have to write the case	• You will need to spend time searching for a case • You may still need to search for new information about the case as the case writer may not have included all relevant information • You may not be able to find a case on the specific company, location, or strategic issue you are interested in	Producing a shortlist of cases after an initial search before filtering; talking to others (including authors and case publishers) about how the case has been used in past analyses – this will help you get a sense of which one can better serve your needs
3 – Developed	You: you are required to research and write your own case, which you will then analyse	• The case can be selected to best fit your personal development and career needs • The case you write could be used in class or published standalone later	• You must write the case (if this is a con!) – this will take time and you need to find the right balance between case writing and case analysis	Checking how your final grade is calculated – how much of the grade is based on the case writing versus the case analysis? Avoid spending too much time on creating a perfect case story, only to rush the analysis

will be ones that companies traditionally had mostly ignored, such as obesity (food com-panies), alcoholism (drinks companies), and gambling (online betting companies).

What will be vital for you when starting out on your quest to choose a case is to engage on a reconnaissance exercise. What are the issues that matter to you, the stakeholders around you, and your longer-term career? You can find out – at a top level – what organ-isations are doing about these issues (positively and negatively) and identify what types of decisions and strategic options they are facing. A lot can be gained by talking to others about these strategic issues and the organisational responses that seem to be apparent. Talking to others allows you to hear different experiences, opinions, and thoughts. You may find consensus amongst the people you talk to. You may also find disagreements and differences of opinion, and opinions that differ from your own. To a large extent it will be good to find differences of opinion – this can form the basis for you to articulate the debates, tensions, or paradoxes that exist around the issue. You can use this process to produce a shortlist of cases with clearly identified strategic issues.

THE DIFFICULTY OF SELECTION CRITERIA

In the situation that you have an opportunity to select or develop your own case (Paths 2 and 3 in Table 2.1), it might be tempting to think that some established, universally accepted criteria for case choice can be applied. Unfortunately, there are no universally agreed selection criteria for choosing a case to select or write, and then analyse. Firstly, what makes an appropriate case for you will likely be very different from what makes a good case for someone else. The career stage you are in, the industry-, country-, and issue-specific factors that are relevant to you will be different to others. Secondly, there is immense diversity in the published body of cases in the world. If you check the collections of case distributors, you will see the vastness of the selection challenge; there are quite literally tens of thousands of cases on many different topics, and of many different types and qualities. And there is an endless – possibly infinite – array of organisations and organ-isational issues in the world that could be scrutinised should you pursue Path 3.

It is rather dangerous to apply a fixed criteria for case choice. Imagine a scenario where students are told to select cases based on: (1) an issue that we think will be around for many decades to come, or (2) a type of organisation that you want to work in in the future. The problem is these types of criteria are highly subjective, and likely to change as the years go on. Ten years ago, issues of how to strategically utilise blockchain, machine learning, and AI were not as prominent as they are now. Five years ago, issues of resilience and survival through global pandemics were not exactly in everybody's minds. They are now. There was a time when working from home was frowned upon; it has now become a norm in many sectors. So, trying to select a case based on a current issue or an assumption about a way of organising that will be around for many years is problematic. They simply may not be relevant in an unpredictable future.

Does this mean that we should not use selection criteria? No. What it means is that selection criteria should be developed with care and attention to individual needs. You could achieve your goals on the strategic business case analysis through several different cases. Your shortlist will contain cases each with pros and cons. You should not regret your choice of case later, wishing you had used an alternative. What is important is that you are in a position where you can provide an immediate and confident answer to the question: "Why did you choose this case to analyse?", and that you can provide this answer in your own words and with your own 'voice' (rather like an elevator pitch).

Several suggestions can help in this deliberate and careful process.

1. *Avoid rushing it:* Admittedly this is all well and good, but students often are under time pressure and strict deadlines. It is essential not to eat into the time allocated for the actual case analysis because of procrastinating on case choice. You can create time before the strategic business case analysis is due to start and begin the process of thinking about what matters to you, checking case libraries and the business press, talking to people, and shortlisting. You will know as soon as you start your management or executive programme that the capstone project will be happening at some point. Create time early to avoid rushing the choice decision later.

2. *Develop your own intuition through case use:* Your 'feeling' for the case subject matters. Use the time on your programme in advance of the strategic business case analysis to develop your intuition about what will make a good case for you. This may come about through your reading and analysis of cases on other modules, not only in strategy, but perhaps also in marketing, leadership, operations, and finance. What were the characteristics of the cases that you enjoyed the most, that you learned the most from, that you were able to use to contribute most to the learning of others? If you identify perhaps 5–10 of these cases, you should be able to form a view of the type of case that is most valuable for you to develop analysis from.

3. *Take a critical approach to best-selling or high-trending cases:* Top selling cases are clearly very useful ones. Professors and instructors around the world gauge their use in class and decide to use them repeatedly. But what may work for class teaching on specific modules will not necessarily work for your longer-term development needs through a capstone project. Don't feel the need to rely on organisations that are household names: they tend to be analysed comprehensively by so many other students, analysts, and commentators that you might not even be able to find a unique angle. You may be working for a relatively unknown organisation that has never had a business case published on it before. And you may derive the most value by casing your own organisation. So be it!

4. *Reflect if stuck:* If you are having any problems with case choice, try and work out why – what is it that is making the choice difficult? Being clear about the reasons for not being able to decide between a shortlist of cases will help you turn indecisiveness to decisiveness. If you become stuck because different advisors are giving you different views, try and identify an adjudicator to help resolve it. If you are stuck because two different cases raise two different strategic issues that both appeal to you, try and find another case where both strategic issues are at play. The point here is that getting unstuck first starts with knowing the reasons for being stuck in the first place.

5. *Finding meaning in the case:* What matters above all is that your case choice has meaning. You will be able to provide a confident answer to the question "Why did you

choose this case to analyse?" if your choice has meaning. You will be able to say: "My case choice means something: it means something to the future of the world we will all live in, and it means something to my own place in that future" – or words to that effect. Meaning is highly subjective and varying from person to person. We discuss here two forms that this can take: being meaningful to global challenges and being meaningful to yourself.

BEING MEANINGFUL TO GLOBAL CHALLENGES

It is worthwhile considering the extent to which you want to include global and grand challenges into your strategic business case analysis. According to George, Howard-Grenville, Joshi and Tihanyi (2016, p. 1880): "'Grand challenges' are formulations of global problems that can be plausibly addressed through coordinated and collaborative effort". This means there are important organisational implications for global challenges, in particular the ways in which organisations understand and interpret them and contribute to resolving them through collaborations with many other types of actors. Global challenges are ones facing us all, not just one organisation or one country. The landscape for these issues is well represented by the United Nations Sustainable Development Goals (SDGs). There are seventeen of these in total: (1) No poverty; (2) Zero hunger; (3) Good health and well-being; (4) Quality education; (5) Gender equality; (6) Clean water and sanitation; (7) Affordable and clean energy; (8) Decent work and economic growth; (9) Industry, innovation and infrastructure; (10) Reduced inequalities; (11) Sustainable cities and communities; (12) Responsible consumption and production; (13) Climate action; (14) Life below water; (15) Life on land; (16) Peace, justice and strong institutions; (17) Partnerships for the goals. And there are 169 targets under these categories.

Many strategic issues facing organisations in the modern era have a social responsibility dimension that aligns with one or more of the UN SDGs. The social issues facing humanity are also ones that have increasingly become strategic concerns for organisations of all shapes and sizes. Bonini et al. (2006) discuss the imperatives of when social issues become strategic. More precisely, they refer to sociopolitical issues: issues that force corporations to consider more than just shareholder returns in their strategic thinking. Business leaders need to understand how the landscape of social and political forces is changing, and they need to lead strategic responses in their organisations appropriately. How they respond has implications for the long-term performance of the firm, as well as the impact on the world around us.

So, the question of global challenges and whether these should be a factor in your case choice needs to be addressed. And it needs to be addressed regardless of whether you are interested in doing your strategic business case analysis on a private sector (for profit) company, or a non-governmental organisation (NGO) or public sector organisation. It may be the case that global challenges are very prominent in your thinking and in your aspirations and goals for your project. Let's consider this to be a 100% commitment to one or more UN SDGs within your work. But it may also be the case that UN SDGs are only part of your thinking and interest. Perhaps they are one of many factors (others could relate to competitive actions, internal modes of organising, leadership issues, and the like). In this scenario, we move down the scale to perhaps a 50% or less weighting on global challenges. It could also be the case that global challenges will not feature at all (i.e., 0%) – in this case please skip to the next section. However, please bear in mind that it is very difficult to find strategic issues today that do not have a social responsibility dimension. Overall, choosing (or writing) a case to analyse that features an issue that is 'meaningful to global challenges' will allow you to contribute to debate and solutions to problems facing business *and* society. This should be considered as it will help to prepare you to contribute to solving these challenges in the years following your immediate studies.

Action box

- Become familiar with the UN SDG list
- Reflect on which area (or areas) – if at all – you find interesting and worthwhile investing your time in
- Where would you position yourself on a notional spectrum of commitment to UN SDGs in your work? (tip: use a scale of 0–100% for each SDG)
- If your commitment to UN SDGs is > 0%, identify the SDGs that mostly closely overlap with your interest (bearing in mind many issues resonate with multiple SDGs).

BEING MEANINGFUL TO YOURSELF

Let's consider how to turn the investment in a strategic business case analysis into one that means something important to you – something that has *intrinsic interest*. This may be linked to the points made above about being meaningful to global challenges. If helping to understand and address global challenges matters to you, then picking a strategic issue in the domain of these challenges for your work on a strategic business case will also be meaningful. But there is another side of case choice that may not necessarily be linked with global challenges that could be intrinsically interesting and 'meaningful to oneself'. This relates to whether the case choice is one that has value and purpose in your life and in your opinion. You may decide that value and purpose of case choice is derived not because the analysis will help contribute to understanding and resolving global grand challenges, but because the issue and/or organisation and/or organisational setting are ones that have value and purpose in your career, in your life. In other words, they have intrinsic value.

Consider some examples in the field of sport. You may be passionate about sport and the role of sport in the community. You may have an opportunity to research a strategic business case on a local community organisation promoting sport as a lifelong endeavour.

The mission of the organisation would be to educate and encourage members of the community of all ages to be involved in sport in whatever capacity they can, and to continue to do so. Perhaps the strategic issue relates to funding gaps, constraints on funding, or how to work collaboratively with many different agencies, given a constrained resource base. Another example could be more global in nature. Perhaps you are passionate about a certain Premier League Football Club that has had some respectable top half of the table finishes in recent years. You are a member of the club's supporters' association and a season ticket holder. You have also invested in some of the shares of the club after it was listed a few years back. The strategic issue is about how the club can compete with the bigger clubs on a global basis, and how it can enter lucrative markets in East Asia in order to build its reputation and fan base, securing new revenues from TV rights and international merchandise sales.

In these examples the value and purpose of the case choice are linked to the intrinsic motivation you would get by spending time on your strategic business case. You get pleasure and personal satisfaction by researching and learning more about sport for life in the community, or your favourite soccer club, about the soccer industry, and about the globalisation of soccer. These types of case choices will add meaning to you because they concern something with which you are personally connected. You like the idea that you can create value for your community. You may add value to your club by sharing your analysis with the supporters' association and the club's executive committee.

Much of this line of argument is linked to the fact that we will enjoy a task more if it has personal meaning and intrinsic value for us. The academic literature on the link between task enjoyment and performance is well established and it covers various scenarios. Task enjoyment is seen as an indicator of intrinsic motivation (Puca & Schmalt, 1999). Studies examine the direct relationship between intrinsic interest/task enjoyment and performance. In a meta-analysis of over 40 years of research on the link between intrinsic motivation and performance, Cerasoli, Nicklin and Ford (2014) confirm intrinsic motivation as a medium-strong predictor of performance. This effect holds even when the levels of extrinsic incentives offered to the individual vary. The hypothesis here is that when people are given tasks (or take on tasks) that they personally enjoy, they are more likely to deliver successful outcomes. This has been shown in many studies based on motivation theory. For instance, Leonard and Weitz (1971) found a positive association between enjoying a task and the successful outcome from that task. They hypothesised that this relationship would depend on whether the individual had high self-esteem or not. However, their findings indicate that the relationship between task enjoyment and performance does not depend on this psychological factor and is robust across high self-esteem and low self-esteem groups. The effect of self-esteem as a moderator of the relationship between task enjoyment (sometimes referred to as 'task-liking' in the literature) is nevertheless confirmed in other studies. For instance, Waters and Roach (1972) found the association between success and task-liking to be only present when the individual had high self-esteem, supporting earlier work by Korman (1968). These studies show what we might reasonably expect to be the case in a strategic business case project – if you enjoy what you are working on, you are more likely than not to achieve a successful outcome.

Studies also have looked at intrinsic interest/task enjoyment as a mediator or moderator between other variables and performance outcomes, i.e., having an indirect effect. For instance, Hirt, Melton, McDonald and Harackiewicz (1996) find that intrinsic interest mediates the relationship between mood and task performance. In their experimental design, participants who were happy at the outset had greater pre-task interest and were more creative. Hirt et al. (1996) also show the role played by the nature of rules associated with the task. Those who were happy would devote more time to a task and generated more output on the task when there was an enjoyment-based stop rule, i.e., a rule in place that directed the participant to stop work on the task once the enjoyment in the task faded. Puca and Schmalt (1999) examine task enjoyment as a mediating factor, altering the relationship between achievement motive and performance. Achievement motive concerns the desire to achieve mastery of a topic and achieve certain learning goals. In their study, this mediation effect was only observed when individuals expected competence feedback, i.e., an evaluation given to them about how well they were doing. This type of feedback fosters positive motivation towards the task. These interaction type studies are more complex than the ones examining intrinsic motivation as a direct effect. They strongly suggest, however, that being engaged in a task that one enjoys and that is intrinsically motivating for the individual will interact with other indicators of a 'healthy' strategic business case analysis. This suggests that you are more likely to feel satisfaction if you are happy with the choice of case and you have an achievement motive. These factors all conspire to influence positive outcomes, underscoring the importance of having intrinsic interest in the case from the outset.

Action box

- Reflect on what matters to you the most in terms of your career and broader life interests
- What kinds of things do you find intrinsically motivating? What kinds of tasks do you enjoy doing?
- Can you identify an organisation with a strategic issue that aligns with the kinds of things you find intrinsically motivating? How do they align?
- If you were to conduct a strategic business case analysis on this organisation and issue, how do you think it would help you in the longer term with your career and life interests
- Engage with others around you about this.

FORMER STUDENT VOICES

Reflection from Nick Waters MBA (airline pilot and lawyer):

My choice to do the MBA was driven by a few factors. I already had around 20 years in business including at senior manager/director level and was eager to put some of my experience into context, to understand what we had done. I had seen companies get into trouble, seen positive and negative outcomes and felt I was missing a common thread to link it all together and learn from it. It gave me additional perspective on how things work that may not be immediately obvious. More than once I had genuine light bulb moments in the MBA, studying some aspect of leadership style or decision theory and thinking back to my own experiences with "*ah, so that's why that happened*".

When first looking at options in strategic case analysis, a few high-level criteria will cross your mind:

Objectives – Do you want to advance in your own industry or transfer to another? Is this a learning opportunity to advance knowledge in those directions by digging into a situation with specific learning points? I chose to look at the events leading to the failure of an organisation within my own industry, to better understand the nature and structure of that industry.

Content – There must be enough material out there to draw upon to support your arguments. High profile cases such as large companies or widespread macroeconomic events naturally give lots of potential to analyse not only what happened, but also the conclusions of others. There may be a natural temptation to look at the Apples and Googles of the world – but these may have been done to death and it's more difficult to make your mark.

If you want to do a study on events in your own business and that has the potential to have real-world impact, have a think about how much information you can draw on to support arguments and make a good case. Examples may be similar studies within your own industry, newspaper, or journal articles and so on.

Relevance – When studying the case options, I kept asking myself "how does this relate to the stuff I have learned so far on the MBA?". This is not only to aid you in making some critical analysis, but also to reinforce learning points you may have come across. This is not an end of term exam where you must shoehorn in an example of every model from each module you did, but equally the story you tell must have some weight, logic, and be supported. All that stuff you studied is a good starting point.

Interest – Don't choose something you think will be easy just because there is a lot of material out there on the event or situation. You will be knee deep in it for quite a while and if you are working full time in a career – as I was – you will need the motivation for weekends and late nights at the keyboard. A genuine interest in 'what happened and why' is invaluable in keeping going.

Reflection from Katherine Neufield MBA (government analyst):

My case pertained to a major AI solution that was being incorporated into operations at a large government department in Canada. My focus was on change management with respect to the AI solution, planning, development, and implementation. The reason why I picked this case topic was my role within the AI space, not as a technician per se, but as a planner, project manager, and strategist. One of my jobs at the time was putting together an AI strategy for the Department of Industry in Canada.

I was originally company agnostic when I decided to choose this topic. I was more concerned with the problem: change management with respect to AI projects and AI implementation. This was an area that really hadn't been addressed very much. What often happened was change management would be done at the very end. The solution was brought in, and then people tried to navigate their way through that change, often with 'interesting' results!

What I looked at was, how is this affecting people? How is this affecting the organisation? And how can we better set up AI implementation in such a way that people understand it and accept it? And also to understand where the division between human decision-making capability is, and where AI decision-making capability is, and make sure that that interface is kept intact. This for me was a burning issue facing many organisations at that moment in time.

KEY TAKEAWAYS

The following are key learning points from this chapter:

- Case choice is vitally important – it will define how you will spend your time and has implications for your enjoyment, learning, and subsequent impact through a strategic business case analysis project
- Cases for a strategic business case analysis may be provided, chosen, or developed – all of these have pros and cons
- Developing your own case for analysis gives you an opportunity to gain in-depth tacit knowledge about the case while selecting the information that you deem most relevant for the subsequent analysis
- Understanding and defining the strategic issue(s) at the heart of the case is a worthwhile task to perform while considering case choice
- Many strategic issues facing organisations are related to global challenges; think clearly about the extent to which global challenges will feature in your analysis
- Intrinsic interest and motivation in the case subject can be established while considering case choice and this can have a strong bearing on ultimate success in the project.

REFLECTIVE PRACTICE TASK

Review the outcomes and your answers to the action boxes above. The first relates to being meaningful to global challenges. The second relates to being meaningful to yourself. Reflect further on the following questions:

1. What?

   What matters to you the most in selecting a case for a strategic business case analysis?

2. So what?

   Why does it matter?

3. Now what?

   What kind of contextual issues are likely to surround the kind of case you are likely to use for your strategic business case analysis? We will discuss the issue of context in the next chapter.

ADDITIONAL READINGS AND RESOURCES

Strategic issues

Nutt, P. C., & Backoff, R. W. (1993). Strategic issues as tensions. *Journal of Management Inquiry*, 2(1), 28–42.

UN SDGs

United Nations: Do you know all 17 SDGs? (https://sdgs.un.org/goals)

Intrinsic motivation

Verywellmind: What is intrinsic motivation? (www.verywellmind.com/what-is-intrinsic-motivation-2795385)

CHAPTER 3

Placing the case in strategic context

HOW DOES MY CASE FIT INTO A BIGGER PICTURE?

Strategic management decisions that organisations make to address or resolve strategic issues occur within context. It is vital to take context into account in a strategic business case analysis. The case itself tells the story of the focal organisation and its strategic issue. It will inevitably include details about the context of the organisation. There will likely be an internal dimension to this: the structure and culture of the organisation, how it is owned and governed, the nature of the leaders and leadership team, perhaps some information about the historical development of the organisation – how it came about in the first place and what the big events were in its past. These are all parts of the organisation's internal context. And there inevitably will be an external dimension to context in the case. This can describe several elements of the external environment: overall industry trends and competitive forces, consumer trends and tastes, government policy and laws, trends in technology and forces and trends in the natural environment. These internal and external dimensions of context are usual features of any business case.

These features are usually descriptive, telling the reader the 'what', 'where', and 'when' rather than the 'why', 'how', and 'what next?'. While the latter are critical questions to answer in a strategic business case analysis, it is necessary to understand how your case fits into context, and what aspects of context will matter when it comes to conducting the analysis. What is the bigger picture that should be highlighted? Perhaps your case fits into a broader narrative about global challenges and problems facing societies around the world. Perhaps it is a case that fits into a narrative about digital transformation and AI. Perhaps it is a bit of both.

Scholars in various subfields of business and management highlight the various types of context in which strategy is embedded. Autio, Kenney, Mustar, Siegel and Wright (2014) in the field of innovation, for instance, describe several contexts that influence entrepreneurial innovation. These include industrial/technological, organisational, social, institutional/policy and geographical (global, national, regional, local) contexts in which entrepreneurial behaviour can occur. They also highlight a temporal context, emphasising how the various other contexts change over time. We will discuss this in the next section. Building on their work, Williams, Hailemariam and Allard (2022) explore entrepreneurial

DOI: 10.4324/9781003288916-4

innovation in one specific geographical context: Ethiopia. They show how the various contexts described by Autio et al. (2014) are at play in Ethiopia, but to differing degrees. The most prominent one was the social context, while the least apparent one was the organisational context. Following calls to identify and explore new contexts in the field of innovation (Welter, Gartner & Wright, 2016), Williams et al. (2022) also identify a 'national citizenship context' specific to Ethiopia. Here they found evidence of individual entrepreneur cognitions set in the challenges facing Ethiopia and the desire to solve these challenges for the improvement of the country.

What this example tells us is that it is not just about internal versus external contexts. There are multiple ways of looking at context, and there may even be new or more nuanced definitions of context that you will find when conducting your strategic business case analysis. Strategic management decisions can be seen as occurring at the centre of overlapping contexts – the various contexts that matter in each case are likely to intersect with one another. It is at this intersection that the strategic issue is placed, and it is at this intersection that strategic decisions will need to be made.

One way of looking at this is through the lens of a *dominant context* (or contexts). A dominant context is one that overshadows the whole case. It is the main environmental domain that influences the strategic issue and phenomenon under investigation. Let's consider some examples. Boubakri, Cosset and Guedhami (2009) examine the privatisation of firms in strategic industries, firms that originally were under state monopoly. The dominant context here relates to privatisation and economic transformation. Carpenter and Westphal (2001) examine different aspects of a board's external social network on its strategic decision-making process. They find that the social context of a board's external network matters to the advice this network delivers for the organisation. The dominant context here relates to social network ties of a board. Judge and Douglas (1998) examine the integration of natural environment concerns into strategic planning processes of firms, showing how this is crucial for both financial and environmental performance. The dominant context here is about the natural environment. In all these examples (privatisation, board interlocks, natural environment), a dominant context can be identified that can help guide the positioning of a case analysis.

Nevertheless, as pointed out above in the Williams et al. (2022) article, various contexts may be at play but in differing degrees. Not all contexts carry the same weight for a given issue or phenomenon. When this happens, we must be more nuanced. The idea of a dominant context can then be relaxed in favour of the idea of dominant *contexts* (plural). An example is the work of Abedin, Kordnaeij, Fard and Hoseini (2015) who explore the determinants of strategic issue identification in organisations. While their qualitative data originates in Iran (a potential candidate for being a dominant context by virtue of geographical demarcation), what they find is that two other internal contexts have a key role to play. These are the management context (including managers' cognition, values, and ethics) and the organisational context (including structure, culture, and information processing). So, we should be attentive to the fact that multiple dominant contexts might be at play and that you need to place your case at the intersection of these.

Action box

- Carefully read your case (or choose one for this exercise if you have not already chosen one)
- Identify as many types of contexts as possible as being present in the case data
- Rank the contexts in order of importance to the strategic issue at the centre of the case
- Consider whether the contexts are internal or external to the organisation
- Identify the dominant context or contexts that you believe will best inform the strategic issue and decision at the heart of the case.

THE TEMPORAL DIMENSION

All cases evolve over time. They depict key events in history. These events may be internal to the focal organisation, they may be external. What they depict is an evolving and changing situation, an organisation interacting with an environment where both are in flux. The case may show how the fundamental nature of the organisation has changed over time. This may be reflected in new and upgraded corporate strategy. The case may reveal how the leadership of the organisation has changed in time. It may also show whether and how the ownership of the organisation might have changed, for instance because of an initial public offering. Externally, there will be changes in many dimensions, often captured in the PESTEL dimensions (political, economic, social, technological, environmental, legal dimensions of the external context). Cases do not show all the change that is happening over a given period, but they should show the most relevant aspects of strategic change, the most pertinent events. What this means is that time is a critical contextual factor in any case, and you need to pay attention to it.

Firstly, define a start point for the case, or perhaps better stated: a *starting point*. In most cases, the origins of the strategic issue facing the focal organisation can be traced back many years, if not decades. The strategic issue may be deeply rooted in the culture of the organisation and has permeated different eras of the organisation. It may be embedded in the fundamental technology and intellectual property of the organisation that was developed many years previously. A starting point then, is where you want to begin the treatment of case data; where you feel the best place to commence the assessment of change. If you want to assess financial performance and growth, what prior period are you comparing to? What changes happened internally and externally over this period? If you want to assess non-financial performance, perhaps the extent to which an organisation meets its sustainability targets, what prior period are you comparing to? So, as you read through your case data (regardless of whether you wrote the case or whether it was assigned to you), be clear in your mind what the starting point for your analysis will be.

Secondly, define the *decision point*. This is the point in time at which a decision needs to be made by the focal organisation, normally by its strategic leaders, to deal with the strategic issue. This is not necessarily the end point of the case, or the date of publication of the case, and it is very likely not the current point in time for the organisation. Decision points can also be set in history. We will find examples of this in the three cases analysed as worked examples in Chapter 7. A case that is assigned to you may have been published many years previously, and the decision point will fall before that publication date. As a case writer and educator, it is often beneficial to set decision points in the past. Doing so means additional information about 'what happened next?' can be included in the teaching note of the case. Instructors can bring data on subsequent events into the class and discuss with students the virtues of the actions or options the decision-maker(s) took, and what the outcomes were. As a case analyst, you can put yourself in the shoes of the decision-maker at the decision point. If you allow yourself to become biased with more recent events, simply because you happen to know what happened and how the organisation evolved within its context subsequently, your analysis will be faulty. You will be drawing on evidence that even the decision-makers did not have at the decision point! Also, the readers (including examiners) of your strategic business case analysis will find it difficult to follow your logic and justification for the points you make in your analysis.

What matters here is the need to respect time as a type of context within your case (Autio et al., 2014). This can be done in various ways; there are many ways in which organisations can be seen from a temporal point of view. Firstly, organisations learn as they go along, and learning is a process that takes place in time. Berends and Antonacopoulou (2014) review the literature on time and organisational learning. They highlight three mechanisms by which organisations learn in time. The first of these is *duration*: it is in the passage of time that experiences are acquired, and outcomes arise. However, this is also a threat to organisations because knowledge can become obsolete, and the content of learning may be forgotten. In relation to this, Williams and Durst (2019) discuss the concept of 'knowledge at risk' within the phenomenon of offshore outsourcing. The gradual transfer of one organisation's knowledge to another (an outsourced vendor), can be seen in terms of knowledge at risk that can lead to underperformance, at least during the transition period. The second of Berends and Antonacopoulou's (2014) mechanisms relates to *timing*: routines for learning happen in time, and learning can be seen as timely and can be synchronised with other activities within the organisation. The third mechanism relates to engagement of learning activity with the *past*, *present*, and *future* of the organisation: the past can be interpreted in different ways and reinterpretation leads to learning. Learning also involves making connections between the past, present, and future.

Secondly, organisations develop capabilities dynamically, and the ability to reconfigure resources in time is a basis for competitive advantage (Eisenhardt & Martin, 2000; Teece, Pisano & Shuen, 1997). Dynamic capabilities are needed by organisations operating in high-velocity and dynamic environments (Wang & Ahmed, 2007). As Wang and Ahmed (2007) note: dynamic capabilities allow new knowledge to be created by the organisation as rapidly as possible and as the situation in which the organisation is in changes. It is about the organisation's ability to reconstruct its resources and capabilities in response to an environment that is changing. Dynamic capabilities, then, lead to new capabilities being developed (Eisenhardt & Martin, 2000; Teece, Pisano & Shuen, 1997). According to Wang and Ahmed (2007), they have certain 'common' features (found across firms), which include adaptive capability (ability to identify and act on new opportunities), absorptive capability (ability to recognise valuable new information, assimilate, and apply it), and innovative capability (ability to develop new products and services). They also involve underlying processes specific to a given organisation, including integration, reconfiguration, renewal, and recreation of resources over time.

Thirdly, organisations – like individuals – are continual information seekers. They seek information from their environments (internal and external) to facilitate learning and make decisions about which capabilities to develop. And they do this on an ongoing basis. Savolainen (2006) discusses time as a context for information seeking. He shows how the information-seeking literature has treated time in three ways: (1) as a fundamental attribute of the context for information seeking, in particular, the social context in which individuals practice information seeking; (2) as a way of qualifying access to information (how much time is available to search for information, is there information overload?), (3) as a way of indicating how the process of information seeking unfolds (including the order in which information is selected and processed).

Action box

- Identify the starting point and decision points for your case (or a case with which you are familiar)
- Reflect and articulate the reasons for choosing those starting and decision points
- Identify the changes in the external context that occurred over the duration of the case
- Identify the key internal changes and events
- Ask yourself whether you think there will be any bias in your analysis, such as being aware of subsequent events after the decision point.

CONTEXT COMPLEXITY

Placing your case into its strategic context is clearly not as simple as identifying the environment of the organisation in industrial (e.g., manufacturing), geographic (e.g., Germany), or organisational characteristics (e.g., small family business) terms. We need to be more nuanced in our thinking about case context as we prepare for a strategic business case analysis. This also means embracing complexity, and in particular the multifaceted nature of overlapping and intersecting contexts. For instance, there may have been one dominant context at the starting point of your case, but, given the passage of time, there were new, different, or more dominant contexts at play by the time the case gets to the decision point. Here we see an intersection between the dominant context and the temporal context. It is this intersection and the interrelationships between various contexts that matter for organisations as they struggle with strategic issues and strategic decision-making.

Scholars from various fields underscore this point.

- In the field of strategy, Lei, Hitt and Bettis (1996) describe the challenge of understanding how firms compete in chaotic environments. They propose the concept of meta-learning: the updating of universal and tacit knowledge in the organisation, a change to its fundamental heuristics. It is this meta-learning that allows new core competences and options for the organisation to develop. The authors provide the following definition: "Meta-learning is the simultaneous conceptualization of different and contradictory forms of knowledge. It integrates information transfers, experimentation, and dynamic routines into a systemic perspective. Meta-learning may create additions to, or substitutions of knowledge (new replacing outmoded knowledge)" (p. 562). This will clearly add to context complexity in strategic business case analysis. It raises questions about not only the 'chaotic' nature of the external environment surrounding the focal organisation, but also the internal environment for continually changing heuristics.

- In the field of information systems management, Hiekkanen, Helenius, Korhonen and Patricio (2013) note how information systems have moved from being an administrative or support function to being tightly coupled into the business fabric of the organisation. This raises questions for the notion of alignment between business (and business strategy) and IT. Both contexts are continually changing, and they are increasingly co-evolving together. They are also co-evolving in a non-linear way, in ways that are difficult to predict. Think of technological breakthroughs, and opportunities and threats that arise because of geopolitical events. The authors highlight the challenges of how to make sense of the increasingly complex strategic context for organisations that has been induced by technology shifts.

- In the field of manufacturing, Malhotra, Steele and Grover (1994) examine the challenges faced by US manufacturers in the 1990s in terms of strategic and tactical areas. At the strategic level, themes including quality management, manufacturing strategy, and process technology were noted. At the tactical level, themes include purchasing, production planning, and workforce supervision. What this shows is two critical contexts within the organisation: one at a strategic level and one at a tactical level. Clearly, one cannot have one without the other. Indeed, at a tactical level, increasingly complex products and how to coordinate their manufacturing are seen as major challenges. The authors note complexity in how to establish manufacturing and organisational systems to address these challenges.

- In the field of climate change, Ulph and Ulph (2007) discuss the complex nature of contexts: the inter-governmental context (because the issue is a global one affecting all nations), the economic context (because cutting emissions comes at a price), and the R&D context (the development of new technology to have an impact on climate change). In addition to these, the authors highlight the temporal context; for instance, the time it takes R&D to bear fruit, and the problems of getting governments (which change over time) to agree on how to address the issues. The authors discuss incentives for both countries and firms within countries to develop and implement environmental policy.

These examples from different literatures serve to illustrate some key points. It will be inevitable that there will be context complexity in your case, the question is: how much? Context complexity may differ from field to field, it will differ from case to case. Appreciating the extent of context complexity in your case as part of the preparation for the analysis that will follow is therefore important. While you will undoubtedly examine the nature of complexity in your case during the actual analysis (more of this in Part 2 of this book), it is useful to get a sense of context complexity as you prepare. An initial reading of your case (if you did not write it yourself) will help you assess the nature of context complexity. You may decide to try and influence case choice (see previous chapter) if you think the nature of context complexity will make it difficult to solve. And if you are writing the case yourself, you will have some discretion over the nature of contexts that you think are relevant; you will directly influence how 'complex' the interacting contexts are in your case as you are the case author. This initial assessment of context complexity will help you prepare for the choice of questions for analysis (next chapter), and it will also help you to remove any sudden surprises later in the case analysis journey.

Action box

- Once you have *identified* the main contexts in your case, including the temporal dimension, spend some time to *understand* the nature of complexity in context:
  - How do the contexts interrelate with each other?
  - How do they change over time?
  - Does context complexity get more acute/less acute as the case moves towards the decision point?

- Draw a graphical depiction that captures context complexity in your case, tools could include:
  - A Venn diagram
  - A path diagram showing dependencies between contexts
  - A series of diagrams at different points in time showing how context complexity evolves in your case

- Produce a list of ways in which defined contexts interact and explain why this complexity presents a challenge to the protagonists in the case, as well as to you, the case analyst.

INTERACTION BETWEEN CASE ORGANISATION AND CONTEXT

Placing your case in strategic context is not only about understanding and specifying the nature of context *per se*. It also involves clarifying the links and interactions between the organisation in your case and the context. As discussed above, the case itself tells its reader the 'what', 'where', and 'when', while the analysis goes into the 'why', 'how', and 'what next?'. It is these more challenging questions that can ultimately only be answered by having an appreciation of the links between the case organisation and its strategic context. Preparing for your strategic business case analysis then, needs to involve an appreciation of how the organisation (together with its strategic issue) at the heart of the case interacts with the strategic context.

There are various ways in which this can happen, and of course these will differ from case to case. Prominent ways may include the following:

- *The case organisation forms a main part of the strategic context of the case*: The internal organisational environment may be the key feature of the case. The case may be about, for instance, how the internal organisational culture inhibits innovation and creativity amongst the employees of the organisation. It may be about how the foreign subsidiaries of the organisation are managed and how communication and information flows are governed across a network of international units. It may be about how the senior management team of the organisation are embroiled in internal disputes that impede the effective functioning of the organisation. It may be about corruption and embezzlement within the organisation. In these kinds of case storylines, the strategic context as it relates to the case analysis is formed mainly by the organisation itself. This does not mean to say the external environment of industry trends, competitor activity, consumer behaviour, and the like do not matter. It simply means the main emphasis in the case is such that internal features of the focal organisation and its strategic issue comprise the basis of context for the case.
- *The case organisation as a key driver of the strategic context*: In this situation, the focal organisation in your case has created or influenced the development of a strategic context that affects other organisations and stakeholders. Perhaps it was a private sector company that acted as the innovative sparkplug behind a new technology that changed the shape of consumer behaviour and technological development for decades to come. Here we can think of companies such as Apple, Microsoft, and Google. Perhaps it was a government that was mired in corruption and mismanagement of public funds, contributing to worsening inequality, poverty, and poor health systems for its citizens. Perhaps it was an NGO or charity operating in a run-down and impoverished part of a developing country helping to alleviate human burden in that location by coordinating efforts across multiple stakeholder groups and organisations. In these types of examples, the case organisation is a force for emergence and change in the strategic context which then has an influence on other organisations and groups.
- *The case organisation as adding complexity to the strategic context*: We could interpret the role of the focal organisation in the case to be one of adding to the complexity of the context. Its actions may be making things more complicated for others operating within the same environment. It may not be a key driver of the emergence of a new type of context, but it may nevertheless be making the nature of context more complex. Examples include: a new competitor entering a market that is challenging incumbents' strategy in some respects but undercutting them on prices (think of low-cost airlines), an activist investor that has managed to acquire a significant ownership stake in a company and is challenging its board to change route – perhaps even threatening to replace the current board with a new one (such as US investor Elliott Management), a government organisation that sends in military force into a disaster relief setting without consulting aid agencies already operating in that setting. In these examples the case storyline will show how the focal organisation adds to the pressures on other stakeholders through its actions.

- *The case organisation being at the mercy of its strategic context*: The focal organisation in your case might not have the power and influence to be a major driving force for change in its industry and environment. Quite the opposite. It might be at the mercy of the external environment. Indeed, that may be the essence of the strategic issue in the case. In this scenario, the organisation is a relatively weak player, it is under threat, and has been challenged to respond to events that were outside of its control. History is littered with companies – large and small – that have collapsed because of not responding appropriately to changes in the external environment. This often relates to industry or technology changes that the company has not been able to keep up with. But it can also happen to NGOs and charities, especially smaller ones that struggle to raise funds amidst a constrained environment for donations, as well as competition within the charity sector. It can also affect government departments and units at national and local levels, especially when central government policy reviews question the performance and cost of departments. In these examples the focal organisation is at the behest of a changing external context.
- *The case organisation changing in fundamental ways over time*: The focal organisation in your case may have changed dramatically between the starting point and the decision point in your case. It may have grown aggressively in terms of employees and numbers of countries in which it operates. It may have multiplied its revenues manyfold. It may have diversified into new product lines, and possibly into completely new lines of business. We can think about a company like IBM that transitioned from mainframe hardware into software and professional services in the 1990s. Or a company like Amazon that started out as an online book retailer but is now a global distributor of almost any type of consumer product, as well as hosting business services such as cloud solutions. Organisations may also have shrunk over time or become more focused and narrower in their offering or services provided. In these examples, the temporal dimension is key. The organisation interacts with time. Certain events and trends that occurred have resulted in major structural changes to the organisation, challenging its original vision and helping to turn it into a different form.

These are just some examples of how a case organisation can interact with strategic context. Being aware of these interactions as part of the preparation for a strategic business case analysis is a very useful step. It will allow you to approach the analysis task with clarity on how your case fits into the 'bigger picture'.

Action box

- Identify which of the ways mentioned above apply to your case within its strategic context
- Think of other ways in which your chosen case organisation interacts with its strategic context
- Make a note of these and reflect upon the nature of context in your case, the role of the temporal dimension, and the nature of complexity.

FORMER STUDENT VOICES

Reflection from Nick Waters MBA (airline pilot and lawyer):

Events or decisions under analysis rarely happen in isolation, there will always be macro and micro factors, perhaps cumulating over years, that influence decisions leading up to the events that form the basis of your case. It's important to understand what these factors are, when did they start, what influenced their development, what were the competition doing?

My case study in the aviation industry really started 20 years before the decision point: deregulation creating an environment for a new type of business model to emerge. As with any industry faced with change, new models emerge, existing businesses may adapt to varying degrees, flail around and fail, or get stuck somewhere in the middle. Those decisions themselves will have a myriad of influencing factors from historical positions, culture, geopolitical factors, leadership styles, and so on. On top of this, you may have macroeconomic or external factors causing shocks, volcanic eruptions, financial crises, and pandemics. It's a constantly changing landscape with many interconnected factors.

Consider not only the historical or current factors influencing the event, what effect did that event itself have in macro or microeconomic terms, on the industry, on competitors? What additional flows could stem from this that have not yet been identified?

I found that once I started taking a wider view of the strategic context, it was fascinating to see the factors that influenced how situations developed and provided useful support for arguments and conclusions.

Reflection from Katherine Neufield MBA (government analyst):

The strategic part of my case analysis concerned how to increase the effectiveness of AI capability in a large complex organisation. There are certain areas where AI does extremely well. If you increase that capability you can increase, for example, the number of clients you can serve and meet increasing demand. That was a strategic problem – trying to meet a massive increase in demand; you couldn't do it with human staff. There was just too much work.

The technology context was important – AI requires lots of data. It needs to be reliable. The technology itself was not that sophisticated in this case – you could barely call it machine learning. The technology comes up with its own rules based on the data that it is fed. But there's the human side too. Humans indicate what's a good rule and what's not a good rule. The organisation started working with developers, eliminating rules that were irrelevant or unhelpful, and keeping the rules that made sense, and adding a few rules that the human officers would normally follow but were not included. So, an important contextual issue was the interface: human–computer interaction.

There's a subfield called human AI interaction, and that was a big part of the change management … creating a culture so people can provide feedback while the technology is in production and people are using the technology in the field. Is there an issue? Was this a good call? This information gets fed back from humans into the existing data set, and the AI model starts to refine.

The regulatory context was also important: the solution needed to pass legal and ethics tests, critical in the regulatory space where I worked. The work was for a government department in the area of immigration. If they made an unfair decision, they could be subject to litigation. As such they are extremely cautious about what decisions they make, especially when there's a machine involved!

KEY TAKEAWAYS

The following are key learning points from this chapter:

- Preparing for a strategic business case analysis can be facilitated by getting a sense of how a chosen or assigned case fits into a broader context
- The strategic context surrounding a focal organisation in a case can consist of any or all of a number of contexts, including:
  - Internal vs. external
  - Technological/industry
  - Social
  - Organisational
  - Institutional/policy
  - Geographical (at different levels)
  - Environmental and natural capital

- These contexts overlap and can influence each other
- There is (are) likely to be one (or several) dominant context(s) – not all contexts will carry the same weight
- The temporal dimension is also a key context in its own right – every case will have one
- The extent to which a given context (including the temporal dimension) will matter to a case organisation will differ from case to case
- Context complexity arises because of the interrelationships between contexts – it is useful to understand this before embarking on more detailed analysis.

REFLECTIVE PRACTICE TASK

Review the outcomes and your answers to the action boxes above. These relate to: (1) identifying the dominant context or contexts; (2) understanding the temporal context; (3) understanding context complexity; (4) clarifying how your case organisation interacts with its context. Reflect further on the following questions:

1. What?

   What are your initial conclusions about the relationship of your case organisation within its context?

2. So what?

   Why does this relationship matter?

3. Now what?

   Think about the kinds of questions you might like to pose as you proceed to analyse your case. We will now discuss the issue of choosing questions for analysis in the next chapter.

ADDITIONAL READINGS AND RESOURCES

Context complexity

Akaka, M. A., Vargo, S. L., & Lusch, R. F. (2013). The complexity of context: A service ecosystems approach for international marketing. *Journal of International Marketing, 21*(4), 1–20.

Vasconcelos, F. C., & Ramirez, R. (2011). Complexity in business environments. *Journal of Business Research, 64*(3), 236–241.

Multisite context research

Yin, R. K. (1982). Studying phenomenon and context across sites. *American Behavioral Scientist, 26*(1), 84–100.

CHAPTER 4

Deciding on the questions for analysis

FORMULATING, CHALLENGING, AND STRUCTURING QUESTIONS

The questions we pose will determine the answers we find, the conclusions we come to, and the impact we make. Research questions matter: they give shape and direction to your work (Agee, 2009). Questions are the very essence of learning (Fraenkel, 1966). In some case analysis assignments, the questions for analysis are pre-decided, typically by the course instructor. In other situations, the student can articulate the key question(s) they want to answer. In the former, understanding why someone else has determined the questions and formulated them in the way they have, and what they may be seeking in return, will be useful. It will be helpful to develop a critical view of the assigned question(s) and be prepared to challenge them as the analysis proceeds. In the latter scenario (the student deciding the questions), one can formulate original, challenging, and probing questions, while appreciating that this itself is a process that will unfold over time. A tentative set of questions can be articulated initially and then modified over time as the analysis unfolds.

In both scenarios it is useful to be inquisitive. You will be inquiring deeply into your case organisation and the strategic issue it is grappling with. You may need to challenge the questions given if they are set by others. This would show a willingness to be curious and proactive. For a project as large as a strategic business case analysis, this can be beneficial because it will enable you to identify analytical nuances and new lenses with which to make sense of your case. Please talk to your supervisor or course instructor if you want to challenge or change the questions given or augment them with new ones; you will need to justify why you are taking this approach. In the scenario that you have freedom to decide your own questions, flexing your curiosity about the case will be equally useful. As the one formulating the questions, you will need to be confident that they will guide the research work that follows in a meaningful way.

The main protagonist in the case, perhaps the CEO or leadership team in the organisation, will clearly have their own questions to answer. The strategic issue and problem facing the organisation will need a solution, it will need an answer. So, in most strategic business cases, at least one of the main questions to be articulated should come directly from the strategic issue in the case. This often takes the form of "What should the

DOI: 10.4324/9781003288916-5

organisation do next?", "Should the organisation pursue option A or option B?", "What should the actions be in the short, medium, and/or long term?". These kinds of questions are normally self-evident and seek a normative answer based on the storyline and decision point set in the case. In this sense, it is neither a course instructor nor the case analyst who is asking the main questions: it is the organisation facing the strategic issue at the heart of the case.

However, we need to be prepared to ask more questions and probe deeper. Strategic business cases are often complex, play out in multiple overlapping contexts, and if there was a self-evident answer, it would have been forthcoming by the time the decision point was reached. In other words, it would have been a no-brainer. So, it is important to formulate multiple questions, all linked to the primary (or root) normative question. While guiding the framing of those sub-questions using the primary question of the case, you can exercise your own creativity and curiosity in generating new questions that ultimately will help answer the question. In doing this, be aware that these questions will structure your overall analytical task. They are not necessarily the same as questions that you would use in an interview, especially a semi-structured or open interview, which may probe into the phenomenon using a wider array of questions.

Table 4.1 shows examples of this, using three primary questions.

TABLE 4.1 Decomposing primary questions

Primary normative[a] question (emanates directly from the case)	Type of question	Examples of sub-questions (not exhaustive)	Examples of counter-questions (not exhaustive)
"What should the organisation do next?"	A general and open question that could apply to almost any case organisation	"What options does the organisation have?" "How is the context likely to change in the future?" "What are the resistance forces or impediments preventing next steps?"	"What shouldn't the organisation do next?"
"Should the organisation pursue option A or option B?"	A closed question referring to two specific options that should be clearly articulated in the case	"What are the capability requirements for A versus B?" "How can the organisation develop or acquire the capabilities required for A versus B?" "What are the costs and risks of pursuing A versus pursuing B?"	"What about option C?"
"What should the actions be in the short, medium, and/or long term?"	A temporally structured question directing the analyst to consider the temporal dimension of context	"What are the path dependencies between actions?" "Why do these dependencies exist?" "What capabilities can be applied for quick wins versus those needed for long-term deployment?"	"Can we ignore the long term for now – after all, the future is difficult to predict?"

[a] Also referred to as a root question.

Action box

- If your case questions have been assigned to you by your course or module instructor, reflect on why they might be formulated the way they are. Try to figure out what is it the instructor is looking for by posing a question in a certain way?
- If you have the freedom to choose or develop your own case and case questions, produce an initial 'back of an envelope' set of questions, before moving on to the next sections.

HOW MANY QUESTIONS MAKE SENSE?

As illustrated in Table 4.1, the top-level primary question of a case can be broken down into sub-questions. These sub-questions can then guide different parts of the analysis during the project. It will be possible to come up with any number of sub-questions for a given primary question. It will also be possible to subdivide sub-questions even further, creating a hierarchy of questions. Such a hierarchy can aid problem solving and is known as a 'question tree'. According to investigationsquality.com, a question tree is a structure:

> for seeing the elements of a problem clearly, and keeping track of different levels of the problem, which we can liken to trunks, branches, twigs, and leaves. You can arrange them from left to right, right to left, or top to bottom— whatever makes the elements easier for you to visualize.[1]

This approach to dissecting the primary question is appealing, especially given complexity in strategic business cases. However, a challenge you will face relates to the total number of questions to formulate within the question tree. Is there an ideal number of questions or levels in a question tree? There is no fixed rule about how many questions in total to aim for. Having too few (e.g., one single question), or too many (e.g., 25 questions scattered over five layers of a question tree) will have negative consequences for your work and for the readers and beneficiaries of your work. Too few questions may lead to the work being unfocused and analytically loose. Examiners and other readers may not find the results coherent. Organisations that could benefit from your work may not be able to follow you clearly; results may not be meaningful. Too many questions could make life difficult for yourself. You may end up with many bundles of discrete analytical work that are difficult to piece together later.

It will be fruitful to find a comfortable middle ground where there is one primary question and a handful of sub-questions, broken down into a second and possibly third layer in a question tree. An example of this is given in Chapter 7 where we analyse the case of Time Out Group. There is no precise number of questions specified in the research methods literature for this. It will be important for you to be comfortable with the total number of questions and avoid creating the conditions for a difficult task for yourself when the analysis starts for real. It is not the total number of questions that matters, but rather the extent to which they have qualities of 'good' questions. We discuss this next.

Action box

- Conduct an initial attempt at a question tree for your assigned case (or another case that you are familiar with) without being restrained by the number of questions
- Reflect on your question tree:
  - Can any questions be removed without harming the primary question?
  - Can any questions be reworded to make them clearer?
  - Can any questions be merged to reduce redundancy?

CHARACTERISTICS OF GOOD CASE QUESTIONS

Various salient points are given in the research methods literature on what constitutes 'good' research questions. These points come from various fields and can be applied to strategic business case analysis projects.

1. *A question must be answerable (Haynes, 2006)*: Writing in the field of clinical epidemiology, Haynes (2006) notes that it is essential to have some knowledge about the problem, and to know that the problem can be answered through analytical research. Avoid questions that cannot be answered within the time frame of your business case analysis, or which are unlikely to lead to a meaningful answer.

2. *A question must be answerable in the time allowed (Agee, 2009)*: Posing a question that is not possible to answer in the time frame of your project is clearly impractical. Agee (2009) notes: "Some questions are simply not answerable given the researcher's time frame and resources" (p. 443). All research is a process, and unforeseen delays and pressures on the researcher's time will impact the plausibility of being able to answer a question before the deadline. Avoid questions that cannot be answered before the deadline of your project.

3. *Poorly conceived and unproductive questions don't help (Agee, 2009; Wasserman, 1992)*: As Agee (2009) notes in the abstract of her article: "Good research questions do not necessarily produce good research, but poorly conceived or constructed questions will likely create problems that affect all subsequent stages of a study" (p. 431). As you review your case questions, ask yourself whether they are poorly devised. Are they created in a way that will lead to answers that will inform the strategic issue at the heart of the case? If not, they are likely to have been poorly conceived. Linked to this is Wassermann's (1992) point that good questions promote reflection and intelligent thinking about the issues at hand. Wassermann shines a spotlight on unproductive – including stupid! – questions. These are useless for promoting intelligent thinking and can even be harmful.

4. *Focus on higher-order explanatory and heuristic questions (Fraenkel, 1966)*: Fraenkel (1966) defines four types of questions: (1) factual questions whose purpose is knowledge acquisition, (2) descriptive questions, which are about knowledge synthesis, (3) explanatory questions, which aim for knowledge analysis, and (4) heuristic questions,

which lead to creative thinking. The first two types (factual and descriptive) are all about remembering, according to Fraenkel. Much of this type of knowledge will already be in the case itself and is not needed in the analysis. Aim for explanatory questions (why? how?) and heuristic questions, which require divergent thinking, and which push the analyst to venture into "uncharted seas" (Fraenkel, 1966, p. 399). A useful source here is Bloom's *Taxonomy of Educational Objectives* (Bloom, 1956) and its revision by Anderson and Krathwohl (2001). These underscore the distinction between lower-order (remembering and understanding) and higher-order questioning (evaluation and creation). Try and focus on higher-order questions.

5. *Questions that encourage integrative thinking (Giurco & Cooper, 2012)*: In the field of minerals engineering, Giurco and Cooper (2012) adopt a broad stakeholder mapping exercise on the case of deep-sea mining in Australia. They show that questions encompassing a wide range of stakeholder concerns and avoiding an overly narrow focus on one part of the problem space will lead to a more integrative perspective on acceptable use deep-sea mining.

6. *Strike a balance between 'big, messy questions' (Kloss, 1988) and overly complex ones (Wassermann, 1992)*: While Kloss (1988) underscores the point made above on avoiding factual and recall types of questions, he also encourages the development of messy questions and being creative about the order in which questions are asked. Although writing in the field of English literature teaching, this principle applies to strategic business case analysis. Big, messy questions can be reserved for higher levels in the question tree, if not the primary level. Sub-questions do not have to follow any order, except that which makes sense to you as you progress through your project. Wassermann (1992) points out that questions that are too complex, however, are unproductive. They can defeat intelligent examination and may require some curtailing or narrowing.

7. *Don't overuse the 'why' question (Reid & Smyth-Renshaw, 2012)*: In various fields ranging from manufacturing engineering to healthcare to the legal profession, root cause analysis (RCA) has become a widely used approach (more precisely, a class of approaches) for solving problems in a structured way. Reid and Smyth-Renshaw (2012) argue that only focusing on the 'why' question can be limiting for the researcher aiming to get to the root cause of a problem. Other question types can be extremely potent if constructed appropriately. Examples include: "What are the reasons?", "What are the value conflicts or assumptions?", "What are the descriptive assumptions?", "Are there any fallacies in the reasoning?", "How good is the evidence?", "Are there any rival causes?" (Reid & Smyth-Renshaw, 2012, p. 538).

8. *Asking questions related to sustainable development goals (Al-Kuwari, Al-Fagih and Koç, 2021)*: Your strategic business case analysis questions may have relevance to global challenges and UN SDGs. Even for cases that seemingly do not appear to be directly concerned with global challenges, critical questions can be posed that will create new knowledge related to global challenges during the analysis. Al-Kuwari et al. (2021) write in the context of education for sustainable development, highlighting the importance of asking the right questions, at the right time, in the right amount, to promote sustainable thinking in students. Questions that promote critical thinking and skills acquisition by students are singled out as suggestions within the education for sustainable development (ESD) space.

Action box

- Apply the criteria and themes discussed here to the questions you formulated in the previous two action boxes – do you think you need to revise your questions? If so, how?
- Can you think of any other criteria that should apply to your questions?

QUESTION DEVELOPMENT AS A PROCESS

Developing questions for any research work is a process. The questions we ask will evolve over time as we learn more about the phenomenon, as new information comes to light, as we challenge our assumptions and develop our own curiosity. While time is a constraint to critical thinking in the classroom (Snyder & Snyder, 2008), with a longer-term research project it is an enabler. Time allows critical thinking to develop, encouraging initial assumptions and questions to be challenged (Lai, 2011). The initial questions are not always the ones that we finally want to use. As Agee (2009) notes: "Many first attempts at question development generate questions that are overly broad and that lack reference to a specific context" (p. 442). When developing questions for a strategic business case analysis try and appreciate this aspect of learning, that it happens in time.

You may not know at the outset that your original questions do not satisfy all the conditions of being 'good' questions for your project, e.g., if they were too broad. You may only realise this as you progress on the analysis journey. Alternatively, it may be that your initial questions are well conceived and not too broad at all, but that your intellectual curiosity changes the more you delve deeper into the substance of your case analysis work. This is completely normal and should not be resisted. It simply means that you sharpen your inquiry as you discover more about the case and what the analysis reveals about the case. This can manifest itself in changes to the wording of your primary question or any sub-question, removing any sub-question, or adding new sub-questions as the wording of the related question changes.

Despite an acceptance that question changes are inevitable during significant research projects, there are also situations to watch out for.

1. *Has the purpose of the project changed?* Question changes that occur during the analysis may change the purpose of the project. This is particularly so when the understanding or definition of the strategic issue at the heart of the case changes. Examples could include: (1) a case analysis initially based on returning a company to profit (financial performance) becoming one of improving the company's reputation for sustainability (non-financial performance), (2) a case analysis on improving the service to patients in one department of a hospital becoming one of efficiency improvements across all the hospitals in the wider trust, (3) a case analysis on corporate governance issues in a large corporation becoming one of dealing with problems in strategic stakeholder relationships. In all these realistic situations the strategic issue as initially defined by the student has evolved, and with it so has the purpose of the analysis.

2. *Is there a need to discuss the questions set with the instructor?* In the situation where the student does not set the initial questions – where they are provided by the institution – it is

entirely possible that the student feels a need to challenge – and change – the questions set. This may not be apparent at the outset. But given the passage of time and the student's engagement with the case material, additional materials, and reassessment of their own interest and objectives with the case, challenging the questions set may be a good thing.

3. *Is significant rework required?* Question changes can lead to significant rework and increase the chances that the project will be delivered late. It may be necessary to collect more data about the case organisation and even rewrite segments of the case itself – in situations where you are responsible for writing the case as well as conducting the analysis. This could be problematic if the realisation of the need to change the questions only comes after a significant passage of time: 30% – 40% – 50% into the project duration. It could mean that segments of text in the case body are discarded, and that components of analytical work already conducted become redundant. It would also mean that the remaining time of the project is spent under considerable time pressure.

4. *Is there a need to change the case completely?* In some situations, the student case analyst may want to change their case organisation and strategic issue, having embarked on the process of developing questions for the case and even conducting some preliminary analysis. Reasons for this are plenty: (1) new information coming to light that alters the considerations for case choice, (2) a change of personal circumstances for the student – such as a change of job – that could impact the meaningfulness of a particular case choice, or (3) new cases or phenomena emerging in the public domain that inspire the student to alter case choice. In these types of scenarios, it is not only the questions for analysis that will change, but the underlying case material and evidence. This is potentially highly risky, especially if it requires the student to develop a completely new case, having already started one. The same issues of time management and time pressure apply as in the previous point. However, it may be the right thing to do, a consequence of a critical reflection and a student who is in touch with their future and the overall role of a strategic business case analysis in that future.

If any of these – or similar – situations occur, it is highly advisable to discuss them with your supervisor or course instructor. Higher education institutions and programmes will have some flexibility and tolerance as far as changes to the delivery date for your work – please check!

Action box

- Can you think of any research projects or consultancy assignments that you have worked on that have required a redevelopment and evolution of questions for analysis? Reflect on an example of this and make a note of the circumstances and how the reformulated questions impacted the final outcomes.
- What potential risks and hazards could arise in your case analysis? Could you put a risk score (e.g., high, medium, low) on the chance of any of the risks mentioned above occurring (changing the purpose of the case, confronting the instructor on any questions set, needing to undertake significant rework of the case, needing to choose an entirely new case)?

FORMER STUDENT VOICES

Reflection from Nick Waters MBA (airline pilot and lawyer):

Our brief was to base the strategic case analysis around a 'decision point', a pivot point or event that the organisation arrived at because of a combination of everything that had gone before, maybe combined with some current circumstances.

Consider it a fork in the road. From the organisation's point of view this point could be a great success, a failure, or a catastrophic failure. It depends on your chosen story but a significant part of the strategic case analysis for me was asking questions about the story up to that decision point – what was happening in the industry, the world, what were its competitors doing, why did my chosen organisation make the decisions it made within that framework, and would I have made the same decisions?

In my chosen case, the organisation did ultimately fail but that was not my decision point. I chose a point several years before where the organisation needed a second round of investment. This enabled me to analyse the industry, competition, and changing business models running up to this point. I probed into what the organisation had done following the first round to improve its competitive position, why had it failed, and what actions were taken following the second round?

Don't worry about setting the questions in stone at the beginning, what you will find is that as you write and dig into the material, further questions arise that may be very interesting. You can always redefine the scope of the work. Just remember to string it all together in the finished document. If you say you are going to analyse A, B, and C, then make sure the answers are for A, B, and C. If you find D interesting on the way, make sure it's clear why!

Reflection from Katherine Neufield MBA (government analyst):

What I did was a lot of background reading on change management. I looked at the work of Julie Hodges and at the Association of Change Management Professionals. Understanding change management frameworks, and then sitting down and trying to figure out the story of what is going on with employees, managers, and executives within the case organisation. I asked the questions: what is the story from beginning to end? And then I queried subsequent performance and outcomes, including how everybody felt about the whole change process.

It was interesting for me because I came from a very quantitative background. And I was coming into this very messy context – a new area for me. I asked about what were the bumps that were happening? And was there something that the organisation could do differently at each step? Projects are often considered as a linear process, whereas AI is a circular process. It is important to know how we deal with that. What did the organisation do to inform employees and management executives? How much engagement was there with the employees, the managers, and the executives? Engagement was a critical problem area in my chosen case to dig deeper into.

What was important was that everybody recognised that there was a need for this case analysis. There was an awareness of why a change needs to be happening. But what had to happen was being willing to accept an AI solution to be brought in to help deal with a deluge of work. The organisation couldn't staff people fast enough to handle this work.

KEY TAKEAWAYS

The following are key learning points from this chapter:

- Be inquisitive as you set out on your strategic business case analysis; this can be formalised and articulated in the activity of question definition
- Deciding the questions for analysis will set the stage for developing critical thinking skills as you progress throughout the project
- Adopting one and only one overarching question – such as the one posed by the protagonists in the case – will limit your inquiry and its impact; it can be valuable to develop a hierarchy of questions in a question tree as part of your preparation work
- There are various characteristics of 'good' case questions identified in the methods literature and from several fields of work, including having questions that are answerable in the time allowed, those that invoke critical and integrative thinking, those that are higher-order, and those that are balanced
- It is worthwhile appreciating that research questions in case analysis projects often evolve over time; be prepared to allow this to happen but also be prepared to manage the risks involved and discuss risk situations with your institution.

REFLECTIVE PRACTICE TASK

Review the outcomes and your answers to the action boxes above. These relate to: (1) formulating questions; (2) how many questions to use; (3) characteristics of 'good' case questions; (4) question development as a process. Reflect further on the following questions:

1. What?
   What do you conclude about question-setting for a strategic business case analysis?
2. So what?
   Why does it matter to both think carefully about your initial questions for analysis while being open to the chance that they will need changing as the project progresses?
3. Now what?
   Now that you have done some preparation work for your strategic business case analysis, you are about to embark on the core analytical work. How should you think about approaching this challenge? The next section of the book will give you guidance in this respect.

ADDITIONAL READINGS AND RESOURCES

Developing research questions

https://research.com/research/how-to-write-a-research-question

Brooks, A. W., & John, L. K. (2018). The surprising power of questions. *Harvard Business Review*, 96(3), 60–67. www.forbes.com/sites/mikemyatt/2016/06/12/the-50-most-powerful-questions-leaders-can-ask

NOTE

1 Tree Analysis – Fault, Cause, Question and Success – Investigations of a Dog (investigationsquality.com), accessed November 24, 2022.

Conducting a strategic business case analysis

CHAPTER 5

The Case Analysis Spectrum

HORSES FOR COURSES

If you have worked through the previous chapters of this book and completed all the action boxes, you should now have: (1) an identified case that you will use as a basis for your strategic business case analysis, (2) a clear definition of the strategic issue at the heart of the case, (3) a firm handle on the nature of context in the case, and (4) a refined set of research questions for your case, structured as a question tree. So, what happens next?

What happens next is that you move from preparation into the analysis stage. Having gone through the preparation of case choice, placing the case in context, and defining the central questions, the jump into analysis should be less of a jump and more like a seamless transition. The careful forethought that you have given to the project will already have got you thinking analytically.

Case studies are a type of research strategy, and there is no one single one way of conducting them (Verschuren, 2003; Yin, 2011). What matters is that there is coherence in how research methods and techniques are used for analysing case material (Verschuren, 2003). It is up to the case analyst to choose which research methods and techniques to utilise within a case study, and how to seek coherence in their use. The approach we will take is to use an overarching framework for analysis that will help generate coherence in case work. This framework provides a basis for understanding fundamentally different approaches for analysing a business case strategically, and for you to make decisions as far as your own research approach is concerned.

Verschuren (2003) notes that cases can be observed "either as a whole or as a conglomeration of different parts or aspects" (p. 124). This distinction is particularly useful as it provides a basis for taking an overall analytical stance towards a case. If we see the case as a conglomeration of different parts, we need to ask ourselves whether all those parts are essential in the analysis. They may be. They may not be. It will depend on the research questions for the case and the analyst's interest in the case. If we see the case as a whole; a single object – albeit a complex one – we will be able to uncover variables omitted by a 'selective parts' approach, and we will be able to trace path dependence over time (Bennett & Elman, 2006). In a nutshell, we can think of our choices for analytical stance being on a spectrum from reductionist on the one hand to holistic on the other.

At one end of the spectrum are *reductionist* approaches for case analysis: dissecting the case into several discrete components and analysing each of those components separately

DOI: 10.4324/9781003288916-7

before connecting the results together to form an overall conclusion. Components can be defined in different ways depending on the nature of the case, the type of organisation and strategic issue, and the time periods in the case. This can be supported by mapping lower levels of the question tree onto discrete analytical units. Another approach is to create components for analysis based on discrete periods of time in the case (e.g., > 3 years before the decision point, < 3 years before the decision point but greater than 1 month, and less than 1 month before the decision point). For a case on an international company, another approach could be to divide the analysis into components for different countries mentioned in the case. In many situations these ways of reducing the case into discrete components of analysis will correspond with the question tree; indeed, it will help if they do.

At the other end of the spectrum are *holistic* approaches for case analysis. This entails viewing the case as a single whole and using a systems approach for analysis. This will emphasise inter-dependency between many and different variables, as well as considering feedback loops and nonlinear relationships when making sense of complexity in the case. Taking a holistic approach pays respect to the uniqueness and complexity of the case. It acknowledges that the lowest level for understanding the case is in its entirety (Hatcher & Tofts, 2004).

At the mid-point are *hybrid* approaches. Here, elements of both reductionist and systems thinking may apply. The logic with hybrid approaches is that benefits of both reductionism and holism can be drawn on without invoking their weaknesses. However, this is not as straightforward as it sounds, and careful consideration should be paid to this stance when evaluating how to proceed with the analysis. These analytical positions are discussed below with reference to the literature, their pros and cons are summarised, and situations in which they may be optimally utilised identified.

REDUCTIONISM

Reductionism involves the breaking down of a larger analytical component into smaller, lower-level units of analysis, and then studying the lower-level parts separately. It has been argued this is a natural way for humans to analyse complex problems as we are naturally reductionist in our sensory observation (Verschuren, 2001). It is deeply embedded in scientific culture (Dongping, 2007). Wood and Caldas (2001) note that the process of reducing complex problems into smaller more manageable chunks is something that has been formatted into our minds as humans. It is not surprising then, that reductionism is discussed in a diverse array of research settings, including life sciences (Kaiser, 2011), chemistry and physics (Chang, 2015), psychology (Richardson, 1979), law (Smith, 1991), as well as in organisational and business settings (Wood and Caldas, 2001).

A central assumption when adopting a reductionist stance for analysis is that the laws that apply at one level also apply at lower levels, even though the terminology used at different levels may differ (Andersen, 2001). Some talk of this in terms of a vertical integration of laws and explanations between levels (Slingerland, 2008). Andersen (2001) argues there are two conditions for the laws applicable at one level (a primary level) to be applicable at a lower (secondary) level. The first of these is a *condition of connectability*. This means that terms used at the primary level are linked to different terms used at a secondary level. The second is the *condition of derivability*. This means that any laws applicable at the secondary level can be derived from laws at the primary level.

Although much of the reductionism literature has been written in natural sciences and medicine (Andersen, 2001; Heng, 2008), these principles can be applied in the social sciences and in the study of strategic business cases. If we take a reductionist stance to analyse a strategic business case, we implicitly accept that concepts of interest and laws (i.e., what we reasonably expect to be the relationship between variables) at a primary level are connected to those at secondary levels. For instance, let's assume we are analysing a multinational enterprise (MNE) that is grappling with how its international human resource management (IHRM) policy can enhance its overall financial performance. If we take a reductionist stance, we can conduct separate analyses in different overseas subsidiaries of the enterprise. We assume that there is a relationship between incentives used for employees in a specific overseas subsidiary and productivity in that subsidiary unit and that this can help explain the relationship between IHRM and financial performance at corporate level. The term we use at a corporate level is IHRM policy, while at the lower level we consider specific incentives used in given locations (pay, bonuses, working environment, training). The condition of connectability is met because the terms used in the analysis at a lower level are connected to the general constructs of interest at the primary level. The condition of derivability is met because the logic for relating HRM practice to performance at a corporate level is used within the separate analyses.

Wimsatt (2006) differentiates between types of reduction. On the one hand, *successional reduction* concerns theory succession on a single level of analysis. It relates to creating explanations 'intra-level', allowing comparisons (approximations) to be made on that level. We could imagine an explanation of market performance of a firm at time t1 and then compare it to an explanation at time t2 in this way. The unit of analysis is the same, the overall firm. On the other hand, *inter-level explanation* is about providing accounts of upper-level phenomena using identities and localisations at lower levels. We could imagine explaining the upper-level sales performance of a whole firm because of the lower-level incentives and motivation of employees in a sales and marketing department in this way. The analogue in science, as described by Wimsatt (2006) would be "explaining the behavior of gases as clouds of colliding molecules" (p. 448).

Reductionists argue a key part of the analytical transition from an upper level to multiple lower levels lies in the *organisation* of those sub-parts. Although many of the examples given by reductionist scholars are in the natural sciences, the principle that the organisation of analytical components into a logical and coherent structure will matter for a strategic business case analysis within management and business studies also applies. As Wimsatt (2006) notes: "One moves to successively smaller parts in successive reductions, but in each transition, much of the explanatory weight is borne by the organization of those parts into larger mechanisms explaining the behaviour of the higher-level system" (p. 458). For reductionism to work in a strategic business case analysis, the case will need to be broken down into sub-parts for individual analysis and then the results of these sub-analyses combined to form an explanation and answer to the questions in the case. This implies a rather linear process of tackling one part at a time and then combining the outcomes of each discrete sub-analysis when considering the overall questions of the case. This linear nature of reductionism is noted in the literature (Verschuren, 2001).

HOLISM

Holism concerns the treatment of a phenomenon as an integrated whole, commonly associated with the familiar expression: 'a whole that is greater than the sum of its parts.' Rather than reducing a case analysis into sub-parts, holistic analysis is conducted at the primary, system level. The term is not new; it was originally coined by the 'Father of Holism', Jan Smuts in 1926. Holism is found in various fields, including medicine – particularly Eastern medicine (McMillan, Stanga & Van Sell, 2018), education (Mahmoudi, Jafari, Nasrabadi & Liaghatdar, 2012), social sciences (Verschuren, 2001), and in organisational fields such as corporate social responsibility (CSR) (Caputo, 2021). In medicine, McMillan et al. (2018) note how "Mind, body, and spirit (MBS) are interconnected elements that make up the person and cannot be separated into individual parts" (p. 2). We can apply this metaphor to the analysis of complex strategic issues in organisations.

Another metaphor we can use is that of the sports team, such as a football team (Verschuren, 2001). As Verschuren notes, even if there are highly talented individuals in a team, it may underperform "because of a lack of team spirit, communication, adequate tactics and strategies and mutual understanding" (p. 401). The team metaphor is very interesting to consider as we are concerned with the analysis of strategic issues in cases that involve organisations. It is interesting for various reasons: the sports team is a social system (just like an organisation), there will be a manager who makes decisions about how to deploy human resources (just like in an organisation), and the team will go up against competitors who also need to abide by the same rules of the game and who pose threats to the team (just like in many organisations). Factors such as team spirit (think organisational culture), communication (think intra-organisational knowledge flows), and mutual understanding (think trust between employees) are all vital to performance in sports teams, just as they are in organisations. These factors, holists would argue, and the relationship between them and with performance, are difficult to assess in a reductionist way as they are all highly interrelated.

Holism is associated with the use of systems thinking, i.e., ways of examining phenomena as complex systems rather than individual parts (Andersen, 2001). Radical transformations in society, including organisational and social change and wicked problems are better understood with systems approaches that capture this complexity (Basile & Caputo, 2017; Dominici, 2012; Grewatsch, Kennedy & Bansal, 2021) rather than with reductionist, causal models. Wicked problems are those complex global challenges such as climate change, inequality, and natural capital degradation that have fundamental implications for humans, but without clear solutions.

Systems thinking is more of a philosophy for analysing problems than a specific collection of tools and methods (Goodman, 1997). According to Goodman (1997), systems thinking involves visualising a problem in as full and complete a way as possible, moving from observation of data and events to a complete understanding of the determinants of patterns that change in time. Systems approaches normally involve the creation of systems diagrams, representations that depict the richness of the phenomenon under scrutiny (Jennings, 1997), including causal loop diagrams that show the interrelationships between variables, including bi-directional and feedback loops that are difficult to model in a reductionist manner (Goodman, 1997). Such diagrams can help in capturing this complexity.

According to Dominici (2012), systems thinking for organisations allows for complex interactions between the internal and external environments of the organisation to be captured. This is very fluid in nature, not well captured with a rigid hierarchy or pyramid metaphor. The requirement to emphasise fluidity is a response to the dynamic and unpredictable nature of the environment. It places an emphasis on intangible assets of the firm (Dominici, 2012). Grewatsch et al. (2021) argue that strategic management scholars need to embrace systems thinking when dealing with wicked problems. It is not just a theory or a paradigm, but also a belief system, a perspective, and a method that has practical relevance. The core principles of systems thinking include: (1) it is a relational view, incorporating interrelationships between many variables within the system being analysed, (2) it is an open view, emphasising multiple open systems interacting with each other, (3) it synthesises multiple emergent properties of a phenomenon into an integrated whole, (4) it allows circularity and feedback loops between variables of interest, (5) it emphasises a hierarchy of nested systems, with higher-order ones changing less frequently than lower-order ones, (6) behaviour within the system is difficult to predict as the system can constantly self-organise (Grewatsch et al., 2021).

In contrast to the linear nature of reductionism, a holistic approach to research strategy is more likely to be 'iterative-parallel' in nature (Verschuren, 2001). This means various distinctive elements of the research process are possible, including: the carrying out of research activities in an unplanned order, the sequence of research activities being dependent on what one finds as one goes along, a reciprocal relationship between case data and theory, and even analysing the research material while writing the report (Verschuren, 2001).

HYBRIDISM

Having reviewed the basic characteristics of reductionism and holism and made the point that both stances are possible to use in a strategic business case analysis, the question arises whether these two poles are really the only options for the case analyst? Is there a middle ground that might combine the benefits of both reductionism and holism? The answer to this will be dependent on the nature of the case being analysed, the strategic issue at the centre of the case, the questions for analysis and the analyst's own preferences. But it is nevertheless an important one to consider for any case analysis because scholars have shown that blending elements of reductionism and holism in the analysis of one case is not only possible … it can lead to fruitful outcomes. We refer to this possibility as a 'hybrid' stance.

Williams and Steriu (2022) use a mixed methods approach for exploring the nature of foreign entry mode and social investment in conflict zones by MNEs, using the case of the Dutch brewer Heineken. The article is essentially a single case of one MNE, and the data used comprises both quantitative and qualitative components. The quantitative component relates to several discrete foreign market entries made by Heineken in developing countries, including war zones, over an 18-year period. This part of the analysis ('Study 1') is very much in the reductionist camp. It examines the effect of violent deaths in the target country on the likelihood of Heineken investing in a wholly owned subsidiary (versus a minority owned investment) as well as the likelihood of it making a greenfield investment as opposed to an acquisition. The key finding from this reductionist approach is that the trend of violent deaths in the host country has a significant impact on the likelihood of investing in a wholly owned subsidiary (a worsening context of violence will lower the propensity for full control).

The qualitative component ('Study 2') is more holistic in nature because it synthesises violent death trend, entry strategy, as well as subsequent social investments in the local communities by Heineken in the years following the entry. Although this part of the analysis was only done for the sub-cases of Heineken Ethiopia and Heineken Myanmar, it emphasises the interrelationships between a broader set of variables that co-evolve over time, the nesting of relationships, and the complex interactions between an organisation and its environment over time. Furthermore, Study 2 helps address a wicked problem (the role of an MNE in contributing to the conditions for peace in a war-torn country).

What this example illustrates is that it is possible to incorporate elements of both reductionism and holism in a single case analysis. While this might not be suitable for all strategic business cases, it is worthwhile considering this stance as a viable option.

Hybridism in a strategic business case analysis will entail elements of both reductionism and holism at some point in the analytical design. It could be that a reductionist study precedes a more holistic analysis (as in Williams & Steriu, 2022). It might also be that a holistic analysis precedes a more reductionist one. In this sense, there can be a sequential ordering of different types of analytical work on the same case – and the same strategic issue – with these different steps being rooted in reductionism and holism respectively. One part will therefore be narrower and more focused, and another part broader and more integrative. It is also possible that both reductionist and holistic techniques are used in parallel to make sense of different aspects of the case alongside each other, rather than one leading to another. For instance, while developing a holistic analysis of a case using qualitative data and systems approaches, the analyst could also collect specific numeric data on organisation-level performance and run a statistical test on a narrow set of variables.

Finally, a more nuanced approach could be to assess the basic tenets of reductionism and holism and decide that, for each of those tenets, a middle-ground is desirable and feasible. Table 5.1 provides an illustration of this. It shows several analytical considerations for the case analyst to deliberate on, along with key features of reductionism and holism for each of those considerations. On the right-hand side, we see how these features could be interpreted as a hybrid form, with the objective of gaining the maximum analytical benefit by combining elements from both.

Attempts to bridge the divide between reductionism and holism have been made in different ways and various fields. In microbiology, it has been noted that it is possible to balance the imperatives for utmost control on the one hand (reductionism) and irreducible complexity (holism) on the other by studying phenomena at medium levels of complexity and establishing the interplay between different types of complexity (Tecon, Mitri, Ciccarese, Or, van der Meer & Johnson, 2019). In the field of supply chain management, scholars have shown how systems can be transitioned from reductionist to holistic supply chain solutions through simulation, while identifying challenges to fully holistic solutions

TABLE 5.1 The Case Analysis Spectrum

Analytical consideration (selected reference)	Reductionist stance	Holistic stance	Hybrid stance: drawing from reductionism and holism
Key objects of interest (Verschuren, 2001)	Narrow set of variables and attributes with uni-directional relationships between them; multiple analytical tasks	Patterns; attributes of groups and larger entities in a synthesised analysis	Expanded set of variables with different types of relationships (uni-, bi-directional, feedback) to understand overall pattern; use of thematic grouping
Level of analysis (Grewatsch et al., 2021)	Firm-level	Macro-level	Elements of both firm- and macro-level, including different measures of performance
Role of researcher (Verschuren, 2001)	Distance from the phenomenon	Interacting with the phenomenon	Maintaining distance on some aspects, being closer or involved with the phenomenon on other aspects
Use of diagrams to make sense of the phenomenon (Jennings, 1997)	Simple diagrams showing direct, mediating, and moderating effects	Complex diagrams with many variables, relationships and depicting evolution over time	Use of both simple and systems level diagrams at different points during the analysis
Laws across levels (Andersen, 2001)	Laws at one level will be applicable to other levels, assuming connectability and derivability	Laws apply to the overall system; however, stochastic unpredictability may mean they break down at lower levels	Accept that some laws may be applicable across levels, other laws might be level-specific
Type of problem most suited (Grewatsch et al., 2021)	Problems that can be logically broken down into sub-parts	Wicked problems; extremely complex and unpredictable environments	Problems that are not necessarily wicked problems but moderate–high in terms of complexity

when collaborations break down (Ponte, Costas, Puche, De la Fuente & Pino, 2016). And in the field of sustainability, Gasparatos, El-Haram and Horner (2008) do not see reductionism as the opposite of holism. The authors make the point that they address different things: holism for understanding a complete system and reductionism for assisting with specific areas of decision-making. Their work on assessing tools to measure environmental impact show different tools embrace criteria for holism to different extents. They point to the criticisms of reductionism for sustainability policy making, while showing that tools that are in place do not fully embrace holism either. Gasparatos et al. (2008) highlight

FIGURE 5.1 Hybridism inherits features of reductionism and holism

how analysts and stakeholders need to understand the assumptions of tools and metrics used for environmental assessment and combine them in appropriate ways. These examples from different fields of literature serve to illustrate the potential bridges that exist in the reductionism–holism debate. For the purpose of performing a strategic business case analysis, a key decision will be how to position the project on the notional spectrum of reductionism–hybridism–holism (Figure 5.1).

POSITIONING YOUR ANALYSIS ON THE SPECTRUM

Returning to the message at the top of this chapter, there is no one single way to analyse complex strategic business cases. There are quite literally hundreds of quantitative and qualitative techniques, many of which serve to reduce the phenomenon to smaller chunks of analysis, and some that act as systems tools for examining cases holistically (Goodman, 1997). Remember, we want the use of research methods and techniques in our case analysis to be coherent (Verschuren, 2003), ultimately providing clear answers to the research questions and justifying those answers.

The purpose of determining a position for your own case analysis in terms of reductionism–hybridism–holism is to allow the analytical tasks that follow to be coherent and for the answers they yield to be justified. As a case analyst, determine where you sit on this spectrum before you invest significant time and effort on analytical tasks. It is worthwhile thinking in advance of analytical tasks about the advantages and disadvantages of each position on the spectrum and answering the question of what it is in your case that makes you lean towards one position over another. This may not be a clear-cut task with overwhelming support for one position over the others. But it should provide a basis on which to proceed, one that you are comfortable with, and one that fits the case data captured in the case.

Table 5.1 shows some basic characteristics of the different stances. It can act as a starting point for positioning your case. Table 5.2 takes this one step further and gives suggestions about when you might want to adopt each stance based on certain features of the case. It also brings in wider considerations, such as the potential impact of the case analysis and the extent to which the analyst is distanced from the case. These are considerations as you determine the overall analytical stance for your work.

Table 5.2 should be seen as a basis for applying certain criteria for deciding which stance to adopt for a strategic business case analysis. It can be developed further and augmented with additional criteria that you consider to be relevant. Qualifiers such as 'high' (versus 'low') and 'some' (versus 'many') are deliberately not measured quantitatively or given

TABLE 5.2 Illustrative scenarios for analytical stance

Criterion	A reductionist stance would be appropriate when …	A holistic stance would be appropriate when …	A hybrid stance would be appropriate when …
Nature of strategic issue at heart of case	• Easily decomposable	• Many, diverse aspects, not easily separated	• Multiple aspects, some of which can be thematically grouped
Nature of contexts in which the case is embedded	• Small number of dominant contexts • Dominant contexts not changing over time during case	• Many overlapping contexts, no one single dominant • High context dynamism	• Moderate number of contexts • Moderate context dynamism
Nature of the question tree	• Clear sequencing and path dependency between questions	• Many branches of the tree • Diverse and open questions	• Some areas of path dependency between questions • Other areas more open and disjointed
Potential impact of case analysis	• The analysis has a narrow purpose to aid a specific decision for the main protagonist	• Case is meaningful to global challenges and UN SDGs • Many stakeholders have interest in case analysis outcome	• Will aid decision-making for core case and address a single SDG or other stakeholders
Position of the analyst relative to the case	• High distance from the case organisation; has not worked or interfaced with the organisation • Does not have access to primary or ethnographic data	• Is an employee, manager, or partner in the value chain of the organisation at the heart of the case • Has access to copious primary or ethnographic data	• Has some experience interacting or working with the case organisation • Has some experience with the strategic issue

fixed numeric limits on which to be applied. This would be very dangerous and potentially erroneous, given the diversity of cases and high variety of strategic issues, contexts, and organisations described in them. When applying Table 5.2, think less in terms of quantifying these boundary points, and more in terms of your own interpretation of where your case would sit, given each criterion. If you end up with some items suggesting a reductionist stance, and some suggesting a holistic stance, then a hybrid stance would make sense as it allows the blending of both reductionist and holistic techniques. In Chapter 6 we will examine common approaches and tools that can be used in each of these stances.

KEY TAKEAWAYS

The following are key learning points from this chapter:

- Reductionism and holism are umbrella terms for collections of techniques that can be used in scientific and social scientific analysis
- They have been debated and applied in various fields, including natural sciences, not just in social sciences and business studies
- Some scholars argue they are opposites, while others see them as being useful for different types of analysis
- We use the term 'hybridism' in this book as a way of combining certain elements of reductionism and holism in the same analysis
- Analysts of complex strategic business cases will benefit by thinking clearly about the pros and cons of reductionism, holism, and hybridism as an overall stance, before embarking on specific analysis tasks
- The choice of overall stance will determine the type of analytical tasks performed in a strategic business case analysis project.

REFLECTIVE PRACTICE TASK

Reflect on the reductionism–hybridism–holism Case Analysis Spectrum and consider each stance as a way of framing the analysis work for your chosen case and strategic issue. Reflect further on the following questions:

1. What?

   What are the relative pros and cons for each stance as far as your chosen case and strategic issue are concerned?
2. So what?

   Why should you weigh these pros and cons carefully before you engage in analytical tasks?
3. Now what?

   Which stance do you feel most comfortable proceeding with? If one stance does not stand out, what other information do you need to obtain to make the decision?

ADDITIONAL READINGS AND RESOURCES

More on holism

Erickson, H. L. (23007). Philosophy and theory of holism. *Nursing Clinics of North America, 42*(2), 139–163.

More on reductionism

Gallagher, R., & Appenzeller, T. (1999). Beyond reductionism. *Science, 284*(5411), 79.

Nagel, T. (2007, September). Reductionism and antireductionism. In *The Limits of Reductionism in Biology: Novartis Foundation Symposium 213* (pp. 3–14). John Wiley & Sons.

More on hybridism

Zhou, Y., Zhang, Y., & Liu, J. (2012). A hybridism model of differentiated human resource management effectiveness in Chinese context. *Human Resource Management Review, 22*(3), 208–219.

CHAPTER 6

Approaches and tools along the Case Analysis Spectrum

DEVELOPING THE TOOLKIT

This chapter discusses examples of tools that may be used in reductionist, holistic, and hybrid modes of strategic business case analysis. While this is not an exhaustive list of analytical tools, it will provide a basis for moving from the analytical positioning of the previous chapter to the more practical phase of conducting analysis work. Think of this as a toolkit for analysis. Some useful approaches are provided here, but many more exist in the universe of analytical work. The case analyst should appreciate the pros and cons of different tools, how they fit with the nature of the underlying data, and how they align with the stance adopted on the Case Analysis Spectrum for a given case and strategic issue. The analyst should also consider their own skill level and prior experience in using these types of tools, as additional training in tool use will be a consideration for managing and progressing through the project. Undertaking new training on tools or software will undoubtedly benefit the analyst and can be seen as an opportunity for human capital development and learning. However, this may come with an upfront price tag in terms of both time and money.

A tool is a device for performing a specific function, 'aiding in the accomplishment of a task'.[1] Humans have evolved over thousands of years by developing and using tools to solve problems. Tools have become more and more sophisticated in this process, guided by advancements in scientific research and knowledge. It is in our fundamental nature to develop and use tools to solve problems facing us. And as we advance and make progress, we find limitations in existing tools and strive to develop new ones. Taking this mindset into the challenge of a strategic business case analysis will be fruitful, especially given case complexity and the fact that no two cases are the same. Some of the tools discussed below might be useful, others not listed may need to be identified and understood. Yet others may need to be adapted or developed for the specific analytical challenge of a given strategic business case.

As part of this process of toolkit development, students should consider conducting an academic literature review to identify research that has already been done on the specific question and strategic issue at the heart of their case. Such a systematic literature review will allow the identification of analytical tools used by academic scholars in research on that specific issue. Systematic literature reviews are a methodology in their own right, common in academic fields with relevance to strategic business cases such as planning research (Xiao & Watson, 2019), entrepreneurship research (Kraus, Breier & Dasí-Rodríguez,

DOI: 10.4324/9781003288916-8

2020), software engineering (Kitchenham, Brereton, Budgen, Turner, Bailey & Linkman, 2009), and healthcare (Purssell & McCrae, 2020). Xiao and Watson (2019) describe eight steps for a systematic literature review: (1) formulating the problem, (2) developing and validating the review protocol, (3) searching the literature, (4) screening for inclusion, (5) assessing quality, (6) extracting data, (7) analysing and synthesising data, and (8) reporting findings. Steps (1) and (2) constitute planning for review, steps (3) to (7) are the conducting of the review, and step (8) is reporting of the review. Other scholars describe similar processes for systematic literature reviews (e.g., Kraus et al., 2020).

Systematic literature reviews in strategic business case analysis can be useful for identifying the types of tools used previously by researchers in analysing case data. In other words, they can be used to gain an overview of the toolkit in use for a given strategic issue. Much academic work is based on case data, and literature reviews can be used to assess the types of tools used in analysing cases by filtering only on articles that use case research. Many research articles use different empirical approaches, including high sample size secondary data and primary data across lower numbers of cases. These types of articles can also be useful to assess analytical tools to use for a strategic issue in a strategic business case analysis. Cases often contain different types of data, including high-n transactional data (e.g., investments made by a focal company over a multi-year period, or performance data on multiple units within a healthcare trust) as well as textual data. So, within the same case analysis, statistical techniques found in high-n studies can be used alongside qualitative techniques.

Approaching the analytical activity for a strategic business case analysis with a mindset for tool development is not only about surveying prior literature to see how others previously have examined the strategic issue. It is possible to get confused and lost in the ocean of published research, and most management and executive students are not (yet) accomplished scholars or users of sophisticated analytical techniques. It will be important to filter out the techniques that do not apply, appraise the ones that might apply, and be ready to augment, combine, or develop new approaches if necessary. This process should be guided by the nature of the strategic issue, the contents of the case at hand (e.g., highly qualitative vs. highly quantitative), and the positioning adopted on the Case Analysis Spectrum. If in doubt, students should seek guidance from their supervisor and institution. It is entirely possible to feel overwhelmed by the volume and complexity of offerings in the 'universe of tools'. Knowing which ones to select and how to apply them can be a daunting task for students who have spent much of their careers managing and leading organisations, rather than analysing them academically. To this end, taking a stance on the Case Analysis Spectrum can be useful as it will help narrow down the array of tools that can be applied in a strategic business case analysis.

APPLYING REDUCTIONISM TO A STRATEGIC BUSINESS CASE ANALYSIS

As noted in the previous chapter, reductionism is all about breaking a problem down into manageable chunks and analysing those chunks separately. It has been argued to be a natural way for humans to analyse problems (Verschuren, 2001), and will come as natural to many. Most academic studies in the field of business and management have a reductionist nature – articles focus on a narrow research question, use a narrow set of data and selection of variables, and a limited set of tools. This does not mean they are invalid or unhelpful. It means that multiple studies need to be combined to establish the overall state of knowledge of a given organisational phenomenon, for instance through a meta-analysis (Field & Gillett, 2010), or a systematic literature review (Kraus et al., 2020; Xiao & Watson, 2019).

To build our toolkit, we consider two families of reductionist tools, one for quantitative data and one for qualitative data.

1. *Quantitative reductionism*: Quantitative data is data that is captured and presented in numeric form. It will contain variables representing different aspects of the phenomenon in the case. The key point from the reductionist standpoint is that the collection of variables will be only a subset of all the information possible in the case. Some variables can be treated as dependent variables – the outcomes we are trying to explain (e.g., performance, growth, carbon emissions). Other variables can be considered independent or explanatory variables – the elements that may cause the outcomes to occur (e.g., marketing investment, R&D investment, number of employees, training). These variables are normally presented in tables in the exhibits and appendices of the case, although they can occur in the body of the case too. Quantitative data might also be the result of additional data collection conducted by the student as part of the analytical work. Tools in this area include visualisation and statistical tools and are available in software packages such as Excel, MATLAB, SAS, SPSS, and Stata. The tools within these software packages allow quantitative data to be understood and relationships (associations) between variables to be established.

    a. *Descriptive statistics*: These allow for the characteristics of the quantitative data to be understood. Variables will have certain characteristics, such as a mean (the average value), a median (the middle value when all the values are sorted), a mode (the most repeated value). They will also have a minimum and maximum value, and a standard deviation around the mean. While many descriptive statistics are calculated as numeric values, visualisation techniques can also be used to understand the nature of variables. These include the plotting of distribution of variables by frequency occurring in the data set – histograms.

    b. *Correlations*: These can be used to show associations between pairs of variables. They can be used in a reductionist stance when focusing on a small number of variables within one sub-analysis. Correlations show the extent to which one variable changes (goes up or down), as another variable changes. Since the correlations are between pairs of variables, these are often referred to as bi-variate correlations. Correlations are captured as a correlation coefficient, and this can have a positive value or a negative value. Correlation coefficients come with a degree of significance attached – indicating the extent to which the association has not occurred by chance. Note that different types of correlation tests exist, depending on the distribution of the underlying data. A Pearson coefficient (known as r) is used when the variables entered are normally distributed. A Kendall *tau* or Spearman *rho* coefficient can be used when the data is ranked (also known as non-parametric). Chi-square tests can be used to analyse contingency tables of two dimensions of categorical variables, where the frequency is known for each combination of the categories.

c. *Comparing groups*: In many instances it is necessary to compare between two or more groups of quantitative data. For instance, the numeric data in a case may include performance in various organisational units before and after a certain event or intervention. It may contain operational information at an individual employee level across different parts of the organisation, such as different foreign subsidiaries of an international company or different doctor surgeries in a hospital trust. A key question for the analyst can relate to whether there are differences between the groups. Different possibilities exist to assess differences between two or more groups. A t-test compares the means between two samples, showing which group, if any, has a higher a mean. An analysis of variance (ANOVA) test also compares means across groups but can also be used for more than two groups. ANOVA also allows relationships between variables to be established based on group composition, and in this respect is considered a form of regression model. Comparing of groups can be seen in a reductionist sense as it necessitates the decomposition of the case into discrete parts (i.e., the groups).

d. *Regression models*: This concerns an extremely wide array of tests that allow for the relationships between multiple variables to be established within the same model. While bivariate correlations only show association between two variables (albeit often tabularised within a set of variables), regression models are multivariate. They are used to establish whether there is a meaningful relationship between a dependent variable (the one we are trying to explain or understand) and one or more independent variables. Quite often we see large numbers of independent variables (including control variables) in regression modelling techniques. Different regression techniques can be used depending on the nature of the dependant variable. For instance, linear regression models work when the dependent variable is continuous in nature, while logistic models work when the dependent variable is binary (multinomial logistic regression when the dependent variable is categorical). The key point about regression modelling from a reductionism standpoint is that it allows for multiple variables to be accounted for at the same time. However, there is usually only one[2] dependent variable, aligning with the tradition of reductionism.

e. *Visualisation techniques*: These support reductionism when basic relationships between small numbers of variables need to be graphically depicted. Anyone familiar with Excel will have come across the charting tools available, including with pivot tables. Similar tools are available in other statistical packages, such as the powerful *twoway* function in Stata. The key point about visualisation techniques is that they allow for an intuitive exploration of the data. They help users to get a feel for the data and the possible relationships that are not apparent by simply looking at a table (or tables) of numbers. They also allow trends to be shown over time. The analyst can create new tables (the output of regression models) that convey the essence of inter-variable relationships to non-statisticians. One can benefit from increasingly sophisticated software to make charts and plots that are highly polished and professional, including the use of colour, annotations, and editing text for axes and legends.

A note on quantitative techniques: the choice of which tool to use will depend on the nature of the quantitative data, including what type of variables are in the data (continuous, categorical, ordinal), as well as the question that guides the analytical activity. Make sure you know what kind of variables you are dealing with and take time to think about what you want to get out of the analytical activity before you begin. If in doubt, consult your supervisor or instructor.

2. *Qualitative reductionism*: Most business cases in strategy will have a qualitative component. Qualitative data consists of text. There is text in the case document itself, describing the storyline of the case organisation within its context. Additional qualitative data will also be available for the case analyst to analyse, including newspaper articles, books, blogs about the focal organisation or the wider issue. Recorded interviews with senior managers, owners, and other stakeholders can also be treated as qualitative data; the same can be said of podcasts from journalists, academics, and subject matter experts. Recordings of these can be transcribed and analysed qualitatively. While qualitative data has more richness in depth and meaning than quantitative data (Ayres, Kavanaugh & Knafl, 2003), it can still be analysed within a reductionist stance. This happens when the data is broken down, coded, thematised, or structured in a way that is consistent with the partitioning of the problem into sub-parts (Wimsatt, 2006). Software packages for handling qualitative data tend to be different to the ones for analysing quantitative data. Popular examples include MAXQDA, QDA Miner, NVivo, and ATLAS.ti. Qualitative reductionism involves a focus on principal themes and variables to simplify and clarify a phenomenon. Unlike the techniques used in quantitative reductionism, the types of tools available to the analyst are very different.

    a. *Quotes*: Quotes are very commonly used in qualitative data analysis. They serve to demonstrate key points in the analysis by making a representation to the reader that the points are backed up by the opinions and experiences of key informants and subject matter experts. In a strategic business case analysis, quoting directly from the case text – or from quotes within the case text – should be cautioned against – at least too frequently – unless it is used to make a key point. It is likely the reader of the analysis will also have read the case and will not appreciate too much duplication. However, if the case analyst has gathered additional data from any of the sources mentioned above (such as additional interviews, publications, podcasts, blogs) then their use can be justified. Quotes do serve to bring the richness and 'reality' of the analysis to the fore. How many quotes to use, and which ones to focus on has not received a great deal of scientific guidance to date (Eldh, Årestedt & Berterö, 2020). Nevertheless, it is acknowledged that they serve less to validate findings and more to illustrate key points of the analysis (Eldh et al., 2020). From a reductionist standpoint, quotes can be used as a way for the analyst to selectively choose the evidence and support the points they want to make.

b.   *Thematic analysis*: Thematic analysis is all about reducing complexity in qualitative data into discrete themes. These themes can then be defined and used as a basis for further treatment, such as ranking and sorting, as well as articulating how the themes relate to each other. In a strategic business case analysis, the themes emanate from the case data (as opposed to, say, from a literature review of previous academic studies). Thematic analysis is not one specific tool – there is a wide range of approaches. Clarke, Braun and Hayfield (2015) describe six different forms: (1) inductive, (2) deductive, (3) semantic, (4) latent, (5) descriptive, and (6) interpretative. They note how thematic analysis can range from "relatively straightforward descriptive overviews of key features in data to more complex, conceptual readings of data that examine the theoretical implications of the analysis" (p. 226). They cite Braun and Clarke's (2006) six steps to conducting a thematic analysis: (1) familiarisation, (2) coding, (3) 'searching' for themes, (4) reviewing themes, (5) defining and naming themes, and (6) writing the report. At the heart of the search for themes is the coding and clustering of data to uncover thematic patterns. The next point on data structures discusses this further.

c.   *Data structures*: Qualitative data can be reduced into themes and depicted as a data structure (Gioia, Corley & Hamilton, 2013). This inductive approach has become very common in qualitative academic research in business and management; it provides a clear hierarchy of data as an output. This aids the reader of the analysis in understanding how the themes were derived. Examples can be found in various management disciplines, including entrepreneurship research (Fisher, Stevenson, Neubert, Burnell & Kuratko, 2020), research on innovation in the developing world (Williams et al., 2022), and complexity in supply chain management (Scheibe & Blackhurst, 2018). The approach is a systematic way for generating higher order themes (fewer in number) from lower order ones (greater in number). The process involves moving from first order codes to second order themes to aggregate dimensions. It serves as a reductionist tool because of this systematic process of theme generation and data structuring from what is typically highly complex and unstructured data.

d.   *Content analysis*: This is a technique for categorising text and allocating codes to the categories so that quantitative techniques can be run on those coded variables. It applies to both the manifest and latent content of the qualitative data. Manifest content is that which is conspicuous in the data and can be added up. Latent content refers to deeper meanings in the qualitative data (Saunders, Lewis & Thornhill, 2019, p. 573). Categories will be elements such as gender, age, unit, location. Counts can then be allocated to each of these categories to allow quantitative analysis and visualisation. When undertaking a content analysis of textual data, it is important to have a clear and transparent coding scheme, one that would yield the same outcome if it were conducted by another researcher. Variables that are allocated to categories should be mutually exclusive to avoid contamination or double counting. For instance, a foreign subsidiary's office building can only have one location, it cannot be in both Paris and London. Content analysis fits within a reductionist stance because it seeks to reduce the richness of latent qualitative data into discrete categories and codes.

e. *Visualising qualitative reductionism*: Visualisation techniques are not solely the purview of quantitative data analysis where the use of bar charts, scatter plots, and pie charts is common (Slone, 2009). Data structures, as noted above, essentially create a visualisation of the hierarchy of themes as interpreted by the analyst. Other visualisation techniques for qualitative data are also aligned with a reductionism stance. Henderson and Segal (2013) provide an excellent map of qualitative visualisation techniques, organised on two dimensions: (1) level of display, ranging from word ⇨ sentence ⇨ theme/narrative; and (2) complexity, ranging from simple to complex. The visualisations that are less complex (i.e., simple, or moderately complex) can be aligned with a reductionist stance as they emphasise key phrases, themes, and excerpts without guiding the viewer to consider the broader system of variables and how they interrelate within this system. The simple techniques include word clouds (at the word level), phrase nets (at the sentence level), and narrative excerpts (at the theme level). The moderately complex techniques include cluster analysis (at the word level), word trees (at the sentence level), and spectrum displays and matrices at the theme level (Henderson & Segal, 2013).

A note on qualitative techniques: as with the use of quantitative techniques for analysis, the choice of tool(s) to use will depend on the nature of the data and the line of questioning you are following. The Henderson and Segal (2013) article provides a useful overview of the types of qualitative techniques that can be used to visualise qualitative data. Techniques for data structuring or content analysis may require some additional reading of the methods literature or training. Don't forget to consult your supervisor or instructor.

APPLYING HOLISM TO A STRATEGIC BUSINESS CASE ANALYSIS

As discussed in the previous chapter, holism is all about treating a phenomenon as an integrated whole. This requires a different mindset to reductionist analysis; it requires systems thinking. With the reductionist techniques (quantitative and qualitative) described above, we break the case into sub-parts to identify and examine selected variables and how they relate to one another. System level analysis requires the analyst to see the case in its entirety and make sense of it 'as a whole'. So, how would one go about this in practice?

To answer this question, we draw from the body of work discussed by Professor Michael C. Jackson in his book *Systems Thinking and the Management of Complexity* (2019). Make no mistake: this is a nearly 700-page book, and we will not do it justice by drawing some of the main ideas from it to help us in our toolkit for a strategic case analysis. However, it represents, in the author's words, a proposition that "systems thinking [is] the only appropriate response to complexity" (Preface, p. xix).

Systems thinking is a range of methodologies that can be used in different types of complex situations. The aim here is to provide a very top-level view of some of the main ones, drawing from Jackson (2019):

1. *Systems thinking approaches*: Jackson (2019) describes the field of systems practice in detail, framing it in terms of a system of systems methodologies (SOSM). This is a framework for understanding different types of systems approaches that have evolved over the decades. SOSM consists of two dimensions: (1) complexity: simple ⇨ complicated ⇨ complex, and (2) stakeholders: unitary (a high degree of shared values) ⇨ pluralist (differences of values, which can be overcome) ⇨ coercive (where compromise is not possible). There are ten methodologies in total, which Jackson divides into six categories. The analyst needs to determine the main source of complexity to choose the appropriate approach and to be in a position to offer guidance on managing the complexity (Jackson, 2019, p. 169).

   a. *Technical complexity*: This relates to a quest for efficiency across all the subcomponents of the system. Tools under this category are rooted in hard systems thinking, systems analysis and operational research. It is necessary to clearly formulate the problem at the outset and then work through a series of stages including model building, scenario formulation, and comparing alternatives, optimisation and testing, and implementation and final operation. Across this somewhat linear project life cycle the analyst needs to engage in clear communications with decision-makers and stakeholders and encourage learning through model development and testing of model assumptions with stakeholders.

   b. *Process complexity*: This concerns the need to "tame complexity" (Jackson, 2019, p. 199) by implementing a process based on actions sequenced to deliver the desired outcomes. There is an emphasis on removing waste and inefficiency from a process, through targeted analysis and solution development. The Vanguard Method requires the analyst to go through three phases of work: (1) check – understanding the current system and causes of waste, (2) plan – deciding on a new purpose and how to improve it, and (3) do – testing and implementation of changes. Specific tools include demand analysis, capability charts, flow charts, systems pictures, and logic pictures.

   c. *Structural complexity*: This occurs when there are many elements making up a complicated system and these elements are inter-connected. The behaviour of the system is then difficult to understand. System dynamics helps the analyst to understand these variables and their interrelationships, including the feedback loops between variables. In contrast to the reductionist tools outlined above, the acceptance of feedback loops in the system is emphasised. A typical analytical process would involve articulating the problem (and identifying the boundaries of the system), dynamic hypotheses (creating initial knowledge on how the parts of the system are interrelated), modelling feedback loops, simulation, and testing, and finally, policy formulation. System dynamics clearly can be used for more complicated systems compared to the tools for purely technical and process complexity. This is a valuable approach in a strategic business case analysis where there are likely to be feedback loops between large numbers of variables in organisational and strategic settings (e.g., innovation ⇨ new products ⇨ sales growth ⇨ profits ⇨ investment in further innovation). Such feedback loops are not adequately treated by quantitative reductionist techniques.

d. *Organisational complexity*: This category of systems problem is not uncommon in a strategic business case analysis. It relates not only to internal interrelationships inside the case organisation, but also the organisation's relationship with the external environment. Jackson (2019) mentions two approaches under this category. The first is socio-technical systems thinking, which stresses both socio- (human) and technical- (non-human) aspects of systems. It draws on open systems theory (Von Bertalanffy, 1950) in viewing the system under scrutiny as part of its environment, receiving inputs from the environment and providing outputs to it in return. Socio-technical systems thinking emphasises this exchange in both socio- and technical- terms. It also stresses purposeful exchange with the environment, honouring human values, granting autonomy to those making the change, and the sharing of an organisation's values with other actors in the environment. The second is organisational cybernetics. This stresses the notion of a 'viable system', one that survives. It argues that centralised systems are too rigid and unable to adapt, while completely decentralised ones cannot act coherently and collapse. Viable systems find a balance between these extremes. There are five features (or sub-parts) of a viable system: (1) implementation – carrying out the tasks that are aligned with the organisation's purpose, (2) co-ordination – reducing conflict between the parts and supporting, not constraining, the parts in their operations, (3) operational control – optimising performance and ensuring synergy between the parts, (4) development – focusing on the future developmental initiatives for the organisation and how it relates to opportunities and threats in the changing environment, and (5) policy – responsible for governance and strategy of the overall system. Using these types of approaches in a strategic business case analysis would involve mapping the detail of the case situation onto these steps and components of analysis to understand how the organisation can change to deal with the strategic issue at hand.

e. *People complexity*: Many strategic business cases will have a significant human side. This may relate to how employees are managed and incentivised internally in the organisation. It may also relate to how the organisation addresses issues related to humanity in the wider world. This is where 'soft systems thinking' comes in. This involves gaining as many perspectives as possible from different constituencies and stakeholders to improve the system as a social system. It seeks to reconcile and find consensus amongst stakeholders such that they are committed to a shared purpose. Strategic assumption surfacing and testing (SAST) is an approach that seeks to acquire useful information from as many viewpoints as possible. Four guiding principles are: to be (1) participative – the needed knowledge is likely to be distributed, (2) adversarial – deliberately seeking to collate opposing viewpoints, (3) integrative – bringing options together, and (4) managerial mind-supporting – exposing managers to different views (Mason & Mitroff, 1981). Interactive planning emphasises viewing organisations as social systems responsible for themselves (the control problem), their parts (humanisation problem), and wider systems (the 'environmentalisation' problem). The method is highly participatory, involving many stakeholders in a planning process that involves (1) formulating the mess – what will the organisation's situation be if it continues its current path? (2) ends planning – specifying purpose and end goals, (3) means planning, (4) resource planning, and (5) implementation design. Soft systems methodology involves multiple stakeholders exploring difficult situations with a learning orientation and common objective to improve it. As an outcome from this participative learning process, soft systems diagrams can be created showing actions and how they interrelate in an organisational setting. The method requires the situation to be acknowledged as problematical and expressed as such before purposeful activity systems are articulated as models. Once these models are in place they are compared with the real world, changed as necessary to be systematically desirable and culturally feasible, before being put into action.

f. *Power (coercive) complexity*: Strategic business cases regularly have a coercive component. They can demonstrate the use of power of one individual, group, or organisation over others. While this is normally concerned with achieving the performance targets and goals of the organisation by exerting control over others, it can also have a negative connotation. Power can be exerted in ways that have a detrimental effect on weaker and disadvantaged actors and communities. We can consider the negative effects of corporate social irresponsibility (CSIR) in this sense. CSIR is defined as a "set of actions that increases externalized costs and/or promotes distributional conflicts" (Kotchen & Moon, 2012, p. 2). Any strategic business case considering global challenges and 'increased externalised costs' may be a suitable candidate for holistic analysis using an approach that emphasises the coercive nature of organisational power. Team syntegrity is a non-hierarchical process involving a set of 30 individuals with interests and opinions on 12 issues or topics (Leonard, 1996). This combination is modelled on an icosahedron (Leonard, 1996), with individuals as edges and topics as nodes. The approach requires participants to agree a protocol for communicating and holding conversations in a distributed way. The process will last for several days and typically has three parts: (1) problem hustle – deciding on an issue list of 12 themes or topics, (2) topic auction – individuals specifying their preferences for topics to define the icosahedron structure, and (3) outcome resolve – a series of meetings on the topics defined by the structure that aim to produce a final statement of importance. Critical systems heuristics is a method with multiple purposes. It aims to create reflective practice, especially around sources of bias that strategic planners tend to adopt. Reflective practice enables greater impartiality. It aims to be dialogical; to improve understanding between individuals with different views. It also seeks to be 'emancipatory', to strengthen those who are disadvantaged by the exertion of power by others. The method involves definition of 12 boundary categories (boundary questions) in three subsystems of interest: (1) social roles: beneficiary, decision-maker, expert, and witness, (2) specific concerns: purpose, resources, expertise, and emancipation, (3) key problems: measure of improvement, decision environment, guarantor, and worldview. Critical systems heuristics is an inclusive approach that allows a questioning of values and interests of those involved in a strategic issue.

TABLE 6.1 A classification of systems approaches

Type/Systems approach for …	Individual methodologies	Requires participation from additional informants?	Examples of strategic issues that could be analysed
Technical complexity	Operational research Systems analysis Systems engineering	Not necessarily	Hard systems thinking requiring mathematical models: optimisation, automation, complex processes
Process complexity	The Vanguard Method	Not necessarily	Efficiency problems, waste reduction, service improvement
Structural complexity	System dynamics	Not necessarily	Relations between management practices, industry pressures, and performance
Organisational complexity	Socio-technical systems thinking Organisational cybernetics	Not necessarily	High-tech manufacturing, implications of AI in the workplace; work design
People complexity	Strategic assumption surfacing and testing Interactive planning Soft systems methodology	Ideally	Soft systems thinking for problems requiring consensus, mutual understanding, cultural change
Power (coercive) complexity	Team syntegrity Critical systems heuristics	Ideally	Problems requiring participation and where implications of strategic decisions on others need to be understood

Source: adapted from Jackson (2019).

Table 6.1 summarises these systems approaches as discussed in Jackson (2019).

2. *Visualising cases as holistic systems:*

   a. *Use of systems diagrams:* These are useful for describing the nature of a case situation holistically. Jennings (1997) shows how systems diagrams are useful in analysing strategic issues in business cases. Firstly, diagramming plays a role in understanding the nature of the problem. As Jennings (1997) notes: "Through constructing the diagram the situations underlying processes become apparent, identifying processes helps to define the problematic nature of the situation" (p. 102). Systems diagrams can be used as a top-level depiction of all the elements in the system, and how they interact or influence each other. Used in an open systems paradigm, they can show the inputs, internal process, and outputs from the case organisation, including feedback loops. In this sense, all the main actors and stakeholders in the context of the organisation can be depicted. Secondly, as

Jennings (1997) notes, such top-level systems diagrams can be used to highlight areas that need further exploration and examination. They can be used towards the start of the strategic business case analysis to anchor the more detailed work that follows. Systems diagrams can take many different forms and can be used in a wide range of contexts and issues. Examples include showing the flow of processes in production control systems (Köhler, Nickel, Niere & Zündorf, 2000), roles and activities in healthcare service delivery (Shukla, Keast & Ceglarek, 2017), in a participatory way in social work (Jackson, 2013), and accounting information systems and auditing education (Bradford, Richtermeyer & Roberts, 2007).

b. *Visualising complexity*: There are several options for deeper analysis of case data in a holistic tradition, going beyond the description of systems diagrams. Writing in the context of qualitative data analysis, Henderson and Segal (2013) describe a range of tools for making sense of qualitative data. Most of these involve visualisation and diagramming. We listed the simple and moderately complex ones above under 'qualitative reductionism'. Henderson and Segal (2013) highlight three useful tools for qualitative analysis in more complex situations. These can be applied in a holistic sense in cases where a large amount of textual data is present. These are: Parallel Tag Cloud/Spark Cloud diagrams (at the level of words), sentiment analysis (at the level of sentences), and graphic recording (at the level of themes and narratives) (Henderson and Segal, 2013). Parallel Tag Cloud and Spark Clouds can be used in a holistic stance because they allow multiple word clouds to be compared. Sentiment analysis can be used holistically because it entails determining if multiple pieces of text are each viewed as positive or negative. There is no theoretical limit to the number of pieces of text that can be assessed (although there is likely to be a practical limit to how many sentiments can be assessed in one diagram). Smith (2011) applies sentiment analysis to the Bible, producing a single visualisation of all the positive and negative effects in the whole work! Graphic recording can be used holistically because it allows group discussion on the findings of a case analysis, helping to translate the analysis into practical implications (Dean-Coffey, 2013). Note that this is a participatory technique involving multiple stakeholders.

A note on systems thinking techniques: if you opt for a holistic stance for your strategic business case analysis it is well worth reviewing Jackson's (2019) book and seeking additional guidance on the most appropriate approach (or combination of approaches) to use. The nature of complexity in your case might not fall neatly into one of the six types in Table 6.1, and a combinative approach might be the best solution. Some of these techniques are participative in nature and require the analyst to coordinate participation with many individuals. Participants may be from the case organisation or otherwise have an interest in the strategic issue. This type of approach would clearly require the analyst to orchestrate additional activity outside of the reading of a single case document as the main source of data. This is likely to be most applicable for analysts already working in the focal organisation or in the domain of the strategic issue. It would require contacting participants, convening meetings, and adhering to ethics guidelines during data collection. The time and resource requirements for this need to be established and factored into the overall project.

APPLYING HYBRIDISM TO A STRATEGIC BUSINESS CASE ANALYSIS

As discussed in the previous chapter, there are situations in which neither purely reductionist nor holistic stances will provide the most optimal insights into a strategic issue facing an organisation. They may reveal some insights, but more could be obtained by combining the best of both worlds and pursuing a design that has elements of both. As shown in Table 5.1 in Chapter 5, this may mean any of the following: a more expanded set of variables than found in a reductionist stance, and different types of relationships between them; elements of both firm and macro-level in the same analysis; the analyst being personally involved with at least some part of the phenomenon but not all; different theory applying at different levels; moderate to high complexity, but not necessarily a wicked problem. This is what we mean by hybridism in this book – a combinative approach – and it finds support in the systems field.

Jackson (2019) shows that all the methodologies and systems approaches (Table 6.1) have received criticisms. He notes: "Given the complexity, turbulence, and diversity of most problem situations confronting decision-makers in the twenty-first century, it is hardly surprising that no one systems approach can supply the answer" (p. 512). He goes on to argue that critical systems thinking (CST) is helpful in this respect. This is about how the different systems tools can be used in combination to "promote more successful interventions in complex organizational and societal problem situations" (p. 512). So, what kinds of tools belong in the toolkit here? We highlight six categories of approaches: CST, fuzzy cognitive mapping (FCM), path analysis, multi-level analysis, process models, noting that each of these comes with capabilities for visualisation. Each of these provides ways of leveraging benefits of reductionism and holism, i.e., they allow the combination and fusion of elements of both stances for a strategic business case analysis.

1. *Critical systems thinking (CST)*: While CST falls within the systems thinking paradigm, we place it as a hybrid stance because of its emphasis on *critical awareness*. As Jackson (1991) notes in his article on the nature of CST, critical awareness is about being cognisant of strengths and weaknesses of individual system approaches and examining the assumptions of any systems design approach. This links to another of the commitments of CST, namely a *complementary use of systems methodologies*. In recognition that no single systems approach will suffice in all situations, particularly where there are different types of contextual complexity (Table 6.1), analysts need to be creative and combine approaches (Jackson, 1991). This is likely to require some elements of system thinking alongside some elements of reductionist techniques, including quantitative and qualitative reductionism. This critical approach could be used in parallel, on different aspects of complexity in the case, or sequentially, one after another. A strategic business case analyst can claim to use CST in a hybrid mode if they surface and articulate their assumptions and criticisms of individual systems techniques to justify a broader analytical framework customised for the situation in the case.

2. *Fuzzy cognitive mapping (FCM):* This is a technique that allows the generation of cognitive maps showing the relationships between variables within a system of variables.

Cognitive mapping was originally used to understand the relationships between place, environment, and human action – people store impressions of their environment cognitively (Kitchin, 1994). However, the FCM technique can be used to generate individual and group level 'mind maps' showing interrelationships in any set of variables, including the types of variables found in a strategic business case. Özesmi and Özesmi (2004) present an excellent overview of how the method works. There is a great deal of flexibility with the approach. Firstly, it allows data collected from different sources to be mapped onto individual cognitive maps. Sources include interviews and textual documents. A case text could be used as a basis for creating a cognitive map, as could further interviews with key informants. Secondly, the technique allows for the maps to be superimposed on each other for a group-level – or social cognitive map – to be generated. This shows the overall pattern of variables in the system. Thirdly, the relationships between variables can be positive, negative, bi-directional, and can have different strengths. Williams, You and Joshua (2020) use FCM in a participatory way to study resilience in small firms on the remote South Atlantic Island of St Helena. The authors co-created individual maps in a participatory way with a small number of micro businesses on the island to generate a condensed social cognitive map of the factors that influence resilience in small firms in such remote places. The technique is hybrid because it allows a system of variables to be identified and interrelated, but also allows thresholds to be placed on the strengths of the interrelationships to eliminate some arrows in the final map. FCM also allows sets of common variables to be grouped.

3. *Path analysis*: This is a technique that allows the statistical testing of cause–effect relations between variables organised in a structural model. The relationships between the variables form the paths – the causes and consequences of changes in each variable on other variables (Tenenhaus, Vinzi, Chatelin & Lauro, 2005). This technique is typically conducted on quantitative data collection through questionnaire surveys of multiple individuals or from other secondary numeric data. The variables are known as latent variables, and they are often comprised of (or indicated by) several underlying items. Different ways can be used to assess path models, including covariance-based (CB) and variance-based partial least squares (PLS). These are both forms of structural equation models (SEM). CB is useful for testing established theory while PLS is part confirmatory and part predictive – useful for exploratory model development (Hair Jr, Matthews, Matthews & Sarstedt, 2017). Once the software has estimated a path model, coefficients are seen to appear on the paths and the strengths and signs of these coefficients are used for analysing the overall model. This is also known as a structural model and differs from a measurement model, which provides key information about the model itself. The path nature of the model has similarities with FCM, although FCM maps are normally generated inductively (i.e., grounded in data that is often qualitative and primary in nature), while path models are specified by the analyst using software, and then assessed in a more deductive manner (i.e., based on some underlying theory or theories). We can consider this technique in a hybrid stance because it opens the analysis up to a potentially large set of variables, and there does not have to be one solitary dependent variable. However, it has elements of reductionism in that the structural model is predefined, often theory driven.

4. *Multilevel qualitative analysis*: Multilevel analysis is commonly used by researchers in a reductionist stance on high sample sizes when the underlying data is quantitative and hierarchically structured, or nested. Data used in this way is often survey generated. However, multilevel analysis can be applied for making sense of cases with more of a qualitative component, and it can be used in a hybrid mode. For instance, Andersen, Bjørnholt, Bro and Holm-Petersen (2018) study the relationship between transformational leadership and professional quality in the context of 16 childcare day centres in Denmark using data at two levels: individual and organisational level. Lapointe and Rivard (2005) conduct an analysis of resistance to IT system implementation using multilevel qualitative data at individual and group level in three hospitals. This approach can be considered hybrid as the issues may not be easily decomposable at the outset, while some thematic grouping will emerge. While they are less meaningful to large-scale grand challenges, they do have implications for multiple stakeholders, including, in these cases, patients.

5. *Analysing process data*: It is not uncommon that strategic business cases depict one or more processes. These may relate to the overall transformation of inputs into outputs, i.e., how the organisation interfaces with its external environment in creating value (Von Bertalanffy, 1950). They also may relate to core internal production processes (Köhler, Nickel, Niere and Zündorf, 2000) or organisation-specific change management processes such as General Electric's change acceleration process (Davids, Aspler & McIvor, 2002). Such processes are often highly strategic and can form one of the (if not the main) areas of focus for a strategic business case analysis. Process data – in quantitative and/or qualitative form can be analysed in several ways. Langley (1999) reviews the literature on process analysis and sums them up into seven approaches for making sense of process data. These are: (1) through narratives – emphasising stories, meanings, and mechanisms, (2) quantification strategy – focusing on events, outcomes, and patterns, (3) alternate templates strategy – focusing on mechanisms, (4) grounded theory – searching for meaning and patterns through incidents and categories in the text, (5) visual mapping of events in sequence, (6) temporal bracketing – dividing into phases, and (7) synthetic strategy – emphasising prediction of processes. There is some overlap across these techniques, and being creative in how to apply them is encouraged. While some of them require data from multiple cases, depending on the nature and structure of a given strategic business case, they can all apply. For instance, the same organisation may have multiple processes for different product lines, and these could be treated as multiple sub-cases with the same case. We consider these types of techniques as part of a hybrid stance because – collectively – they are part holistic and part reductionist. As Langley (1999) says about these tools: "Some strategies favor accuracy, remaining more deeply rooted in the raw data (narrative strategy and grounded theory). Others are more reductionist, although they allow the development and testing of parsimonious theoretical generalizations (quantification, synthetic strategy, and simulation)" (p. 706).

6. *Visualisation in a hybrid mode*: The hybrid approaches listed above all yield a diagram to visualise the analysis. In CST, one or more types of system thinking techniques would be applied, each with its own type of diagram. In FCM, a map of variables and their interrelationships (with strengths and directions) is produced and indeed simplified when moving from the initial social cognitive map to the condensed map (Williams et al., 2020). Similarly, in path analysis a path model is specified and portrayed in software.

In multilevel analysis, nested relationships can be shown in a hierarchical diagram. And in the analysis of process data, different types of process diagrams can be drawn. Just as with the holistic diagramming, the tools one finds in hybrid approaches also allow effective visualisation as a basis for communicating results and making sense of the case.

ANALYSIS PRESENTATION, DERIVING IMPLICATIONS AND DEVELOPING NEW TOOLS

In addition to the application of the types of tools mentioned above on case data, additional capabilities need to be applied to deliver an impactful strategic business case analysis. Analysis will need to be presented coherently and transparently. Implications for all interested parties will need to be derived. And new tools may need to be developed along the way.

Firstly, a clear and well-justified presentation of results is vital. Applying tools to case data – wherever they may be positioned along the Case Analysis Spectrum – will usually result in the generation of copious tables, diagrams, spreadsheets, and text. Output from tools may not be the same as the input into the final report. What is required from an analytical point of view is to carefully review these outputs and select those (and the parts of those) that will be most meaningful for the final report. Use can be made of appendices or supplementary documents for analyses with large volumes of supporting evidence. What is usually required in the main report or body of the main report are the key pieces of analysis ('centrepieces') that fulfil the criteria of answering the research questions and addressing the strategic issues set out. This requires a careful filtering and transformation step by the analyst. Centrepiece exhibits are then referred to and discussed by the analyst in the body of text in the final report. In some circumstances the output from a software package may be used as a figure in the body of the final report. In most cases though, the analyst will need to select only those elements of the output that matter and that can be understood by the reader of the report.

Secondly, it is important to derive implications and recommendations from the strategic business case analysis and for these to be relevant and helpful to different stakeholders. As noted in Figure 1.1 in Chapter 1, stakeholders in business case production and analysis can be divided into: the practitioners affected by the strategic issue, the case writer telling the story of the strategic issue, the academic system in which the analysis report will be assessed and graded, and the student performing the analytical work. When it comes to deriving implications from the analysis, we need to dig deeper into the question of: implications for whom? First and foremost, a strategic business case analysis should have *implications for practice*. However, the word 'practitioner' – often used by academics – is a very high-level and even loose label. There are many types of practitioners in the world of business and public administration that could have an interest in the results of the analysis. The ones that matter will vary from case to case. In general, they can be divided into two camps: (1) executives, managers, and associates working within the case organisation itself, and (2) executives, managers, and associates working in other organisations but with an interest in the strategic issue examined in the analysis. Wherever possible, implications derived through the analysis should specify precisely which set of practitioners might benefit by taking note of the findings. Shrivastava (1987) specifies criteria for rigor and relevance in the field of strategy. In terms of scientific rigor, criteria include conceptual adequacy, methodological rigour, and accumulated empirical evidence. In terms of practical usefulness (or relevance), Shrivastava (1987) draws from Thomas and Tymon (1982) to specify the following criteria:

1. *Meaningfulness*: are the implications comprehensible to managers?
2. *Goal relevance*: are the variables analysed aligned with the goals of the organisation?
3. *Operational validity*: are the recommendations actionable in practice?
4. *Innovativeness*: are there new and non-obvious results that will make managers think in new ways about the strategic issue and its solution?
5. *Cost of implementation*: are the recommendations feasible in terms of cost and time?

These five criteria can form a useful guide for analysts as they articulate implications for practice based on their case analysis work.

In terms of *implications for theory*, strategic business case analysis can critique or extend existing theory or develop new theory. The requirement for delving into the world of academic theory will vary from institution to institution. In some situations, the emphasis will be more on actionable recommendations. In others, a balance between recommendations and theoretical discussion will be required. Cases in strategy do lend themselves to theory development. They are often highly inductive, and no *a priori* theoretical assumptions need to be made before the analysis begins. If the analyst adopts a holistic or hybrid stance and draws from systems thinking or the multitude of tools that allow the emergence of path diagrams and maps depicting the interrelationships between many variables, the basis for new theory will be readily forthcoming. Propositions can be articulated based on the strongest relationships between variables that emerge in the analysis. Reductionist stances with quantitative or qualitative tests of relationships between smaller numbers of variables can be used as a basis of making an informed discussion on the utility of any given theory. Overall, while the focus should be on generating an answer to the strategic issue in the case for the benefit of stakeholders in the world of practice, analysts should expect to be able to make informed comments on the usefulness of theory as well. We will discuss in more depth how to maximise impact from a strategic business case analysis in Chapters 8 and 9.

Thirdly, the case analyst might need to develop new tools to strengthen the toolkit for a strategic business case analysis project. One might expect this to be a rare occurrence, as so many tools already exist for making sense of case data. But creativity in methods for case analysis is not uncommon and should be considered as part of the arsenal for approaching complex cases. As Jackson (2019) notes, all techniques have pros and cons; the savvy analyst should always be prepared to innovate. Being a creative analyst of case data is arguably more applicable to the qualitative side of case data rather than the quantitative side. It is highly unlikely that a case analyst will develop new quantitative techniques, along with the mathematical foundation for the technique, let alone doing this over the duration of a strategic business case project. However, in the analysis of qualitative case data, creativity in methods is not implausible and may be highly appropriate. Nevertheless, we should be wary of calling this fundamental innovation in qualitative analysis. Wiles, Crow and Pain (2011) reviewed 57 articles claiming to have performed an innovation in qualitative analysis, only to conclude that most were not innovative at all, but were rather based on adapting existing methods, or transferring methods from other disciplines. So, what we mean when we refer to developing the toolkit for strategic business case analysis is more likely to involve an ability to adapt and/or transfer methods from other disciplines. The analyst can consider this if, after evaluation of other known techniques along the Case Analysis Spectrum, no suitable approach is found, or at least there is a belief that optimisation and improvement can be made. The search for new methods from other disciplines is likely to be way costlier in terms of time, compared to adapting or combining already-known techniques. Other disciplines will be unfamiliar territory, with their own sets of journals and books, and it will take some considerable effort and time to become familiar with them. Supervisor guidance can be important in this respect.

TOOLS AND THE CASE ANALYSIS SPECTRUM

Table 6.2 provides an overview of the tool families discussed in this chapter.

TABLE 6.2 Examples of popular tools along the Case Analysis Spectrum

Reductionist	Hybrid	Holistic
Quantitative: • Descriptive statistics • Correlations • Comparing groups • Regression models Qualitative: • Quotes • Thematic analysis • Data structures • Content analysis	Fuzzy cognitive mapping Path analysis Qualitative multilevel analysis Process analysis on qualitative data	Systems thinking: • Operational research • Systems analysis • Systems engineering • Vanguard Method • Systems dynamics • Socio-technical systems thinking • Organisational cybernetics • Strategic assumption surfacing and testing • Interactive planning • Soft systems methodology • Team syntegrity • Critical systems heuristics
	<------- Critical systems thinking ------->	
Visualisation: Quantitative: • Charts (including bar, line, scatter, pie, histograms, box plots, contour maps) Qualitative: • Word clouds, phrase nets, narrative excerpts, cluster analysis, word trees, spectrum displays and matrices	Visualisation: • Bespoke techniques • Path diagrams • Nested tree diagrams • Process diagrams	Visualisation: • Systems diagrams • Parallel Tag Cloud/Spark Cloud diagrams • Sentiment analysis • Graphic recording

KEY TAKEAWAYS

The following are key learning points from this chapter:

- The analytical tools highlighted in this chapter do not represent an exhaustive list; they include some of the most common families of techniques that allow analysts to make sense of different types of case data
- Different tools will be appropriate depending on the stance adopted for the strategic business case analysis
- Techniques used in a reductionist stance will be vastly different to those used in a holistic stance, while a hybrid stance may involve a combination of approaches
- Choice of technique will be dependent on the nature of the underlying data captured in the case, whether it is in the actual published or written case document, or in additional data about the case organisation collected by the analyst
- Visualisation techniques are encouraged and can be used across the Case Analysis Spectrum; they are not constrained to reductionism, holism, or hybridism.

REFLECTIVE PRACTICE TASK

Reflect on the different approaches and tools along the Case Analysis Spectrum and consider how they might apply to your chosen case and strategic issue. Reflect further on the following questions:

1. What?

   Create a table indicating which approaches and tools are (1) not applicable and (2) possibly applicable to your case and chosen stance. Conduct further research into the ones that are possibly applicable – including discussion with your supervisor – to narrow down on the tool/tools you consider most likely to provide the insights required. What are the pros and cons of each?

2. So what?

   Write a justification statement for your choice of tools. Why is it important to provide a methodological justification for your choice of tools?

3. Now what?

   Which tools will you proceed with? Do you need to conduct an additional search for other tools, combine or develop new tools to proceed? Do you need to undertake training to understand how to use the tool or relevant software?

ADDITIONAL READINGS AND RESOURCES

A list of statistical packages

https://psychology.fandom.com/wiki/List_of_statistical_packages

A list of qualitative data analysis tools

www.indeed.com/career-advice/career-development/tools-for-qualitative-data-analysis

Background to Professor Michael C. Jackson

https://en.wikipedia.org/wiki/Mike_Jackson_(systems_scientist)

Top level information on PLS-SEM

https://studybuff.com/what-is-pls-sem-used-for/

Common strategy analysis tools

www.visual-paradigm.com/guide/strategic-analysis/utilizing-the-various-strategic-analysis-tools/

NOTES

1   www.merriam-webster.com/dictionary/tool, accessed 25 December 2022.
2   Exceptions to this are regression techniques using multiple equations. In these instances, more than one dependent variable can be specified. However, this is typically only a small, finite number – aligning their use with the reductionist stance.

CHAPTER 7

Worked examples of strategic business case analysis

This chapter provides an illustrative analysis of strategic business cases using each of the three stances described in Chapters 5 and 6. The cases are also reproduced here in full, and you are encouraged to read them through before reading the analysis of each one. Each of the cases is aligned to one of the three stances. Table 7.1 shows an overview of the case selection and justification for the stance adopted. Different case analysts may interpret the storyline and strategic issue in the case differently, and it is entirely plausible to attempt an analysis on each case using a different stance. While the analyses presented here are for illustration only, and do not represent a specific academic outcome on any given programme module, they do show how to use the analytical toolkit to provide answers to the questions set. They all reflect strategic issues for the organisations and protagonists involved, and they are all set in a complex environment with multiple contexts.

We use the case on *Time Out: A New Global Strategy to Bring Back Profit* to illustrate how to apply a reductionist stance to a strategic business case analysis. The case concerns corporate strategy in a multi-business line small-medium sized enterprise (SME) that had been established for many years and that had a presence in many foreign markets. At the time of the decision point, despite its diversification abroad, it was making a financial loss. It was faced by multiple severe threats in the external environment, including from competition, technological disruption, and shareholder pressure following a recent initial public offering (IPO). There is a strong digital transformation aspect to this case, as it is set in the media space, and at the same time there is a 'bricks-versus-clicks' aspect too (how much strategic emphasis to place on e-commerce versus physical delivery of experiences for customers). A reductionist stance can provide answers for the decision-makers in this case.

We use the case on *Brightwater: Clean Water from Broken Wells* to show an application of a holistic stance to a strategic business case analysis. The case concerns a social enterprise in Dilla, Ethiopia called Brightwater that was set up to provide clean drinking water to the local community while also providing career and training opportunities for girls. The enterprise was established in part through an initiative involving MBA students from IE Business School in Madrid, and through funding from an American-based NGO called Wuhu Sira (www.wuhasira.org/). After two years of operation in the context of Covid-19 and civil war in the country, Brightwater was already making a small profit while delivering on its social objectives. The social entrepreneur at the heart of the case was now interested in expanding across Ethiopia, was considering expanding into plastic bottling, and wanted to break away from the NGO and reduce its dependence on it. A holistic stance can provide answers in a highly complex situation of diverging interests and tensions in this case.

DOI: 10.4324/9781003288916-9

TABLE 7.1 Case selection for worked examples

Case/ Decision point	Country/Size/Industry	Case development	Main protagonist	Dominant contexts	Root question	Analytical stance taken
Time Out 2016	UK HQ, presence globally Medium (<250 employees) Media and entertainment	Primary data (interviews) Secondary data (company documents, media, and investor documents) 6 Exhibits	CEO, Julio Bruno	Technology, especially internet and e-commerce Organisational, including entrepreneurial culture Financial, pressure following IPO	What decisions should Bruno make to bring sustainable profit back to the company?	Reductionist
Brightwater 2022	Ethiopia Small (<10 employees) Social enterprise (clean water)	Primary data (interviews) Secondary data (social and health conditions in Ethiopia) 7 Exhibits	Social entrepreneur, Berhanu Gebeyehu	Developing country UN SDGs (clean water, gender equality) Technology, solar powered pumps Organisational, especially arrangements for finance and dependence on foreign NGO	How should Gebeyehu proceed to expand, move into plastic bottling, and reduce dependence on the foreign NGO?	Holistic
Olympus 2011	Japan Large (>10,000 employees) Electronics and optical instruments	Secondary data (media reports, company documents) 6 Exhibits	COO, Michael Woodford	Institutional, especially informal norms in Japan Organisational, corporate governance Legal, evidence of fraud	How should Woodford influence the Japanese board in terms of short-term and long-term change?	Hybrid

We use the case on *Olympus and the Whistleblower President* to illustrate the application of a hybrid stance to strategic business case analysis. The case is set in corporate Japan and describes the corporate governance situation involving a newly appointed British president and Chief Operating Officer (COO) of the company confronting a Japanese board as irregularities and evidence of fraud were uncovered. Efforts to establish the facts and resolve the issues were met with resistance by senior members of the Japanese board. While the case has a corporate governance theme, it also highlights cultural differences in leadership teams in international companies, including the role of deeply entrenched values and ways of working. As an outsider, the British COO now must decide how to proceed and influence the board in the direction he sees appropriate. A hybrid stance helps us to develop answers for him in this situation.

CASE 1

☒IVEY | Publishing   **Time Out: A New Global Strategy to Bring Back Profit**

9B17M063

TIME OUT: A NEW GLOBAL STRATEGY TO BRING BACK PROFIT

Christopher Williams and Umair Shafique wrote this case solely to provide material for class discussion. The authors do not intend to illustrate either effective or ineffective handling of a managerial situation. The authors may have disguised certain names and other identifying information to protect confidentiality.

Julio Bruno, chief executive officer (CEO) of United Kingdom-based Time Out Group PLC (Time Out), had been busy since overseeing the company's initial public offering (IPO) in June 2016. From his office in the heart of London's West End, Bruno, 51, reflected on this recent success. The IPO, which had been achieved in an eye-catching two and a half months, had raised much-needed capital for investment and growth, and all eyes were now on Bruno.

Before the IPO, the company had reported adjusted earnings before interest, tax, depreciation, and amortization (EBITDA) losses of £5.5 million[1] in 2014 and £12.4

million in 2015. Revenues had been flat in traditional areas of print advertising and circulation, and they were falling slightly in international licensing. However, there was momentum in new market areas: digital advertising and e-commerce revenue had grown 19 per cent, to £11.7 million, between 2014 and 2015. In addition, the company had recently launched a physical Time Out Market in Lisbon, Portugal, and this had seen revenue growth of 67 per cent, from £1.2 million to £2.0 million, between 2014 and 2015.

Now, with £59 million in proceeds from the IPO to invest, Bruno needed to decide how he should lead the newly public company back to profitability. How should he balance foreign direct investment in physical Time Out Markets around the world with investments in digital transformation and the company's global online presence?

TIME OUT GROUP: BACKGROUND

Time Out began as a print publication created by student Tony Elliott with £70 during a summer break from Keele University in 1968. The first two issues were folded-down posters that Elliott distributed himself on the streets of London. By its third issue, the publication had become an A5-sized saddle-stitched magazine. Time Out's contents included information about the events Elliott considered to be the best among those happening in London during the late 1960s. Bands such as the Animals, the Who, the Beatles, the Kinks and the Rolling Stones were in their prime, and London was seen as the epicentre of all things "hip and fashionable." As well as cultural content and listings about events, the magazine also had articles on the issues of the day. The magazine, which evolved into a weekly in April 1971, became an enduring and iconic brand with both a print and online presence.

Elliott internationalized the business in two stages—first, introducing a Time Out publishing operation in Paris in 1989–1991, and then launching Time Out New York in the United States in 1995. The company's first website was launched in the late 1990s, before the peak of the dot-com boom, and the Time Out brand continued to internationalize its presence principally through the Internet. By 2013, the company had set up websites for locations as diverse as São Paulo, Brazil, and Tokyo, Japan. By 2016, the company was present in 108 cities across 39 countries, had a global monthly audience reach of 156 million, and was generating over 1 billion page views per year. The vast majority of Time Out's publications and websites were in English, but by 2016, the company had websites in 11 other languages for 16 other locations (see Exhibit 1). Time Out also had multiple strategic partnerships with web-based service providers, including Uber Technologies Inc., Viator Inc., Broadway.com, Booking.com, and TicketNetwork Inc.

In 2010, after looking for a new investor for Time Out for nearly a decade, Elliott sold 50 per cent of the company to Oakley Capital Limited and retained 50 per cent himself. The company was valued at £20 million, and Elliot intended to use the capital to accelerate its online and digital expansion. This came at a difficult time for the company, which had experienced pre-tax losses of £1.3 million in 2007 and £3 million in 2008, and declining sales in printed circulation. The weekly London edition, which had reportedly peaked at 105,000 copies in the late 1990s, was at around 60,000 per week by 2010.[2] By 2013, Elliott had sold more of his stake and retained a small minority holding.

Due to the growth of the Internet and consumers' preference for web-based content, the Time Out print magazine became a free publication in London (in 2012), in New York and Chicago (in 2015), and in Los Angeles and Miami (in 2016). Launching free magazines across key cities was part of Time Out's unique approach to print distribution, which it used to grow its brand, audience, engagement, and reach. This approach also provided increasing value to advertisers, who could connect through new creative opportunities across the brand's global print, digital, mobile, and event platforms. By 2016, the printed Time Out magazines had a total weekly circulation reach of approximately 600,000 in the company's owned and operated territories, and approximately 260,000 in those territories where it carried on business through international licensing agreements. By 2016, there were 39 magazines available—seven through owned and operated businesses and 32 through international licensing agreements. The company had also offered printed Time Out city guides, but these were discontinued in 2015, and outsourced to another publisher for a few select cities.

Time Out became active in staging live events, putting on over 400 curated events in London and New York every year. These included "Silent Disco" events at the Natural History Museum and the Shard in London, and "Battle of the Burger" contests, sponsored by Amstel in New York[3] and by Guinness in Chicago. In 2016, the group also ran a number of global campaigns, including the Time Out Love City Awards, an annual campaign that ran in seven cities worldwide: London, Lisbon, New York, Chicago, Los Angeles, Tokyo, and Paris. The campaign encouraged customers to vote for their favourite local businesses such as attractions, coffee shops, bars, shops, and restaurants.

The company was the recipient of four Professional Publishers Association (PPA) awards between 2010 and 2014: the International Magazine Brand of the Year in 2010 and 2011, and the International Consumer Media Brand of the Year in 2013 and 2014.[4] In awarding Time Out the International Consumer Media Brand of the Year award in 2014, the PPA judges noted, "The sheer scale of launches across multiple territories and platforms made it hard to look anywhere other than Time Out. A powerful global proposition."[5] Nevertheless, despite these accolades from the PPA and the earlier cash injection from Oakley Capital Limited, the newly formed Time Out Group[6] had consecutive losses in the years ending December 31, 2014, and December 31, 2015 (see Exhibit 2). Group revenues for 2014 and 2015 were £26.9 million and £28.5 million, respectively, while adjusted EBITDA losses for the same two years were £5.5 million and £12.4 million, respectively.

Bruno joined Time Out Group as executive chairman in September 2015. Bruno had previously served as global vice-president of sales at TripAdvisor and had held senior executive roles at Travelport, Regus Group Companies, and Diageo. He had been based in New York and was looking for a new leadership challenge back in

Europe in the media, travel, and entertainment space when he had singled the company out, later commenting, "They didn't find me . . . I found them." He was particularly interested in the challenge of transforming the company from print to digital, and had expressed his ideas for growing the company to Oakley Capital Limited, convincing the firm to appoint him as executive chairman. The intention was for Bruno to be based between London and New York.[7]

Bruno spearheaded the group's IPO on the Alternative Investment Market, a sub-market of the London Stock Exchange. The IPO, which became effective on June 14, 2016, was completed in a record two and a half months under the leadership of Bruno, who became group CEO at that time. The company had £59 million net after paying off shareholder debt;[8] it used the IPO not only to pay off debt but also to raise funds for continued investment and transformation into digital and e-commerce initiatives. Statements in the IPO admission document indicated five areas of investment: expansion of Time Out Market to other locations, sales and marketing, technology and product, commercial teams, and general corporate purposes (see Exhibit 3). While the largest single item for post-IPO investment was related to Time Out Market (£20 million), digital and e-commerce investments together added up to over £30 million.

TIME OUT DIGITAL

Time Out had been engaged in a process of digital transformation since 2010, and had attained a monthly global audience reach of 111 million, growing to 137 million in June 2016. It had started to move away from a reliance on revenue from printed materials to new revenue sources based on the Internet and online technologies. Continued investment in developing the company's technology and sales and marketing of new digital products was seen as an important driver for growth and profitability (see Exhibit 3). For example, in 2015, the company had sold 262,000 tickets through a combination of click-throughs and direct sales via its own and other systems.[9] Bruno commented that "we need to invest in 'clicks and mortar' . . . our customer can be digital [clicks] or physical [mortar] by visiting a live event or the Time Out Market."

Development of new and enhanced digital platforms was central to Time Out's post-IPO strategy. It would provide new capabilities such as content offerings and social media functionality that would result in an increase in the number of transacting users. While these technology developments were aimed at increasing revenue from users, they also provided opportunities for the company to grow revenue from advertisers by enhancing advertising solutions on its platforms. Innovations in video and social media and creative applications of technology would broaden the appeal of Time Out as a platform for advertisers around the world. The company also wanted to improve its electronic interface with local business partners, offering them self-service solutions such as the ability to list their own events and issue electronic discount vouchers, which would make interacting with the Time Out platform more attractive.

While Bruno continued to drive the company's efforts in digital products, he also provided fresh impetus for a new venture that had been successfully launched in Lisbon, Portugal, in May 2014. This new venture was known as Time Out Market.

TIME OUT MARKET

Time Out Market brought together the best of a city, based on Time Out's editorial curation, under one roof. It was a market-style food-hall space within a fashionable area of a well-known global city, where consumers were offered food, drink, and cultural experiences. It was first launched and trialled in the Mercado da Ribeira, in Lisbon, Portugal, in May 2014. In addition to the physical experience, the market had its own website (in Portuguese and English), which informed consumers on the latest chefs, menus, and cultural experiences; consumers could also get information via the market's email address and direct telephone line. The Lisbon market offered an open space for consumers to enjoy dining experiences from 14 chefs in 30 restaurants.[10] It was open from 10:00 a.m. to 12:00 a.m. from Sunday to Wednesday, and from 10:00 a.m. to 2:00 a.m. from Thursday to Saturday. The market included a cooking academy as well—a space in which consumers could "learn, perfect, and share" their love of food.[11]

The initial results were highly encouraging for Time Out. The market received 1.9 million visitors in 2015, which was noteworthy because the population of the greater Lisbon area was 2.8 million people. The company also reported receiving 1.3 million visitors in the first half of 2016, and 3.1 million for the full year. The Lisbon market showed a positive EBITDA within 18 months of opening.

Bruno and the board of Time Out felt that the Time Out Market was a scalable opportunity. Bruno believed the company's early experiences from the Lisbon market would allow it to build and develop successful markets in other locations around the world. He saw this as a way of differentiating the company from the competition, noting, "Time Out sells experiences . . . our markets are experiences . . . who else out there is doing this?"

Based on these experiences with the Lisbon market, the company considered expanding the Time Out Market. First, it considered further penetrating Portugal with a market in Porto, in Northern Portugal. It also considered London in the United Kingdom and Miami in the United States. Other possible locations considered for opening within the following two years were Berlin in Germany and New York City in the United States. Bruno noted, "We receive requests from around the world—places such as Sydney, Tel Aviv, and Tokyo, and many more—to come and set this up as they would love to have a Time Out Market there. If we could accelerate this using management contracts, then great . . . the scalability is there."

Given these possibilities, Bruno decided to focus on opening new Time Out Markets in Porto, London, and Miami in 2017 and early 2018, and having a dedicated CEO responsible for setting up in these locations. This resulted in plans to open a new Time Out Market in the iconic São Bento train station in Porto in 2017, subject to planning permission. This market would provide 500 seats over 2,043 square metres, and would include 15 restaurants, four bars, four shops, one café, and an art gallery. The London site, which was also subject to planning permission, would be a converted Victorian stable in Shoreditch, close to the famous Old Spitalfields Market. It would be 1,788 square metres and would accommodate 450 seats surrounded by 17 food stalls, four bars, a permanent shop, an art gallery, and a cooking academy.[12] Shoreditch was seen as a trendy area of London. In December 2016, a conditional lease agreement was signed for a Time Out Market in South Beach, Miami. A number of people in Time Out Market's central team, including designers, architects, and operations specialists, worked closely with local designers and architects in each location.

GOVERNANCE OF TIME OUT GROUP

At the time of the IPO in June 2016, the group's board consisted of Bruno, Peter Dubens (non-executive chairman and partner in Oakley Capital), Richard Boult (chief financial officer), and non-executive directors Lord Rose of Monewden, Alexander Collins, Christine Petersen, and Tony Elliott. Only Elliott, the founder, had been involved in the company since its early days. Dubens and Collins had joined the group in 2010; Bruno and Lord Rose of Monewden joined in 2015; and Bruno recruited Petersen, his boss at TripAdvisor, in 2016.

In terms of operating structure, Time Out Group was divided into two subgroups: Time Out Digital (TOD) and Time Out Market (TOM). While Bruno was CEO of the combined group, each subgroup had its own CEO, who reported to Bruno. TOD was further divided into Europe, North America, International, Content/Editorial, Marketing, E-commerce, Engineering, and Product. The CEO of TOM had four direct reports from Time Out Markets in Lisbon, Porto, London, and Miami, as well as central support groups (see Exhibit 4).

In 2016, the group owned and operated business in 65 cities and 14 countries. In 25 other countries (43 cities), the group used international licensing arrangements with partners (see Exhibits 5 and 6). Under the licensing model, Time Out Group retained ownership of rights, title, and interest in the brand and content. The majority of revenue in owned and operated business came from the United Kingdom and the United States, which represented 59.6 per cent and 32.1 per cent of group revenue in 2015. The group generated £26.7 million in revenue through the owned and operated models in 2015, compared to £1.7 million in fees and royalties revenues in 2015 from international licensing arrangements. The international licensing arrangements were made with local media companies and provided between 7 and 15 per cent of revenue generated through the licence. These were all fixed-term agreements.

ORGANIZATIONAL CULTURE

Bruno strongly believed that the company's employees needed to be content and happy themselves in order for this to translate into satisfied consumer experiences. He said, "We sell happiness, so we need happy people." Recalling the atmosphere around the time he joined the company, he noted a "need to nurture our culture . . . it was a big problem . . . . [There was] no clear sense of purpose and a lack of entrepreneurial spirit." In his view, the company was a "48-year old start-up," and he wanted to inject the kind of entrepreneurial culture that he had experienced working in start-ups in the United States. He felt there had been a silo mentality in the organization, with departments not communicating effectively and some employees not understanding the company's strategy. Bruno was concerned about mistrust and suspicion between departments, and a lack of creativity and innovation.

In order to address profitability concerns as well as concerns about the company's culture, Bruno laid off around 20 per cent of staff globally in November and December 2015. Throughout 2016, Bruno established a number of new organizational routines designed as opportunities for employees to socialize, be recognized, and develop a common sense of purpose around the company's new vision. He set up Time Out café/bar areas within the offices in London and New York. Every week, external contacts and representatives from the wider entertainment and media sectors would be invited to showcase their brands and companies, and socialize with Time Out staff in the café/bar area. Music, pizza, alcohol, and soft drinks were served for free. These external representatives included distributors, entrepreneurs, and founders of other companies (for example, the founder of a new vodka company based in London) who would then get exposure for their products among the staff at Time Out.

Bruno also established a variety of meeting types for the key offices in major cities. "Stand-up" meetings took place every two weeks and allowed all employees to stand up and give a short presentation on their current projects. New joiners were introduced to the rest of the team in the location at these meetings. "Shout-outs," whereby employees gave accolades regarding the quality and impact of their colleagues' work, were encouraged, and staff could also anonymously submit questions to be read out and answered by the senior executives. "Town hall" meetings were also run by Bruno, who visited every major city office once every three months throughout 2016 to share the company's new mission and vision. These formal meetings took place in the United Kingdom, the United States, Spain, Portugal, and France. Finally, "show and tell" meetings involved product demonstrations by the technology (engineering and product) team. In these meetings, staff could show what they were actually working on and elicit feedback from all others in attendance.

COMPETITION AND DIGITAL DISRUPTION

Time Out Group faced competition from different sources and industries. The company was present not only in e-commerce and digital advertising but also in the area of offering experiences to customers through live events produced and sold by Time Out and Time Out Market. Bruno emphasized that his vision for the company did not align Time Out Group with a single traditional industry: "We don't consider ourselves publishers . . . Time Out is the only global brand you can read, eat, drink, and enjoy."

On the content side (events and culture), Time Out Group faced competition from traditional and new publishers of content. The publishing industry for entertainment, culture, and events was broadly defined as including publishers that provided information or content related to events, travel, food, art, theatre, lifestyle, and so on. However, this industry had been affected by digital disruption with competitors that increasingly offered content online. Digital disruption meant that publishers now had to contend with a much bigger field of competition. Several other companies offered similar content and information online and for free, competing for the audience's attention and advertisers' budgets.

Direct competition came from companies such as TripAdvisor and Yelp, which had become well-known and established online platforms for users to gain information and provide reviews about businesses offering services in the travel, entertainment, and hospitality sectors. By 2016, TripAdvisor, with 3,000 employees, had reached 390 million average monthly unique visitors and operated in 49 countries. Yelp, with 4,050 employees, had a mission to "connect people with great local businesses." By 2016, it had a monthly average of 25 million unique visitors via its app, and 72 million visitors to its mobile web platform.[13] Competition came from other magazine publishers who utilized the "freemium" business model (that is, they complemented free print publications with an online presence and mobile applications) and who shared a similar or overlapping audience with Time Out. These included general news and lifestyle magazines like *Metro*, *Evening Standard*, *ShortList*, and *Stylist* in the United Kingdom, and *Billboard*, *Entertainment Weekly*, and *The New Yorker* in the United States. Competition also came from websites such as Vice, Buzzfeed, and New York Magazine.

Indirect competition came from a range of sources, including technology and social media companies like Google and Facebook, which had entered the entertainment, culture, and events markets and were solidifying their presence there. Such companies had introduced applications (apps) such as Google Trips, Google Maps' "explore" features, and Facebook's events features and new "Events" app. Further, travel and online booking companies like Expedia, Ticketmaster, and StubHub competed for revenue from e-commerce commissions and offered ticketing options that were similar to those of Time Out. Despite this competition, there was a trend towards co-opetition[14] in the industry: Time Out Group sold tickets through Facebook, and consumers came to the Time Out web pages through Google searches.

Print magazine publishers had been forced to transform themselves into primarily digital publishers and to adopt a freemium model—offering high-quality content for free and using digital advertising and e-commerce for revenue. Publishing no longer focused on a product but on a user-centric platform that provided content from contributors and advertisers (e.g., retailers), and publishers' audiences were no longer seen as readers but instead as consumers. These new breeds of publishers competed for consumers to interact with their sites and worked to monetize their website traffic through e-commerce activity and digital advertisements that influenced their consumers' purchasing behaviour.

Digital disruption had also given rise to the phenomenon of "big data," as publishers tried to use data to understand consumer behaviour and optimize and personalize content according to consumers' profiles and needs. Big data could further be used to develop key performance indicators to demonstrate the value of websites to digital advertisers.

Changes in consumer behaviour also affected the publishing industry. As a result of digital disruption, the publishing industry's audience increasingly overlapped with the audience of companies that offered information and content related to entertainment, events, and culture. Consumers became frustrated by advertising attempts such as pop-up advertisements, and native advertising and sophisticated content marketing, which could be used to discreetly advertise and market services or products without impeding a user's experience, were seen as the way forward.[15] Consumers favoured mobile apps that provided real-time events, culture, travel, and entertainment information using location-based services, and allowed them to make reservations or book tickets for events very quickly.

Many consumers had started to prioritize experiences over material goods, and they increasingly wanted to experience new cuisines, events, and cultures, and to share these experiences with others. This desire took the form of consumers exploring their own cities, as well as tourists exploring new places by touring as locals. Airbnb recognized this trend in its marketing, which promised to provide tourists with local, cultural experiences. Consumers flocked to trendy locations that were in the news, including countries such as Brazil, which hosted the FIFA World Cup in 2014 and was the first South American country to host the Olympic Games in 2016. At the same time, consumers from emerging economies such as China were starting to explore the Western world.

As the market became increasingly congested with information and content related to entertainment, culture, and events, consumers relied on trusted user-generated reviews. Companies such as TripAdvisor emerged as leading providers of such reviews. Analysts had observed that consumers increasingly demanded a seamless and tailored user experience,[16] and they were loyal to trusted and well-known brands that provided tailored and personalized content. Companies tried to build relationships with individual consumers rather than trying to reach out to the masses.

While there was no direct competition for the specific format used by Time Out Market, this new and relatively unique format faced competition from a wide range of restaurant types, particularly those that offered local or trendy new styles of cuisines. Restaurants that were local favourites or offered unique dining experiences—those places with good reviews that offered quick and efficient dining experiences in close proximity to shops and creative zones such as art galleries—were seen as potential competition to the Time Out Market.

JULIO BRUNO'S VISION

At the time of his appointment in 2015, Bruno explained his vision:

> I believe that the Time Out brand and our unique content approach will reach an even larger audience. Over the next few years, we have exciting plans to roll

out our digital products globally as well as our unique Time Out Market. As I see it, Time Out is the global source for local entertainment, and I am very pleased to be joining at this exciting moment in time to lead this organization to greater heights.[17]

It was clear that Bruno no longer saw Time Out simply as a publisher. He later commented that he saw "the magazines as a marketing channel." In his view, Time Out was the global media and entertainment business, creating value through clicks and mortar. He also observed that "the consumer is not unidimensional," and that creating value from the entertainment needs of global consumers would require simultaneous competition and co-operation with other companies. In his view, the basis of competition had changed. In addition, Bruno was highly aware of the importance of carefully balancing global capabilities with local needs. For instance, when reflecting on Time Out Market, he observed that "the best of Porto is not the best of Lisbon . . . and the same for London. It's a city-by-city model. Brand colours may be the same, but tables and chairing are different and unique to that place. That's why it takes time."

BREXIT

On June 23, 2016, one week after Time Out Group's IPO, the United Kingdom held a referendum on its European Union (EU) membership—a democratic decision made by the British electorate on whether to withdraw from the EU, commonly known as the "Brexit" decision. The country voted to leave the EU by 17,410,742 votes to 16,141,241 votes. The result took many by surprise, including currency markets. Within days of the vote, the United Kingdom's currency, the pound, had fallen to a 31-year low against the U.S. dollar, and the Financial Times Stock Exchange 100 Index had lost £100 billion in value amidst market volatility.[18] While stock indices recovered in subsequent weeks, the pound remained suppressed, and the outlook for pound-to-dollar and pound-to-euro exchange rates remained uncertain. Imports into the United Kingdom became more expensive, and foreign direct investments in U.S. dollars or euros could be up to 30 per cent more expensive than they were before Brexit, all other factors remaining equal. Uncertainty over the impact of Brexit on British businesses remained.

Prior to the IPO, Time Out Group had not developed a currency hedging strategy and had not believed the Brexit vote would materially impact its strategy. However, the company had bought modest amounts (low millions) of U.S. and European currencies before June 23 in order to cover ongoing operating expenses in those currencies.

STATUS AND DECISION POINT

Bruno was facing challenges in multiple areas. There had been overall losses in 2014 and 2015, and flat or even declining revenue in traditional lines of business. Some good news had come from the growing revenue in digital and e-commerce and from Time Out Market, the fastest growth area in the non-digital and non-traditional area of the company. Indeed, by the middle of 2016, Bruno's work appeared to be having a positive effect on the company's bottom line. Figures for the first half of 2016 were £16.6 million in revenue with a loss (adjusted EBITDA) of £4.8 million.[19] This was encouraging news for the company: for the first half of 2016, pro forma revenue was up 16 per cent, and losses improved by £0.8 million.

Yet Bruno was mindful of potential hazards. While he had £59 million to invest, he was aware of the risks of rushing into overseas investment. "I want to spend it very carefully," he commented. "Even if you gave me £200 million right now and said, 'Go and open 20 new Time Out Markets,' I wouldn't because of the amount of management resources and curation needed to open one market, let alone 20. We will eventually open many, but not in one go. It takes time and expertise, not just money." Nevertheless, competition remained fierce, and the effect of Brexit on the attractiveness of foreign investment opportunities was unclear.

Returning to Profitability

This was the biggest challenge. Bruno was under pressure to get Time Out back to a position of sustainable profitability quickly. How should he lead the recently listed company back to profitability? How should he balance foreign direct investment in physical Time Out Markets around the world with investments in digital transformation and the company's global online presence? Did the areas for investment indicated in the pre-Brexit IPO admission document (see Exhibit 2) make sense in light of the post-Brexit impact on the pound?

Reinforcing Culture and Staff Satisfaction

Bruno had started to build a new organizational culture within Time Out through new meeting formats, socialization activities, and café/bar areas within the offices in London and New York. What else could he consider doing in order to promote the type of internal culture needed to fulfil the corporate vision?

Maintaining the Vision

Bruno was acutely aware of the fast pace of change and levels of disruption in the industry. He himself saw Time Out Group's new strategy as a disruptive force—but was his vision sustainable? How should it change going forward, and how could he revise the vision in line with changing events?

EXHIBIT 1 List of time out's non-english website locations and languages

Location	Language
Paris	French
Barcelona, Madrid, Girona, Mexico City	Spanish, Catalan (Barcelona only)
Lisbon, Sao Paolo, Rio	Portuguese
Moscow	Russian
Istanbul	Turkish
Tel Aviv	Hebrew
Beijing, Shanghai	Chinese
Bangkok	Thai
Tokyo	Japanese
Seoul	Korean

Source: Created by the case authors based on company documents.

EXHIBIT 2 Time out—segment revenue 2014–2015 (in £ millions)

Segment	2014	2015
Digital advertising and e-commerce	£9.8	£11.7
Print advertising and circulation	£15.0	£15.0
Other, principally international licensing	£2.1	£1.8

Note: Figures were for years ending December 31.

Source: Created by the case authors based on Time Out Group, *Time Out Admission Document*, 2016, 74, accessed November 17, 2016, http://media.timeout.com/www_timeout_com_uploads/wp-content/up-loads/2016/06/Admission-Document.pdf.

EXHIBIT 3 Time out—indicated areas for investment (in £ millions)

Area of Investment	Amount
Capital expenditure to roll out Time Out Market: • geographical expansion of the concept to new cities • sourcing and design of new leased premises • physical infrastructure improvements • recruitment of local management teams • local marketing • technology, including point of sale and free wi-fi	£20

Investment in sales and marketing for e-commerce offerings: • increasing in-house headcount • engaging in paid social media • increasing use of direct advertising and Google Ad Awards • enhancing "gamification" (rewards via membership and mobile app) • developing customer relationship management tool	£15
Investment in technology and product: • expansion into new product verticals • development of new user interface • improvement of premium profiles service • development of data warehouse • improvement of user integration and integration of Flypay • development of management information system (MIS)	£10
Commercial teams: • expansion of teams, focusing on premium profiles, brand solutions, creative solutions, content moderation, and e-commerce partner acquisitions	£5
General corporate purposes	£8

Source: Created by the case authors based on Time Out Group, *Time Out Admission Document*, 2016, 32, accessed November 17, 2016, http://media.timeout.com/www_timeout_com_uploads/wp-content/uploads/2016/06/Admission-Document.pdf.

EXHIBIT 4 Time out—company structure

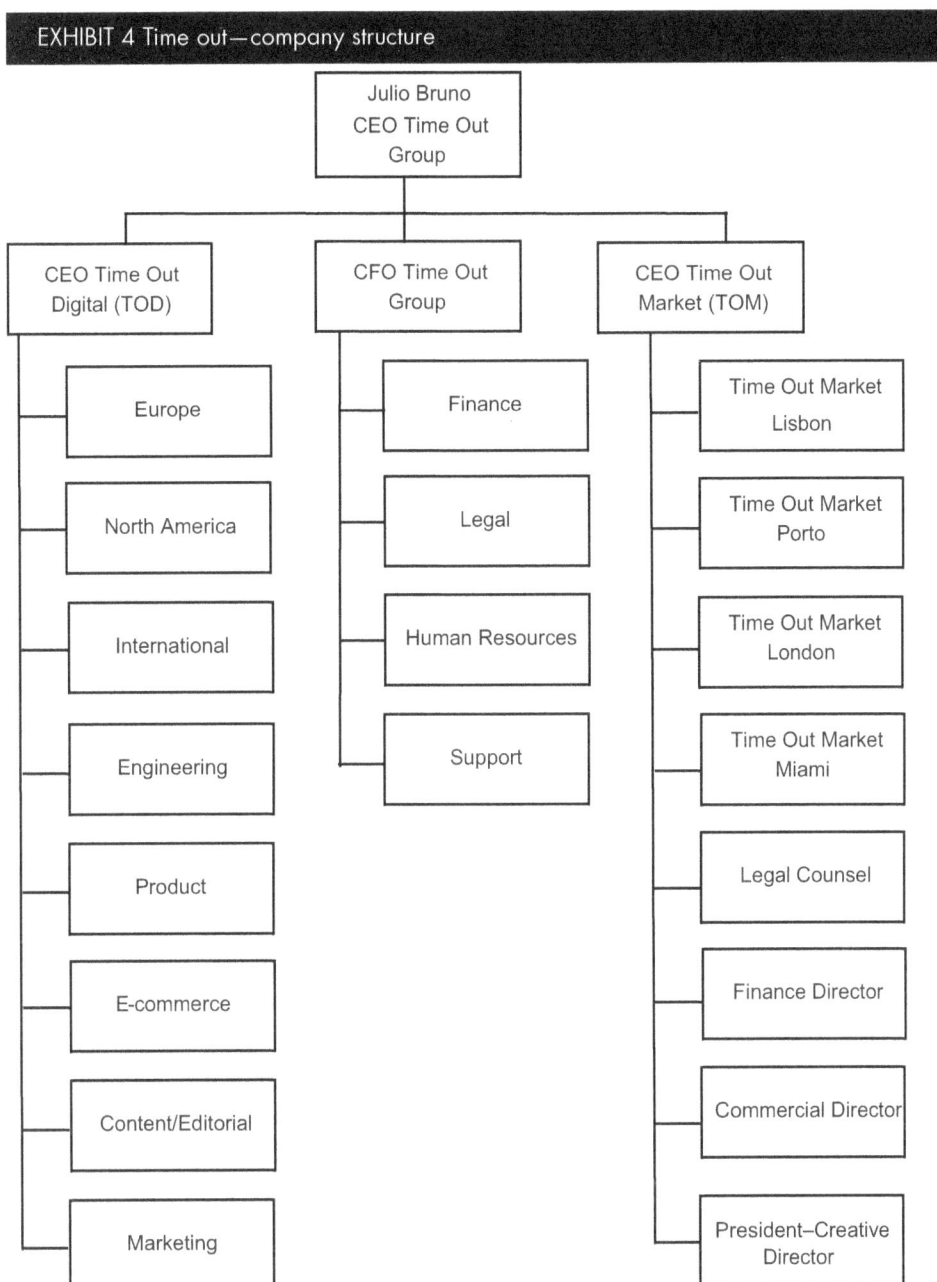

Source: Created by the case authors.

EXHIBIT 5 Time out—owned and operated businesses

Region	Countries
Americas	United States, Canada, Argentina
Europe	United Kingdom, France, Germany, Portugal, Netherlands, Czech Republic, Sweden, Ireland, Italy
Africa	South Africa
Middle East	None
Australasia	None
Asia	India

Source: Adapted from Time Out Group, *Time Out Admission Document*, 2016, 14, accessed November 17, 2016, http://media.timeout.com/www_timeout_com_uploads/wp-content/uploads/2016/06/Admission-Document.pdf, and company input.

EXHIBIT 6 Time out—international licensing arrangements

Region	Countries
Americas	Mexico, Brazil
Europe	Croatia, Spain, Switzerland, Turkey, Russia, Cyprus, Malta
Africa	Ghana
Middle East	United Arab Emirates, Lebanon, Oman, Bahrain, Qatar, Israel
Australasia	Australia (includes the right to operate in New Zealand)
Asia	Japan, China, Malaysia, Singapore, Sri Lanka, Korea, Hong Kong, Thailand

Source: Adapted from Time Out Group, *Time Out Admission Document*, 2016, 15, accessed November 17, 2016, http://media.timeout.com/www_timeout_com_uploads/wp-content/uploads/2016/06/Admission-Document.pdf, and company input.

ANALYSIS OF TIME OUT CASE USING A REDUCTIONIST APPROACH

The primary issue in this case is returning the company to profitability, as indicated in the title of the case! The fact that a singular primary issue can be identified quickly lends itself to considering a reductionist approach. As an analyst, you can ask the question: "given the presence of a clear primary issue, how can this be broken down into sub-parts for further analysis?" If the answer to this question was "not easily", or "it can't", then a holistic or hybrid approach should be considered. But in this case, there are several ways of subdividing the problem.

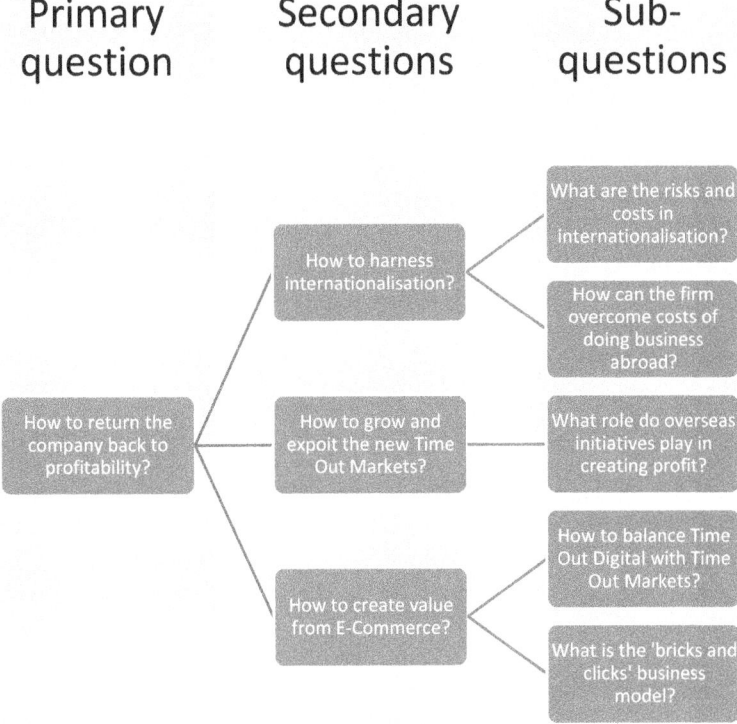

Primary question · Secondary questions · Sub-questions

- How to return the company back to profitability?
  - How to harness internationalisation?
    - What are the risks and costs in internationalisation?
    - How can the firm overcome costs of doing business abroad?
  - How to grow and expoit the new Time Out Markets?
    - What role do overseas initiatives play in creating profit?
  - How to create value from E-Commerce?
    - How to balance Time Out Digital with Time Out Markets?
    - What is the 'bricks and clicks' business model?

FIGURE 7.1 Question tree for the Time Out case

A question tree can be derived relatively easily in this case and can act as a tool to guide the reductionist process. Figure 7.1 shows a question tree for the Time Out case. Several secondary questions arise. In this worked example, we opt for three secondary questions. In your own reading of the case, it may be that a different number of secondary questions are identified. It may be that they are different in substance. In this example, we opt for three because: (1) each represents a clear context of the case (i.e., there is sufficient evidence in the case that each constitutes a dominant context), (2) they are sufficiently distinct to warrant being reduced and separated in this way, and (3) they are all linked to the issue of profitability. But this is not a fixed rule; what matters is that you are able to justify your choice of secondary questions.

Firstly, we consider the issue of *internationalisation*. This is an interesting and challenging context in this case. When a company ventures abroad, it encounters new sources of risk. In the Time Out case, the firm's core offerings (information about events and entertainment) are very much embedded in the local culture. They are immersed in the unique characteristics of cities in host countries. Indeed, it was a strategic focus of Time Out to concentrate on the 'best of a city'. At the same time, venturing abroad comes with the risk of being seen as an 'outsider'; discussed in the academic literature on internationalisation as 'liability of foreignness' (Eden & Miller, 2004). This liability of foreignness could put Time Out at a disadvantage compared to other local competitors and substitute offerings that have a trusted brand image and detailed cultural knowledge of the city in the host country. The question then arises whether and how the use of partners can help to overcome the liability of foreignness. If partners can be found and used to help Time Out achieve sales abroad, they will also be expecting to take a share of the revenues and profits. This will put pressure on the profitability of the focal company in foreign markets and question its viability as a global brand. According to Exhibits 4 and 5 in the case, most wholly owned businesses of the company were in the UK, US and Canada, and Europe. Most international licensing agreements were in countries further afield, geographically, and culturally (including Africa, the Middle East, and Asia).

Secondly, we consider the issue of *corporate entrepreneurship*, defined as the creation of a new business within an existing business. We see this very conspicuously in the Time Out case in the form of Time Out Markets (TOM). The first Time Out Market started in Lisbon, Portugal. It was not an HQ-driven initiative that had been tried and tested in the home country and then rolled out to other countries around the world. Quite the opposite. It was what academics refer to as a 'subsidiary initiative', a business initiative that was identified and exploited in a host country. One interesting point about subsidiary initiatives is that they can be used to create new knowledge about a new market space for the whole organisation, not just the local part of it (Williams & Lee, 2011). They can form the basis of new businesses within the corporation that then take on a life of their own when they are diffused across other countries. Innovative dynamics and entrepreneurialism that take place in the overseas subsidiary can form the basis of sustained competitive advantage for the whole MNE (Birkinshaw, 1997). But how easy is this to pull off? Just because an initiative in one country is profitable, it does not mean to say that it is necessarily profitable in another.

Thirdly, we consider the issue of *E-commerce* and the fact that Time Out had invested over the previous years in the digital space. Indeed, it had reduced its strategic emphasis on printing and paper publications distributed and sold in cities. The traditional *Time Out* magazine had not been sold any more in paper format and had only been distributed on a free basis with advertisers providing a source of revenue. The big strategic thrust for the organisation here was in the form of the Time Out Digital division (TOD). Unlike the TOM in Lisbon, which was a host country initiative, TOD was an ongoing centrally driven strategic transformation for Time Out. According to Exhibit 2 in the case, revenue from the E-commerce segment had increased from £9.8m to £11.7m between 2014 and 2015. However, losses for the overall enterprise continued. The case also shows how competitive and disruptive the digital space had become. The key question within the E-commerce area is how to balance TOD with TOM. TOM related to actual experiences that customers received. TOD related to online interfaces in cyberspace, allowing customers, for instance, to search for information, read reviews, comment on their experiences, and book tickets for events. The problem was that these same customers were not necessarily locked-in to Time Out's online offering. There were many other appealing and therefore competing offerings for customers to use, some of which were highly disruptive. And the same customers that used both TOM and TOD would not necessarily stay loyal to TOM and TOD. At the heart of the issue here is the fundamental business model that the company needed to develop that would generate sustainable profits.

We can see several dominant contexts in this case. There is an internationalisation context – the company has already expanded into many markets around the world, either through wholly owned subsidiaries or through licensing agreements. And it achieved this despite its relatively small size. The internationalisation context is a source of opportunity for the firm, but also a source of risk. Then there is the organisational context – the CEO, Julio Bruno, has started to change the organisational culture to be more entrepreneurial and cross-disciplinary. He has set up organisational structures for both TOM and TOD (Exhibit 4 in the case), and the company has a corporate governance set-up that includes outside directors with plenty of experience. This is important, given the recent IPO that occurred and that has placed a great deal of scrutiny on the leadership team as it seeks to drive performance for a new set of shareholders. Arguably, the cyberspace context is also a dominant context for the case. We noted the importance of TOD in an increasingly disruptive space and the need to develop a business model that has TOD at its heart, but which also appreciates the complementarity to TOM. How this cyberspace can be understood and utilised strategically seems to be critical, especially given the trends towards the use of smartphones in researching, booking, paying for, and commenting on entertainment in cities. And finally, one can see a clear temporal context – the case presents some history to the company and shows how it has evolved over the recent past from being owned by founder Tony Elliott to now being at a post-IPO point with a broad and diverse shareholder base at the decision point. We see how many of the other dominant contexts have evolved over time. The internationalisation context has resulted in the emergence of a new subsidiary initiative that may give new possibilities for profitability based on a new business model yet to be fully designed and established. The organisational context has also changed enormously, especially with the new leadership team on the run up to the IPO. And the context for internet transactions and client engagement is one that did not even exist in the first three decades of the firm's existence.

We use a reductionist approach because of the way in which this case can be decomposed into smaller, lower-level parts for a series of discrete analyses. It is the type of problem well-suited to reductionism (Grewatsch et al., 2021). In the approach conducted here, these analytical chunks – internationalisation, corporate entrepreneurship (in the subsidiary), and E-commerce – make the overall analytical task manageable. While ultimately these chunks are all interrelated at the firm strategy level, there are different bodies of academic literature that look at them. More precisely, it will be possible to draw from these different bodies of literature to understand determinants of performance and profitability. This will help us evaluate what has been going wrong in the case from a profitability point of view, and then generate recommendations for future strategic action. Reductionism is supported because of the possibility that laws that apply at one level also apply at other levels (Andersen, 2001) (i.e., the fundamental relationship between the firm's capabilities and financial performance). This means the condition of connectability is satisfied. We can also seek to establish the connection between capabilities and financial performance at both primary and secondary levels, meaning the condition of derivability is satisfied (Andersen, 2001). If either or both conditions are not satisfied, or it is unclear how they would be satisfied, it does not necessarily mean a reductionist approach cannot be applied. The key point is that the organisation of the sub-parts into the overall primary question makes sense and that we can justify our answer to the overall primary question through the organisation of the sub-parts (Wimsatt, 2006). Another basis to justify the reductionist approach is that we are distanced from the phenomenon (Verschuren, 2001); we are not consultants, employees, or managers working in Time Out itself.

To aid us with the analysis of each sub-part and the reintegration of findings into the overall primary question we will draw on one seminal article from the academic literature relating to each sub-part, before synthesising the results using the Matrix of Principles approach (Henderson & Segal, 2013). The Matrix of Principles approach allows the integration of major elements that make up one theoretically based principle (in this case, that there will be a relationship between firm capabilities and financial performance) into an overall visualisation. We use this technique to summarise the evidence for this relationship across the sub-parts. Reintegrating analytical output from different sub-components is essential in a reductionist approach. First, we will conduct the three sub-analyses. Second, we will produce the matrix showing the integration of the elements.

Sub-analysis #1: Internationalisation

The principle in the first sub-analysis is that there is a relationship between the internationalisation of the firm and its financial performance. Several theories are shown by the international business (IB) literature to be useful in understanding performance outcomes, including cost efficiencies, exploiting cross-national distances, flexibility in location choice and internal cross-border learning advantages, as well as risks and costs of coordination and communication highlighted by transaction costs theory (Pangarkar, 2008). We use the 'OLI' (eclectic) paradigm pioneered by John H. Dunning over many years since the 1960s. We will draw on one article: Dunning (2000), as it does a good job at explaining the motives for internationalising and the way three different theoretical lenses (O – Ownership advantages, L – Locational advantages, I – Internalisation advantages) can be used to help us understand what it is about internationalisation that can lead to (or undermine) profitability. In this sense, Dunning (2000) helps us to be even more reductionist: breaking down the secondary layer under internationalisation into three more sub-questions (O, L, and I).

Ownership advantages relate to assets (tangible and intangible) under the firm's control that it can use to overcome liability of foreignness in overseas markets. The Time Out case reveals several assets here. It has an established brand, a strong and evolving entrepreneurial culture, and importantly, financial capital raised through the recent IPO. The latter totals £59 million and the indicated areas for investment are revealed in the information for investors at the time of the IPO – shown in case Exhibit 3. Another positive revolves around the launch of TOM in Lisbon, an asset that has shown itself to be profitable in the first year of operation. However, we note from the case that the technology used by the company is still evolving and this is clearly a competitive space for servicing the market. Indeed, a large part of the indicated areas for investment of the proceeds from the IPO are in new technology. And it is not clear how new technology can be utilised profitably across large numbers of foreign markets. Overall, the link between ownership advantages is partially evident, but opaque in many respects.

Localisation advantages relate to features of the countries in which the firm has a presence, which will support above-normal returns. Exhibit 4 in the Time Out case shows 13 countries in which the company has owned and operated businesses. One could argue that this is high, given the size of the company, which is still an SME. Wholly owned foreign subsidiaries will incur greater costs, including costs of coordinating knowledge about the local market conditions and requirements for service delivery. The principle that a small company should focus on a small number of countries is raised in this case. On this basis we attribute a "not evident" to this element. Clearly, there will be certain locational attractions as advantages in each country, otherwise Time Out would not have entered in the first place. Chief amongst these will be presence of cities, market size in those cities, and level of economic development. While these can be seen as location advantages per se, when one looks at the number of countries with wholly owned subsidiaries, and the geographical spread of those countries, it is not clear how coordination costs and localisation advantages are being exploited.

Internalisation advantages are the gains accrued to the firm by internalisation of transactions (such as by setting up or acquiring a wholly owned subsidiary in another country), compared to carrying out those transactions on the open market (Dunning, 2000, p. 164). Here we find some strong evidence that the principle of internalisation theory has been applied in practice. One finds the evidence for this in case Exhibits 5 and 6. Transactions are internalised (Exhibit 5) in countries that are closer, either culturally, linguistically, or geographically. Transactions appear to be externalised through licensing (Exhibit 6) in countries that are culturally, institutionally, and geographically further from the home country. This is suggestive of the fact that the former Time Out strategy has taken various forms of transaction cost into consideration when assessing the risks of doing business in this industry in these 'further away' locations. For this reason, we note that the principle of internalisation advantages is evident in the actual corporate strategy of the firm.

Sub-analysis #2: Corporate entrepreneurship (in the subsidiary)

The principle in the second sub-analysis is that there is a relationship between entrepreneurial initiative arising in an overseas subsidiary, the development of that subsidiary, and the overall competitiveness of the corporation. So, we frame this according to subsidiary initiative and development. There is a large and established literature on the topic of subsidiary initiatives in international firms (Strutzenberger & Ambos, 2014). It has been seen as a distinct context for the creation of entrepreneurial knowledge in the firm, and a major source of competitiveness for the firm (Williams & Lee, 2011). We choose one seminal article to conduct the sub-analysis here, using the work of Birkinshaw and Hood (1998). The authors develop a model to understand the factors that determine the role development of an overseas subsidiary. The important point relating to TOM in the Time Out case is the fact that Portugal as a host country saw an evolving role as soon as TOM was established and took off. The specific business that the Portuguese subsidiary was involved with changed dramatically once TOM was established. The implications of this for the overall Time Out Group was not only immediate revenues. It was also the generation of entrepreneurial knowledge for this new business segment, knowledge that could then be applied in other markets around the world in order to seek new revenues and profits.

Birkinshaw and Hood's (1998) model sets out some theoretically grounded elements for us to understand this. First, decisions made by headquarters managers allow the new TOM activities to be performed by the subsidiary, this requiring the allocation of appropriate decision rights to the subsidiary. This is referred to as head-office assignment by Birkinshaw and Hood (1998). Second, the subsidiary also has a choice in the activities it takes on. We can assume that subsidiary managers were confident to pursue the TOM initiative, but their activities on the ground (see section on Time Out Market in the case), were likely ones that could not have been effectively taken by HQ managers (including decisions on the specific location of TOM, searching and contracting for chefs and artists, selection and management of architects for the market). The local capabilities for local delivery of experiences for customers is essential. Third, there is a local environment determinism that influences the evolving subsidiary's role. In the case, this would have included the existence of a market comprised of local consumers and international tourists that would want to visit the TOM. On the supply side, it would have included the existence of sufficient high-quality and well-known local chefs that could offer the 'best of the city'. In all these areas we find evidence of the existence of the theoretical element required for the Matrix of Principles. In line with sub-analysis #1, we also see a further decomposition of theoretical principles into lower-level constructs, reinforcing the reductionist stance for analysing this case.

Sub-analysis #3: E-commerce (TOD)

The principle in the third sub-analysis is that value can be created through E-commerce and that this value is created through the fundamental business model in use. The topic of value creation and business models based on E-commerce has received a high level of attention by academics (Paredes, Barrutia & Echebarria, 2014). In the case, we are particularly interested in TOD, and the sub-question of how TOD and TOM can complement each other. We select the seminal work of Amit and Zott (2001) to examine this. Amit and Zott (2001) develop a model of how value is created in e-business, derived inductively from a study of 59 cases. Four interrelated factors are shown to be relevant. The first of these is novelty: e-businesses create value when they enable new transaction structures and content, and new participants to transactions. We do not see a great amount of novelty in the digital transformation described in the Time Out case; much of the functionality (listings, bookings) had already been done by alternative providers at that time. However, the new areas of functionality, such as pay-at-table using the Time Out app, were potentially novel. So, there is mixed evidence here. The second relates to lock-in: the extent to which there are costs for customers if they switch to using the services of alternative providers of information about entertainment and events. We attribute this as not present in the case. There are really no switching costs for customers. The third relates to complementarities: the extent to which value is created by combining products with services, or between online and physical assets. TOD and TOM are clearly distinct but, apart from an org chart showing how they are organisationally related (case Exhibit 4), there is not a great deal of information in the case on how complementarity features in the strategy of the company. Fourthly, efficiency of the platform can be a source of value creation. This may mean reducing search costs for customers, which TOD clearly does. The platform is also likely to be simple to use and offers information in a speedy fashion. These are positives as far as efficiency is concerned. However, whether the platform can achieve economies of scale is not clear in the case. For instance, there are many market segments that do not have coverage with the Time Out model (such as provincial cities), and the reporting of content will be at the discretion of writers and editors working for – or contracted to – the company. So, the verdict for efficiency is also one of partial evidence.

Table 7.2 shows the Matrix of Principles for the sub-analyses, including sub-elements within each analysis. This reductionist approach breaks down the primary question into three main sub-analyses, but then into ten elements in total. The approach involves seeking

TABLE 7.2 Matrix of Principles for profitability in the Time Out case

Theoretically based principle	Elements		Evidence of elements	Evidence of principles
1. Internationalisation needs to overcome costs of doing business abroad	1.1	*Ownership advantages:* Time Out has firm-specific advantages in brand, technology, TOM, organisational culture, knowledge, financial capital that overcomes liability of foreignness	⊖	• ⊖ ∅
	1.2	*Location advantages:* For an SME of Time Out's size and asset base, a focus on quality services in low numbers of countries makes sense	∅	
	1.3	*Internalisation advantages:* Wholly owned operations make sense in developed/culturally closer countries – easier to control these firm-specific assets; partner arrangements make sense in more distant countries	•	
2. Subsidiary initiatives can form the basis of competitive advantage	2.1	*Autonomy:* Most decisions made centrally in London, but increasing autonomy given to TOMs, starting with Portugal	•	•
	2.2	*A source of best practice:* TOM in Lisbon has moved from exploration to exploitation with outstanding results – this will be a source of best practice and a model to build on for future TOMs in other locations	•	
	2.3	*Location assets:* Has appropriate cultural resources (cuisine/dining/entertainment) and client base (business, locals, and tourists)	•	
3. Value can be created through e-business and digitalisation	3.1	*Novelty:* Online listings are not novel but new tech in bookings and pay-at-table are relatively new to the market	⊖	⊖ ∅
	3.2	*Lock-in:* Ideally, customers cannot switch easily; in practice, they do	∅	
	3.3	*Complementarities:* TOM and digital offerings are distinct but it is not clear how they complement each other	∅	
	3.4	*Efficiency:* This is provided through up-to-date information and simplifying transactions, but unclear how scalable this will be for the company if customers are able to switch easily	⊖	

Note: Evident = •; Partially-evident = ⊖; Not evident/countervailing evidence = ∅.

information and insights from the case to establish evidence for each of the elements. The result, as seen in Table 7.2, is very mixed. There are four elements where we find support for the principle that the company's capabilities will drive profitability. There are three elements where we claim partial support for this. And there are three further elements where we claim there is no support.

In conclusion, we can say the following: the situation is mixed with respect to internationalisation and digital transformation. In these two areas there is not overwhelming evidence that the theoretical principles for value creation are present. Subsidiary initiatives, on the other hand, are a strong area for value creation. This will be contingent on how they can be diffused to other countries appropriately, following the initial TOM in Portugal. Strategic attention should be paid to re-balancing international presence with a scaling down and re-focusing of wholly owned operations to countries with the highest level of locational advantages. The company's leaders should work urgently on finding ways to improve novelty and lock-in within TOD as well as complementarities for the strategic integration between TOD and TOM.

CASE 2

☒ IVEY | Publishing **Brightwater: Clean Water from Broken Wells**

W29898

BRIGHTWATER ETHIOPIA: CLEAN WATER FROM BROKEN WELLS

Christopher Williams, Gayle Allard, and Atsede Tesfaye wrote this case solely to provide material for class discussion. The authors do not intend to illustrate either effective or ineffective handling of a managerial situation. The authors may have disguised certain names and other identifying information to protect confidentiality.

In May 2022, Ethiopian social entrepreneur Berhanu Gebeyehu had to decide on next steps for his clean drinking water business, Brightwater Ethiopia (Brightwater), which he had begun in 2019 in the southern town of Dilla. Gebeyehu noted that

96 per cent of Dilla's households had reported on surveys that the clean water available in the town was inadequate for their needs and that school-aged girls regularly missed class because they bore the burden of collecting water, often from unsafe sources.[1] Following two successful years of business, during which Gebeyehu had striven to contribute to the United Nations (UN) sustainable development goals (SDGs) by providing clean drinking water and boosting gender equality while also making a profit, Gebeyehu wanted to reduce his business's dependency on the foreign non-governmental organization (NGO) that had helped fund and set up the business. He was also considering expanding his social enterprise's model across Ethiopia as well as developing a capability that would deliver clean water in plastic bottles.

ETHIOPIA AND SAFE DRINKING WATER

Ethiopia had a unique and fascinating ancient history. It was one of only two countries never colonized in a continent once parcelled out by Europeans. Its language, alphabet, and even its calendar were unique, and it was the world's largest land-locked nation and the second most populous country in Africa. It was also known for the profound poverty suffered by its people as well as the scarcity of clean water available for daily use. Despite having been one of the world's fastest-growing nations in the twenty-first century, Ethiopia's personal income was still very low. Most standard-of-living indicators ranked Ethiopia near the bottom of the global scale (see Exhibit 1).

One of the most serious manifestations of poverty in Ethiopia was the dearth of basic resources such as drinking water. Low incomes and insufficient government funding meant there was little or no investment in the infrastructure and treatment processes needed to give the population access to sufficient clean water for drinking, cooking, bathing, and washing. In addition to a lack of investment in water development projects, continued droughts also contributed to water scarcity, which had serious implications for health. In Ethiopia, up to 80 per cent of communicable diseases were due to unsafe drinking water (see Exhibit 2), leading to stunting, malnutrition, and high mortality rates in children.

Only 7 per cent of the water supply outside of the capital, Addis Ababa, was low risk. When clean water was not readily available, the welfare of the local population was affected in additional ways. Unless the water was piped directly into homes or was available in sufficient amounts very close by, family members had to invest time in carrying water home for household use. A report by the We Are Water Foundation noted that this was particularly true for women and girls, who "have to travel huge distances to fetch water... [and] consequently, have no time to go to school or participate in community life."[2] Community life extended to economic activities as well as schooling, which girls frequently missed part or all of while carrying water for their families (see Exhibit 3).

These implications were so far-reaching that the UN included water access as one of their SDGs (Goal 6). An academic paper on the water situation in southern

Ethiopia stated the issue very simply: "No other single intervention is more likely to have a significant impact on global poverty than the provision of safe water."[3]

WATER SHORTAGES IN DILLA AND THE RESPONSE OF NGO$_s$

A city of just under one hundred thousand people, Dilla was located in a lush tropical area of southern Ethiopia in a region called the Southern Nations, Nationalities and Peoples' Region. Although Dilla was less than four hundred kilometres south of Addis Ababa, travelling to Dilla was difficult due to the extremely poor condition of the roads. In Dilla, poverty was higher and incomes were lower than the national average.

Dilla was situated between two rivers. A city water facility treated the river water and piped it to community faucets in many of the areas where people lived. However, the water did not flow regularly. Sometimes it only came out of the faucet once a month, and people in the surrounding area hurried to fill any containers they had to store water for coming weeks. The city water flowing from the faucets was often cloudy, making it possibly unsafe. Other sources of water, for those not living near a city faucet, were hand pumps at wells and taps at local springs. Children would wait in line for hours to fill jerry cans with clean water from these sources; a joint monitoring project by the World Health Organization (WHO) and UNICEF that analyzed data from twenty-five countries in sub-Saharan Africa noted, "It is estimated that women spend a combined total of at least 16 million hours each day collecting drinking water; men spend 6 million hours; and children, 4 million hours."[4] Water could also be drawn straight from the rivers, although the water was usually unsafe. Rivers were often used for bathing and for washing clothing and vehicles, and animals and people would sometimes defecate in the water. Some families bought jerry cans of water from local vendors or hired home delivery of water on donkey carts. The jerry cans could be dirty, contaminating otherwise clean water when it was poured inside.

Higher-income families with access to city water often had water tanks at home in which to fill and store water. Sometimes they would resell this water at high prices during the dry season. Many higher-income families also had expensive water filters that processed the water they purchased or collected, to ensure its safety.

In response to the dire water needs of Dilla, in the late twentieth and early twenty-first centuries, large NGOs invested in building wells around Dilla, to bring clean water to the population. One of the largest global water NGOs was Charity: water, which had spent about US$100 million digging wells in Ethiopia.[5] World Vision and Water.org were also active there. A total of eleven boreholes were dug in various areas of the city where underground water was available, with hand pumps installed on the surface enabling people to draw water into jerry cans for home use. However, the pumps broke down over time, and the town had neither the resources nor the expertise to repair them. By 2015, some of the boreholes had lain unused for decades.

In a survey carried out by Dilla University in 2015, the vast majority of families reported that (a) their main water source was over one hundred metres from home (with 52 per cent being over two hundred metres from home); (b) 48 per cent of households invested more than thirty minutes a day collecting water; and (c) water use for the average family was less than twenty litres per person per day (67 per cent of households).[6] This was compared with a WHO minimum standard of fifty to one hundred litres per day "to ensure that most basic needs are met and few health concerns arise."[7] Just under half of the surveyed population was able to obtain water from a city faucet (see Exhibit 4). In the same survey, 96 per cent of respondents indicated that they were not satisfied with the current water supply to the town, and 93 per cent indicated that distribution of water was not fair.[8]

In an academic paper based on the 2015 survey, Mandefro Chala Debela and Habtamu Kassa Muhye concluded that there was a "huge gap" between the town's water supply and the city's need for water, for various reasons.[9] Shortages had occurred because of problems with malfunctioning water pumps, unreliable power supply, and weak institutional structures. At the same time, the population had increased from 73,361 inhabitants in 2011 to 91,029 in 2015. In essence, the water supply infrastructure had become obsolete, resulting in interruptions to its supply and a perception amongst the population that water distribution was unfair.[10]

DEVELOPMENT OF THE DILLA INITIATIVE FOR SOLAR-POWERED PUMPS

Gayle Allard, an economics professor at IE Business School (IE) in Madrid, began taking master of business administration students to Dilla, Ethiopia, in 2013. Her initial objective was simply to visit a country that fascinated her. As she became familiar with Ethiopia, she spent more and more time pondering how to help address some of the serious economic problems that she saw there. Initially, she and her students organized intensive English courses for the girls in town who were impoverished, in hopes of supporting their education. But the water problem was visible everywhere in Dilla—the need for it, the time invested in obtaining it, and the lack of government spending and other efforts to address the problem. Allard and successive groups of IE students began working with water experts and researching possible solutions, and Allard created an NGO called the Wuha Sira Initiative (Wuha Sira) to raise funds for a possible project. Wuha Sira's mission was to promote the education of young women in Ethiopia and enhance the provision of access to clean water. Their donations came from individual contributors, many of whom had travelled with Allard to Ethiopia, and an annual grant from the IE Foundation. As Allard and her students worked, they always came up against the same set of obstacles: insufficient government involvement and funding, no trusted local partner on the ground, and no capacity to supervise projects from Madrid, with only one trip to the site per year.

The IE visits to Dilla did not go unnoticed, however. One summer, a local entrepreneur, Berhanu Gebeyehu, requested a meeting with Allard to discuss his own interest in doing something to help his city alleviate its water shortage. Gebeyehu, a native of Dilla who first studied to become a priest before deciding to complete law school and work for the local government on social issues, was something of a serial entrepreneur. Besides his law practice in Dilla, he had been involved in a landscaping company and a local transport company. While he had no formal business training, he had a passion for the welfare of his community and had decided that alleviating the water problem should be a key objective of his professional life.

Gebeyehu and Allard began looking for a small, feasible project that would generate sufficient returns to enable Gebeyehu, as a social entrepreneur, to cover operating costs. Meanwhile, the local government, which had also heard about IE's efforts and Gebeyehu's interest, made Gebeyehu an offer: he could operate the eleven city-owned boreholes that were non-functional, and collect revenues from them, if he could find a way to repair their pumps and make the water flow again for the community. Allard and the IE students drew up a business plan with precise technical specifications: Solar power would be used to power new pumps that would be installed on the old boreholes. The water would be piped into large storage tanks and sold at an affordable price to the people of Dilla. There would be branded green jerry cans that Gebeyehu's new company, Brightwater, would collect from consumers when they were brought for refill, so that they could be sanitized, keeping the water clean. Gebeyehu agreed to give preference to female employees, and he accepted a government requirement to give the water for free to the lowest-income consumers, who would bring an official card when they came to collect their water. Allard's NGO, Wuha Sira, would provide a grant covering the start-up costs for the project (see Exhibit 5).

OPERATIONAL AND FUNDING MODEL

Brightwater began operating in late 2019 with a pilot project at a single borehole in a neighbourhood called Lottery. Gebeyehu set a low price for the water due to his concern for the community and had difficulty covering costs at the outset. As the COVID-19 pandemic reached Dilla, he built small handwashing centres and showers and, to the displeasure of Wuha Sira, diverted some of the water there to help with local sanitation efforts and boost his revenues. He initially subcontracted home water delivery for some clients to donkey cart operators who traditionally provided water door to door to customers, but he suspended this service when he discovered that the donkey cart operators were selling the water elsewhere at higher prices and keeping the revenues. Other challenges were related to developing capability in water management. These were partly addressed through hands-on trial and error and partly through knowledge transfer from Wuha Sira. Gebeyehu said:

> Factors that hindered us initially were a gap of skill and knowledge all about
> water management, water quality, sharing experiences with other companies,

water filtering systems (to train staff as well as customers), managing the water sources (to know when the water level is low or high), and how to manage other water sources (spring water) if I was to expand into other towns. This is very important to expand my water business and give more services for customers.

Brightwater managed to break even over the first year, partly because prices rose with demand in the dry season (see Exhibit 6). The largest line of business in terms of revenue was through provision of the handwashing and shower services. These services proved to be particularly in demand during the first year of the COVID-19 outbreak.

After a year of operation with the successful pilot, Gebeyehu wanted to continue expanding. Two more boreholes were selected, Wuha Sira raised an additional $4,000 in funding and provided it as a grant to Brightwater, and Gebeyehu followed the same template: replacing the non-functional hand pump with a usable solar-powered pump, building a storage platform for five-thousand-litre tanks to store the water in, and buying new green jerry cans to fill and sell in the surrounding neighbourhood. In the second year of operation, Brightwater's clean water revenue increased by almost 50 per cent, while the shower service decreased by almost the same amount. This reflected the expansion to new boreholes and capacity, and less demand for washing (see Exhibit 7).

As he expanded to three boreholes, Gebeyehu also wanted to begin home water delivery to have a greater impact and boost revenues. In order to license Gebeyehu to deliver Brightwater jerry cans to houses, the local government administration required Brightwater to use a vehicle rather than a donkey cart; doing so would indicate a higher-level product and fully reliable, clean water. Gebeyehu approached a local microfinance institution and a bank for a loan to buy a car for water delivery. He projected that with three boreholes and home water delivery, his profits would be large enough to cover the loan payment for the car at 12 per cent interest. Gebeyehu said:

> Say, if we could have three or four systems set up, everything can be loaded at once in a car. We can arrange for five thousand litres of water to be poured into all the tankers, and people can get the water right where they are instead of having to always come to us. Our employees will be posted in every village; there will be one mother as a representative, and one big tanker will be bought for her. She can then make all the sales needed and make profit for herself as well.

STATUS AND DECISION POINT

By the middle of 2022, the third borehole was just becoming operational, but the price of the car Gebeyehu had planned to buy had tripled due to supply-chain problems and the plummeting local currency, the Ethiopian birr. As such, he had to abandon plans for home delivery using a vehicle. However, there were five permanent employees, and the impact of the business on the community was becoming clear. As Gebeyehu recounted:

My satisfaction is when people are drinking water from my Brightwater company, when some workers are employed having job opportunity, and, financially, I am getting income from the business. I have employed a [young woman] as sales for the second site. Her salary is not enough to pay for her accounting course in a private college during a weekend program. So I am paying her ETB 500 more every month.[11] She is good with her academics and her job. She is also working on additional tasks in my business, such as pump operating and managing water quantity in the storages. I plan to hire [young women] who are in need of school fees and interested in attending private colleges. It is difficult to have [young women] pass to university, so better to support those who want to attend private and government colleges.

At that time, Gebeyehu had a new objective in mind: to further expand his business without depending on Wuha Sira for additional grant funding. He did not want to continue to rely on foreign charity to run his business. He had also considered expanding his product range to include plastic bottling and to sell the Brightwater product in smaller plastic bottles that would be more convenient for customers and could be sold in different outlets. Establishing a plastic bottling plant in Ethiopia would require obtaining land and machinery and meeting the local administration requirements for a manufacturing plant. Gebeyehu had done some research and discovered that the cost of the machinery was not out of reach. He estimated that for less than $10,000 he could obtain the equipment needed to produce approximately sixty bottles per hour, which could then be distributed across the country. However, he knew that to import equipment he would need a loan for this amount, which would be difficult to obtain in Ethiopia due to the civil war and economic downturn. He would also need the permission of the Dilla administration zone to bottle city water and sell it elsewhere—an idea that they might not support. He also faced objections from Wuha Sira, which expressed to him that they preferred not to see the business that they had financed expand into plastic water bottling due to the environmental impact of such an undertaking.

After two and a half years of successful operations with solid financial and non-financial results, Gebeyehu mulled over the next steps for his social enterprise. The first option was for Gebeyehu to continue as before, accepting funding from Wuha Sira to continue to expand until all eleven broken wells in Dilla were providing clean water to the community at a reasonable price. As a second option, Gebeyehu could expand without support from a foreign NGO by seeking local funding and continuing to provide more clean water to the local community as he successively opened broken wells. The last option was for Gebeyehu to go forward with his idea to shift from jerry cans to plastic bottles for drinking water, possibly expanding his reach beyond Dilla into surrounding areas. What option would Gebeyehu choose?

EXHIBIT 1 Selected quality of life indicators, ethiopia versus other countries and country groups

Indicator	Ethiopia	Kenya	Nigeria	Zambia	Uganda	Ghana	DRC	SSA	Canada	World
GNI per capita (US$; Atlas method)	890	1,760	2,000	1,190	800	2,230	550	1,480	43,530	11,057
Population growth (%)	2.58	2.27	2.56	2.89	3.54	2.16	3.19	2.66	1.41	1.07
Poverty (% of population living on less than US$1.90/day PPPs)	30.8	37.1	39.1	58.7	41.3	12.7	77.2	42	0.2	10.1
Life expectancy at birth (years)	66.6	66.7	54.7	63.9	63.4	64.1	60.7	57.8	82.0	72.7
Primary completion rate (%)	68.1	99.7	NA	80	52.7	93.8	69.9	70.4	100	90.1
Under-five mortality rate (per 1,000 births)	50.7	43.2	117.2	61.7	45.8	46.2	84.8	75.8	4.9	37.7
Electric power consumption (kWh per capita)	69.2	164.3	144.5	717.3	....	391.3	108.5	487.3	15,588.5	3,131.7

Note: GNI = gross national income; PPP = purchasing power parity; kWh = kilowatt hour; DRC = Democratic Republic of Congo; SSA = sub-Saharan Africa.

Sources: "Ethiopia," The World Bank, accessed August 25, 2022, https://data.worldbank.org/country/ethiopia; "Kenya," The World Bank, accessed August 25, 2022, https://data.worldbank.org/country/kenya; "Nigeria," The World Bank, accessed August 25, 2022, https://data.worldbank.org/country/nigeria; "Zambia," The World Bank, accessed August 25, 2022, https://data.worldbank.org/country/zambia; "Uganda," The World Bank, accessed August 25, 2022, https://data.worldbank.org/country/uganda; "Ghana," The World Bank, accessed August 25, 2022, https://data.worldbank.org/country/ghana; "Congo, Dem. Rep.," The World Bank, accessed August 25, 2022, https://data.worldbank.org/country/congo-dem-rep; "Sub-Saharan Africa," The World Bank, accessed August 25, 2022, https://data.worldbank.org/country/sub-saharan-africa; "Canada," The World Bank, accessed August 25, 2022, https://data.worldbank.org/country/canada; "World," The World Bank, accessed August 25, 2022, https://data.worldbank.org/country/world.

EXHIBIT 2 Basic water indicators, ethiopia and selected countries (in percentages)

Indicator	Ethiopia	Kenya	Nigeria	Zambia	Uganda	Ghana	DRC	SSA	Canada	World
People using at least basic drinking water services	48.1	60.9	75.8	64.6	54.2	84.7	45.2	40.8	99.2	89.7
People in rural areas using at least basic drinking water services	38.5	51.1	60.0	47.3	46.5	70.9	21.7	33.6	99.1	81.1
People with basic hand-washing facilities	8.1	26.7	33.1	17.8	22.5	41.5	19.1	…	…	…
People using safely man-aged drinking water services	12.0	NA	21.3	NA	15.7	39.7	18.4	NA	99.0	73.7
Mortality rate per 100,000 from unsafe water, sanitation, and lack of hygiene	43.7	51.2	68.6	34.9	31.6	18.8	59.8	63.3	0.4	11.8

Note: DRC = Democratic Republic of Congo; SSA = sub-Saharan Africa.

Sources: "Ethiopia," The World Bank, accessed August 25, 2022, https://data.worldbank.org/country/ethiopia; "Kenya," The World Bank, accessed August 25, 2022, https://data.worldbank.org/country/kenya; "Nigeria," The World Bank, accessed August 25, 2022, https://data.worldbank.org/country/nigeria; "Zambia," The World Bank, accessed August 25, 2022, https://data.worldbank.org/country/zambia; "Uganda," The World Bank, accessed August 25, 2022, https://data.worldbank.org/country/uganda; "Ghana," The World Bank, accessed August 25, 2022, https://data.worldbank.org/country/ghana; "Congo, Dem. Rep.," The World Bank, accessed August 25, 2022, https://data.worldbank.org/country/congo-dem-rep; "Sub-Saharan Africa," The World Bank, accessed August 25, 2022, https://data.worldbank.org/country/sub-saharan-africa; "Canada," The World Bank, accessed August 25, 2022, https://data.worldbank.org/country/canada; "World," The World Bank, accessed August 25, 2022, https://data.worldbank.org/country/world.

EXHIBIT 3 Water collection and transport in Dilla, Ethiopia

Sources: Photographs taken by the case authors in August 2019.

EXHIBIT 4: Water use in Dilla, Ethiopia, 2015

	Source	Percentage (%)
Primary water source for the household	Pipeline	49
	Public tap	39
	Water vendors	12
Distance from water source to residence (metres)	Up to 10	4
	10–50	7
	50–100	14
	100–200	23
	>200	52
Average time spent collecting water (minutes)	<5	13
	5–30	39
	>30	48
Average water use per person per day (litres)	<20	67
	20–30	30
	30–50	3

Source: Created by the case authors based on Mandefro Chala Debela and Habtamu Kassa Muhye, "Water Supply and Demand Scenario of Dilla Town, Southern Ethiopia," *International Journal of Water Resources and Environmental Engineering* 9, no. 12 (December 2017): 270–76, https://doi.org/10.5897/IJWREE2017.0748.

EXHIBIT 5: Brightwater Ethiopia start-up costs, 2019

Start-up expenses	(ETB)	(US$)
Storage construction	34,400	669.69
Contingency	116	2.26
Prepaid labour expenses	7,685	149.61
Solar panels	44,800	872.15
Water pump, plumber	40,000	778.71
Storage, 5,000 litres (2)	36,000	700.83
Jerry cans	40,000	778.71
Total initial investment	203,001	3,951.95

Note: ETB = Ethiopian birr; USD 1 = ETB 51.3850 on May 1, 2022.

Source: Created by the case authors based on data provided by Brightwater Ethiopia.

EXHIBIT 6: Brightwater Ethiopia income statement, 2020 and 2021 (ETB)

	2020	2021
Number of jerry cans sold	10,242.00	13,739.00
Clean water revenue	22,713.00	34,917.00
Shower service revenue	31,653.00	16,687.00
Total net revenue	54,366.00	51,604.00
Cost of goods sold	620.00	1,960.00
Gross profit	53,746.00	49,644.00
Operating expenses	53,521.50	38,550.00
Earnings before interest and taxes	224.50	11,094.00
Interest expense	0.00	0.00
Income taxes	0.00	0.00
Net earnings	224.50	11,094.00
Net earnings (US$)	4.37	215.96

Note: ETB = Ethiopian birr; USD 1 = ETB 51.3850 on May 1, 2022.

Source: Created by the case authors based on data provided by Brightwater Ethiopia.

EXHIBIT 7: Brightwater Ethiopia balance sheet, 2020 and 2021 (ETB)

	2020	2021
Assets		
Current assets		
Cash	225	35,524
Property and equipment		
Solar panels	44,800	42,560
Water pump	40,000	36,000
Storage, 5,000 litres (2)	36,000	28,800
Jerry cans	40,000	26,667
Total assets	161,025	169,551

Liabilities		
Current liabilities	0	0
Long-term debt	0	0
Total liabilities	0	0
Shareholders' equity		
Retained earnings	161,025	169,551
Total liabilities	161,025	169,551

Note: ETB = Ethiopian birr; USD 1 = ETB 51.3850 on May 1, 2022. Depreciation: Solar panels, 20 years; water pump, 10 years; storage, 5 years; jerry cans, 3 years.

Source: Created by the case authors based on data provided by Brightwater Ethiopia.

ANALYSIS OF BRIGHTWATER CASE USING A HOLISTIC APPROACH

The primary issue in this case concerns the situation facing social entrepreneur Berhanu Gebeyehu in Dilla, Ethiopia, and how he should proceed with his social enterprise for clean water. The decision point concerns the proposal to move into plastic bottling following two years of successful operation of Brightwater. He was also considering whether to reduce dependence on the foreign NGO that helped to establish the social enterprise. This is a contentious proposition for two reasons. Firstly, moving into small plastic bottles in a location that does not have an established infrastructure for plastics processing and recycling could create plastic waste and cause damage to the natural environment. Secondly, the NGO – Wuhu Sira – is opposed to this and would still like to have some influence over how the social enterprise decides on its next strategic moves, especially in terms of gender equality in education and providing clean water.

There are various dominant contexts at play in this case. Firstly, there is the developing world context; an economically poor urban area where even the provision of clean water to the population has failed the government. International water charities had stepped in many years earlier to dig boreholes and install water pumps, but these had fallen into a state of disrepair. As noted in the case, the town of Dilla had higher poverty than the national average for Ethiopia, itself one of the world's poorest countries. Water usage in Dilla per family was reported at being less than 20 litres per day. This was less than the level recommended by the World Health Organization (WHO) which is between 50 and 100 litres per person per day.[1] While access to clean drinking water was declared a human right by the United Nations in 2010 (Resolution A/RES/64/292), it is a right not enjoyed in much of the developing world.

Secondly, there is a social enterprise context in the case. A social enterprise is an organisation that aims to promote social or environmental welfare over solely profit maximisation. In the Brightwater case, the company managed to break even in the first year and make a small profit in the second year. The company was not guided by profit maximisation, and it wanted to deliver a desperately needed service to Dilla residents. We note that prior efforts by international NGOs to solve the water access issue had resulted in boreholes and pumps that had become unusable. So, there is a social enterprise context here that involves different waves of attention to the issue. The learning that was generated following the former NGO strategy influenced a new approach by a new external actor in collaboration with Gebeyehu.

Thirdly, there is a technological/non-human context. Central to the solution identified by the IE MBA students on their assignment to Dilla and used by Brightwater was the solar powered pumps to replace the hand-operated ones that had fallen into disrepair. There was also the more basic technology used for container (jerrycan) sanitisation. Additionally, there was the new infrastructure required for piping water and storing it in large storage tanks. There were also the showers that were set up by Brightwater during the pandemic to help maintain cleanliness amongst the residents. Distribution remained an issue: donkey cart operators were initially used, and this was a problem when Gebeyehu found out they were acting opportunistically and selling the water at higher prices for their own personal gain. Gebeyehu was looking to invest in a car for distribution.

We position the analysis using holism because of the presence of multiple dominant contexts that overlap very tightly and that cannot be easily separated. The developing country context has had a major influence over the technology that was previously used and what is now possible. It meant social enterprises needed to step in and play a role in filling institutional weaknesses. There is no one single dominant context in the case, and there is a degree of dynamism, particularly in terms of the role foreign NGOs play. The case is certainly meaningful to UN SDGs, and there are many stakeholders involved. Finally, primary data was used in developing the case, meaning the case authors were close to the phenomenon. These are all criteria for holism that are satisfied in this case (see Table 5.2, Chapter 5).

We use a socio-technical systems (STS) approach for demonstrating holism with the Brightwater case. The main reason for this is that STS incorporates both human and non-human aspects. The human aspects are most prominent in the developing country and social enterprise contexts. They include the families affected, the girls who were disadvantaged and used as water collectors, the NGO (Wuhu Sira) and the IE students, the local government, donkey cart operators, and Gebeyehu himself. The non-human aspects are prominent in the technological context; the solution involved a range of low-tech interventions arranged in a new way. These included new solar-powered pumps, new pipes, water storage, new jerrycans, shower centres, and technology to replace and clean jerrycans.

Trist (1981) argues that STS studies need to be performed at three inter-connected levels: (1) a primary work system level (how people are working with technology to transform inputs into outputs), (2) a whole organisation systems level (such as whole plants), and (3) at a macrosocial systems level (which include communities and society). We combine elements of all levels here for two reasons. Firstly, we do not have complete operational information in the case to be able to depict only a primary work system level analysis for Dilla. This is certainly possible but would need additional primary data collection on the ground in Dilla. Secondly, we have data at all levels in the case – some information on how people work with technology, some information on the whole production system, and some information on how the community is affected.

STS can be used to analyse complex issues in environmental sustainability. Dwyer (2011) argues STS is applicable to challenges in climate change and mankind's impact on the environment. This is because STS emphasises two relevant aspects: a system goal related to sustainable development, and a feedback loop comparing actual outputs to desired outputs. There are two types of components within an STS analysis that aid this: (1) *components* that are based on humans and their social existence, and (2) *artefacts* that are technical in nature. Following this approach, we represent the former using a solid line box, and the latter with a dotted line box in Figures 7.2 and Figure 7.3. Dotted lines show the social relationships between human actors. These figures show our depiction of the socio-technical system for the Brightwater case before and after the Brightwater intervention in Dilla.

Before the intervention (Figure 7.2), there was a range of external influences, including poverty in Ethiopia, a backdrop of climate issues and drought, and the fact that the local and national governments have not solved the issue of clean water for much of the country's population. Brightwater's intervention was then associated with new external influences: the role of Wuhu Sira, and an awareness of the existence and availability of solar technology for water pumps (Figure 7.3). External outcomes beyond the main aim of providing clean water for Dilla include improved prospects for girls, especially in relation to education – a desired goal of Wuhu Sira, and the profitability of the enterprise (Figure 7.3).

Prior to the intervention, the main interdependencies in the technical subsystem are between derelict boreholes and delivery mechanisms through the water collectors (including young girls). The latter were tasked with transportation of dirty water to families although donkey carts were also used (Figure 7.2). The local government had social connections with families in Dilla and was aware of derelict boreholes and pumps, although had not solved the problem. After the intervention, the socio-technical system becomes more complex (Figure 7.3). Firstly, the existing subsystem shown in Figure 7.2 still exists, but we move it to one side of the diagram to make space for a new constellation of human and non-human objects. We retain this subsystem because of inertia; the previous system of water collection is still being used to some extent and Brightwater has not replaced all these norms. Secondly, we have new human components in the system as part of the intervention. These include the IE students, Brightwater itself, and loan providers. We position loan providers at the blurry boundary of the system as they had not made a concrete contribution to Brightwater at the time the case was written – whether for new infrastructure, expansion, or car acquisition. There are infrastructural artefacts such as new pipes, storage containers, facilities for cleaning jerrycans, and showers deployed during the Covid-19 pandemic. These are all shown on the right-hand side using dashed line boxes. There is also a new water access card that allows certain low-income families to have access to clean water for free. This was because of pressure from the local government, hence a social interdependency between Brightwater and the local government.

We see how Brightwater assumes a central position at the heart of the new socio-technical system in Figure 7.3. It relates socially to families, the IE students (and Wuhu Sira), as well as the local government. It interacts with many non-human artefacts, including the new solar powered pumps, the new pipes and shower centres, the jerrycans and their cleaning. It also has an interdependency with the donkey carts as a means for delivery, although this interdependency was challenged as noted in the case.

The main imperative when using STS in this way is to determine whether the system performance is reaching the system goal (Dwyer, 2011). There is clear evidence in the case that the clean water supply for Dilla has improved since Brightwater started operating. However, we do not have a follow-on study akin to the Debela and Muhye (2017) review of the water situation in Dilla, which is referred to in the case. Such a study could show the change in terms of key indicators such as time spent on water collection per day, cleanliness of the water consumed, and broader social impact. Nevertheless, Exhibit 6 in the case does show over 10,000 jerrycans sold in 2020 and nearly 14,000 in 2021. This is clear evidence of an impact and a new supply of clean water into the community.

As far as the decision point is concerned, the socio-technical system lens helps us consider the subsequent impact if Brightwater then reduced dependency on Wuhu Sira and/or sought funding to venture into plastic bottle use and distribution. If the interdependencies with Wuhu Sira were cut, the role of the IE students in future assessment and assistance would be threatened. Future grants (not loans) might not be possible. Figure 7.3 reminds us of the importance of the IE students (and the associated grant as indicated in the case) in establishing new technological artefacts that were at the heart of the solution and the business model for the social enterprise. There would be no point in even attempting to expand into plastic bottles if assistance and funding for new solar powered pumps and new boreholes was not forthcoming. The expansion of capacity would not be possible unless Brightwater was able to manage the continuation of solar powered pump installation itself, in addition to all the other operational activities taking place. Figure 7.3 also reminds us how complex these existing activities are. The ability of Brightwater to secure funding and assistance from other sources is contingent on its ability to demonstrate that the existing intervention has worked on a sustainable basis. We know that it has started to make an impact after two years of operation. But we do not yet know the extent of the diffusion of clean water throughout the community and its effects on local society over the longer term. The lack of information in this respect could deter other investors. Finally, introducing plastic bottle production and distribution into the frame would make the interaction between human and non-human objects in the socio-technical system even more complex. External outcomes so far have been positive. A proliferation of plastic bottles into the natural environment would threaten this.

In conclusion, we can say the following: Brightwater has created an initial solution to the dire water problems of Dilla, Ethiopia, under the external influence of a foreign NGO and students from IE Business School in Spain. The intervention has involved the establishment of a new socio-technical system, one that is more complex than the previous system, but also one that works financially and has started to have an impact. The system is working as expected although there are fine-tuning opportunities. Brightwater should continue its relationship with the external NGO to conduct this fine-tuning. It should not pursue plastic bottling because of the effect this would have on a socio-technical system that is performing adequately. Strategic effort should be made instead on repeating the analysis conducted in 2015 by Dilla University (Debela & Muhye, 2017) to independently assess the impact on the community of the new clean water system. This will provide a stronger measure of system performance and will allow the feedback loop to be more comprehensively completed before any further system interventions are made.

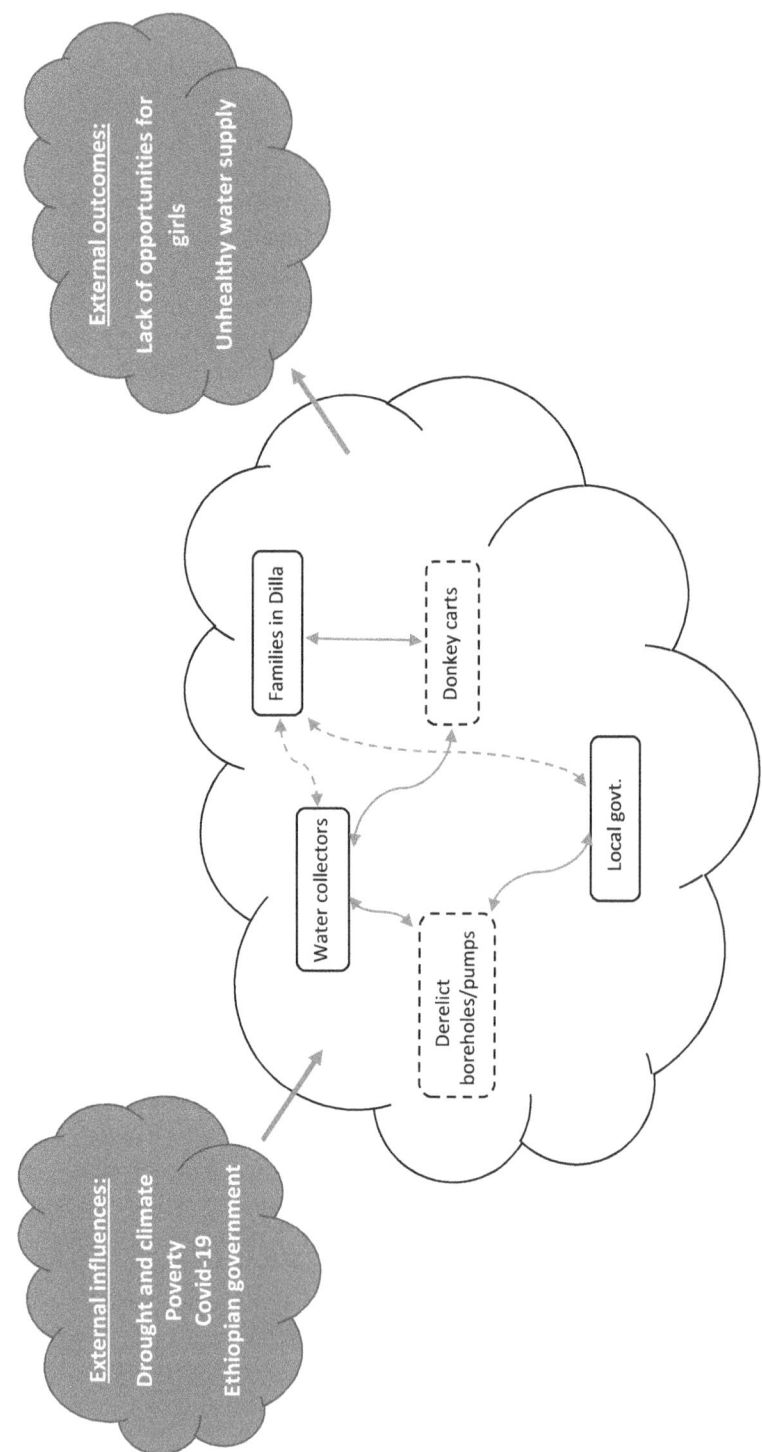

FIGURE 7.2 Socio-technical system for the Brightwater case (original situation)

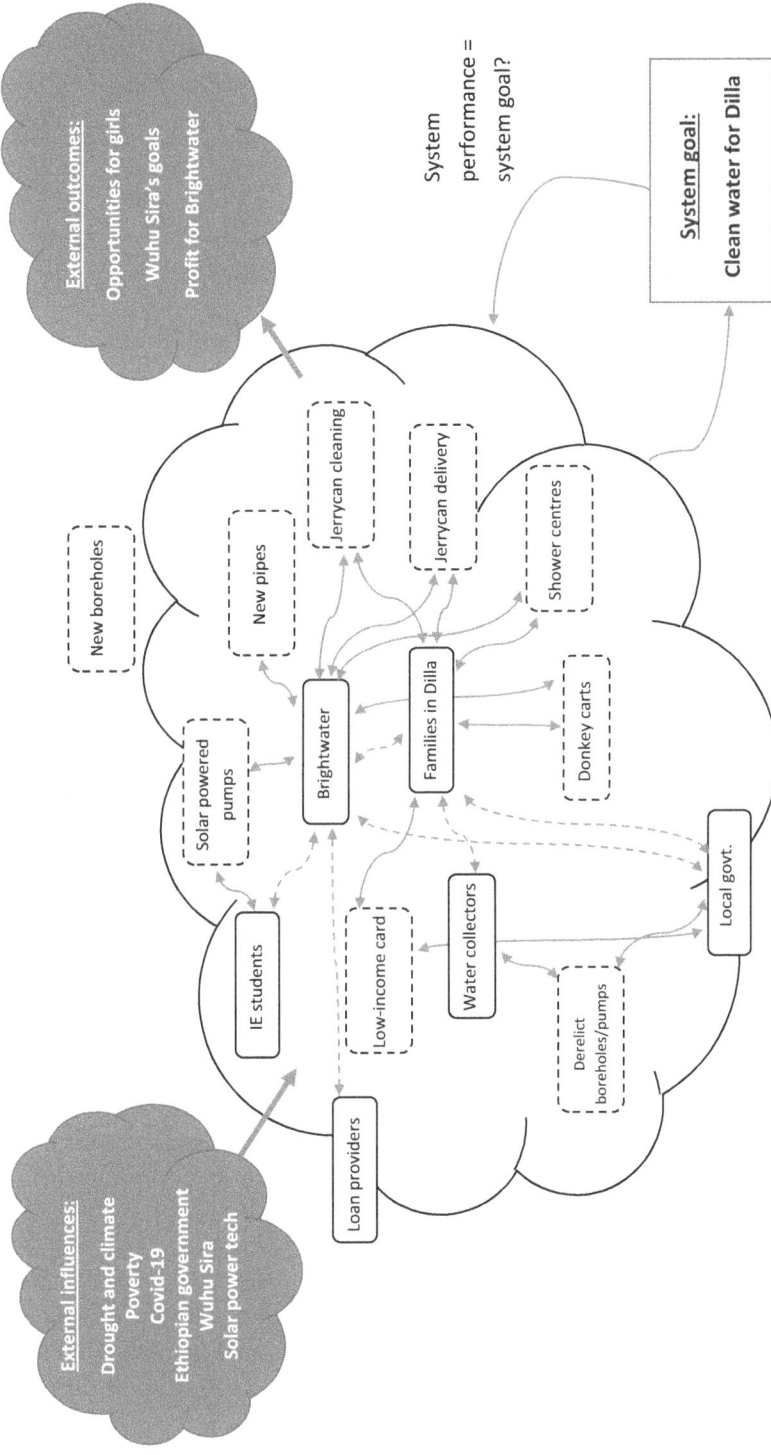

External outcomes:

Opportunities for girls

Wuhu Sira's goals

Profit for Brightwater

System performance = system goal?

System goal:

Clean water for Dilla

New boreholes

New pipes

Jerrycan cleaning

Jerrycan delivery

Shower centres

Solar powered pumps

Brightwater

Families in Dilla

Donkey carts

IE students

Low-income card

Water collectors

Local govt.

Derelict boreholes/pumps

Loan providers

External influences:

Drought and climate

Poverty

Covid-19

Ethiopian government

Wuhu Sira

Solar power tech

FIGURE 7.3 Socio-technical system for the Brightwater case (intervention by Brightwater)

CASE 3

Ivey | Publishing   **Olympus and the Whistleblower President**

9B12M012

OLYMPUS AND THE WHISTLEBLOWER PRESIDENT[1]

Seijiro Takeshita and Christopher Williams wrote this case to provide material for class discussion. The authors do not intend to illustrate either effective or ineffective handling of a managerial situation. The authors may have disguised certain names and other identifying information to protect confidentiality.

In mid-October, 2011, Michael Woodford, the newly appointed president and chief operating officer (COO) of Olympus Corporation of Japan, was called to an emergency board meeting. The meeting would take place at the corporate headquarters in Japan on October 14. Woodford was a British national who had joined the company by virtue of an acquisition it had made 25 years earlier, in 1986. The purpose of the meeting was to discuss governance issues regarding corporate mergers and acquisitions (M&A). However, it would be no ordinary meeting. Since assuming the role of president in April 2011, Woodford had discovered evidence of corporate fraud on a large scale. He had commissioned an external auditor's report that showed a significant loss of shareholder value. His call for changes to be made to the Japanese board of directors had been met by resistance. From his office in London, he sat and pondered. How should he plan for the meeting? What could he expect? What position should he take? How should he influence decisions regarding the company's immediate problems and its longer-term corporate governance?

BACKGROUND

Olympus Corporation of Japan (Olympus) was established in October 1919.[2] It developed and marketed its first microscope in 1920, and entered into the camera market in 1936.[3] In 1950, it developed the world's first commercial-use endoscopes.[4] By 2011, Olympus was one of Japan's leading firms listed on the Nikkei

225 index. The company held 70 per cent global market share in endoscopes, [5] but also had actively diversified into areas such as information-related businesses.[6] In the year ending March 2011, 42 per cent of the company's consolidated sales were derived from medical products, 12 per cent from life science and industrial appliances, 16 per cent from imaging equipment, 25 per cent from information and communications and 6 per cent from other areas.[7] The company, which was considered "an international blue chip, [8] had nearly 40,000 employees throughout the world, with 50 per cent of sales in Japan, 23 per cent in the United States, 19 per cent in Europe and 8 per cent in Asia/Oceania, as of March 31, 2011.[9] Consolidated sales reached ¥847,105 million (US$11,019 million at ¥76.87/US$), and the company had capital of ¥48,322 million (US$628 million) at end of March 2011.[10]

Olympus's strength lay in its dominant position in the endoscope market.[11] The company held a colossal 70 per cent global market share. In this market, Olympus faced two main competitors: Pentax (owned by Hoya) and Fuji Film. These competitors had difficulty catching up with Olympus.[12] In March 2011, Olympus's consolidated operating profit was ¥35.3 billion (US$459.2 million). However, its medical division churned ¥69.3 billion (US$901.5 million), indicating that it supported other loss-making divisions, such as the imaging business, which had incurred a loss of ¥15.0 billion (US$195.1 million).[13]

Exhibit 1 shows the company's segment sales in 2011, and Exhibit 2 shows operating profit change by segment between 2010 and 2011.

The core product in the company's imaging business was digital cameras. Olympus was a medium-sized player in this field.[14] Polarization was taking place in the digital camera market, where larger players such as Canon and Nikon were steady, but medium-sized competitors such as Casio and Olympus were suffering.[15] To sustain stable earnings in digital cameras, players in this market needed to sustain sales of more than 10 million units to cover their costs.[16] Competitors also needed to have a strong brand image through high-value-added products such as SLR (single lens reflex) cameras.[17] Olympus's annual output of digital and SLR cameras was 7.6 million units and 0.5 million units respectively, for the year ending March 2011. The company was aiming for sales of 8.7 million and 0.8 million units respectively, for March 2012, although such figures were seen by some as optimistic.[18] One concern was that compact digital camera prices had plummeted to less than half in just five years: from ¥21,300 (US$277) in 2005 to ¥10,500 (US$137) in 2010.[19] Olympus was trying to break through by introducing a strong product line into the emerging mirrorless camera market.[20] It was only matter of time, however, until strong competitors such as Canon and Nikon entered the market.[21] A recovery of Olympus's imaging business was described as unlikely in the foreseeable future — and this part of its business had become a heavy burden for the firm.[22]

EXPANSION UNDER KIKUKAWA (1996–2001)

Tsuyoshi Kikukawa, who had served as chairman and president of Olympus for 11 years, had expanded Olympus's digital camera business.[23] In the five years from 1996 to 2001, Kikukawa had boosted this division's annual sales to more than ¥100.0 billion (US$1.3 billion). This achievement had led to Kikukawa's promotion to a senior managing director position in 1998 and to president in 2001. Kikukawa had made it clear that it was his dream to lead a firm with sales of ¥1.0 trillion (US$13.0 billion). Reaching this goal meant virtually doubling the March 2001 sales of ¥466.7 billion (US$6.0 billion), by creating new pillars of growth.[24] Under Kikukawa's leadership, Olympus started to diversify intensively, including into areas that had little relationship with Olympus's existing businesses.[25]

In May 2010, Olympus established Olympus Business Create (OBC). This venturing unit administered many of its new businesses, including a pet service firm and a DVD manufacturing firm. These businesses had little relationship with Olympus's core businesses of endoscopes and digital cameras.[26] The vast majority of approximately 100 firms under OBC were unlisted, and hence it was difficult for outsiders to see details of their business and management.[27] In March 2001, just before Kikukawa became president, Olympus had 71 subsidiaries and affiliates. This figure grew to 1,999 in March 2011, just before Kikukawa became chairman.[28] One of his reasons for diversifying into new venture businesses was the slowdown of the digital camera business.[29]

Under Kikukawa's aggressive expansion, interest-bearing debt had reached ¥648.8 billion (US$8.4 billion) by the end of March 2011. The capital adequacy ratio was at 13.5 per cent at end of June 2011, far below the 30 per cent level that was the rule of thumb for blue chips in Japan.[30] The company's debt to equity ratio was 432 per cent at end of September 2011, the 12th largest among the Nikkei 225 and the 6th largest among the ex-financials.[31]

ENTER WOODFORD (2011)

On February 11, 2011, Olympus announced that its non-managing director and European president, Michael Woodford, would become president and COO of Olympus. Tsuyoshi Kikukawa was to become chairman and the chief executive officer (CEO) on April 1.[32] It was rare to have a foreigner as president of a large Japanese corporation, especially a foreigner who had previously been an employee in an overseas subsidiary. Most foreign company presidents were either at a firm that a Japanese company had acquired or at a firm that had strong capital ties and relationships.[33] For example, Howard Stringer of Sony was well known as a foreign president in Japan, former president Stuart Chambers of Asahi Glass was from Pilkington Japan (Pilkington had been bought by Asahi Glass in 2006) and Carlos Ghosn of Nissan had come from Renault (Nissan had become a part of Renault group in 1999, with 44.4 per cent holdings in Nissan), which had a strong capital relationship.[34]

Many in the boardroom had gasped when they heard that a foreign national — merely 50 years of age — would be assuming the role of the next president (in effect, "jumping the queue" of 25 directors ahead of him).[35] On April 1, 2011, Michael Woodford, a British national, was named president of a 92-year-old optoelectronic/medical equipment firm in Japan, Olympus Corporation.

Woodford had started his career in 1981, as a salesman in KeyMed, [36] a British surgical instrument manufacturer, which became a wholly owned subsidiary of Olympus Corporation Japan in 1986.[37] Woodford was happy to assume the role of president. He had never even been elected as a managing director of the main board, although he had been president and chairman of Olympus Europe.[38] When asked what type of management he aimed for, Woodford replied that he would like to create a corporate culture where confrontation should not be feared.[39] Woodford, however, was reminded by Kikukawa that personnel matters, including the salaries and bonuses of managing directors and those immediately below them, were up to Kikukawa, not to Woodford.[40]

Exhibit 3 shows the composition of the board of directors in June 2011. Exhibit 4 shows the corporate governance structure as reported in the company's annual report in 2011. Exhibit 5 shows the company's group organizational chart.

The share price of Olympus shot up 5 per cent on February 14, the first trading day after the announcement of the new president. Many expected that restructuring would take place.[41] On taking up his new position in April, Woodford issued a plan to significantly reduce selling, general and administrative expenses (SGA) to sales ratio in four years; from 34 per cent in March 2011 to 27 per cent in March 2015.[42] He also stated that he would consider folding the digital camera division should it continue to drain deficits.[43]

Although foreign presidents often struggled in Japan, many expected them to be ruthless in making massive restructuring changes.[44] Olympus's share price remained firm, as the market expected further rationalization (particularly of the camera division) by Woodford.[45] Olympus's share price was rising thanks to the expected contribution of new endoscope products and cost cuts by the new president.[46] The buying mainly consisted of those items that expected a quick recovery of earnings.[47]

Exhibit 6 shows the company's share price movements since the announcement of Woodford's promotion.

SURPRISE REVELATIONS AND WOODFORD'S SHOCK

In July, a friend of Woodford handed him a translated version of a magazine article to read, insisting to him that "it's serious."[48] The article about Olympus was from an August 2011 issue of a magazine called *FACTA*. It provided details of a series of large embezzlements at Olympus that went back for years.

The *FACTA* article[49] revealed four issues.

1. Concealment of three large acquisitions
    Olympus bought three venture firms totaling more than ¥70.0 billion (US$910.6 million) that had little to do with its core businesses throughout 2006 to 2008 and then wrote off virtually all of the sale the following year.[50] None of the three firms had sales greater than ¥200 million (US$2.6 million). Taking into account the shares outstanding, the PER (price-to-earnings ratio) and the purchase price, analysts had concluded that Olympus was expecting sales from

these three firms to multiply between several tenfold and several hundredfold within four to five years after the acquisitions.

Nothing had been disclosed in regards to the acquisition of these three firms. The Tokyo Stock Exchange did not enforce disclosure if the ratio of profits or net asset of the acquired firm was small in comparison to that of the purchasers. At the same time, the Lehman crisis in September 2008 had also helped Olympus to conceal its acquisitions, as it was not rare to see a firm that had to clear half of its capital at the time.

2. Mystery of ¥270 billion (US$3.5 billion) purchase of a British firm

Olympus's purchase of the British medical equipment firm Gyrus in February 2008 had left many unanswered questions. Olympus bought Gyrus with a 40 per cent premium at ¥211.7 billion (US$2.7 billion) when it was listed in London. This sale price had been seen as a very expensive purchase at the time. Surprisingly, Olympus also bought Gyrus's preferred shares during March 2010, by churning another ¥59.9 billion (US$779.2 million). From whom Olympus acquired these preferred shares remained a mystery. Gyrus did have high profitability (and was a medical equipment firm), but its sales were merely ¥50.0 billion (US$650.4 million) per annum with total assets of ¥100.0 billion (US$1.3 billion) at the time of purchase. Many outsiders had considered the purchase price of ¥270.0 billion (US$3.5 billion) as having had no rationale. In addition, half of the total asset base of Gyrus was goodwill.[51] Many in the market stated that they had never seen a company that had a block of goodwill that was covered further by more goodwill.

Olympus disclosed Gyrus's sales but no further information. Olympus had goodwill of approximately ¥100.0 billion (US$1.3 billion). In addition, Gyrus had invested in M&A with goodwill and trademarks totaling ¥60.0 billion (US$780.5 million). These figures were not accounted for as goodwill under intangible fixed assets, but had possibly been hidden under the "other" category. If Olympus wrote off this goodwill in one go, then it would virtually wipe out Olympus's consolidated capital. Such reckless management had already resulted in hurting Olympus's financial footing: its consolidated capital of ¥334.2 billion (US$4.3 billion) at March 2007 had shrunk to ¥163.7 billion (US$2.1 billion) by the end of March 2011.

3. Suspicious relationships with consultants

Olympus had suspicious and complicated relationships with its consulting firm, Global Company (GC), which seemed to have engaged in most of the M&A undertaken by Olympus. GC acted as Olympus's advisor, but also sold venture capital (VC) to Olympus. GC was virtually another arm of ITX (a 100 per cent owned subsidiary of Olympus that administered venture business investments). The president of GC, an ex-Nomura man was a brother of the president of ITX at the time it had accelerated its venture investments. Many of these VC investments were unsuccessful and were administered under the Olympus Business Create (OBC) initiative, which had now become a "Pandora's box" for the company.

4. Doubts in the financial market

   Foreign currency translation adjustments had reached a negative of ¥100.8 billion (US$1.3 billion) for the year ending March 2011. This loss was far greater than firms of the same size in the same industry (e.g., Nikon). Analysts expressed doubt over possible further losses that had not been revealed.

   The news of Michael Woodford becoming president attracted attention because he was a non-executive foreign director surpassing 25 ahead of him. The next candidate in line was the executive vice president in charge of medical equipment. However, this shift of presidency did not put an end to the Kikukawa era. Kikukawa had not given up his stance as a CEO.

In Japan, several criteria led to corporations being delisted because of wrongdoing. Falsified reporting of accounts was one such criterion.[52] Many such cases had lead to criminal prosecutions and arrests.[53]

Woodford left Japan for two weeks, returning on August 1.[54] He learned that Kikukawa had instructed other employees to not to talk to Woodford about the article.[55] The next day, when confronted by Woodford, Kikukawa had told Woodford that there was nothing to worry about, attributing the story to typical sensationalism by a tabloid paper.[56] Woodford sensed, however, that a big fabrication was going on behind the scenes in the boardroom.[57] Woodford confronted Mori (the vice president) and pressed for a response. He received only vague replies without any specific or meaningful answers.[58] Woodford started to lose his temper, and asked Mori who he thought his boss was. Mori replied "Chairman Kikukawa."[59] Woodford then left Japan again for a business trip and summer vacation.[60]

FURTHER REVELATIONS AND BOARDROOM ISSUES

On September 20, the Japanese magazine *FACTA* (which had published the initial exposé two months earlier) came out with its October edition, providing more revelations about Olympus. Woodford made a statement that it was he who would sign off on the statement of accounts, and that he needed all information on any trades that had accommodated risk and the process those trades had followed.[61]

On September 29, Woodford and an English colleague met with Kikukawa and Mori.[62] Woodford asked for the role of CEO to be handed to him. He felt that his authority was insufficient to fulfill his role as president. He also demanded that Kikukawa not attend any further managerial meetings in the company.[63] Kikukawa rebutted, but Woodford stated that he would step down as president if he did not become CEO.[64] If Woodford resigned, Olympus's governance problems would be exposed to the public.[65]

On September 30, the Olympus board appointed Woodford as CEO.[66] However, during the board meeting, the other directors questioned Woodford: "You also must have known about Gyrus, so why do you want to bring it up again?" and "You cc-ed all the mail and materials to the auditors — why did you do such a thing?" Woodford suspected that the board of directors still was working under orders from Kikukawa.[67]

That night, Woodford headed for London and decided to ask Pricewaterhouse-Coopers (PwC) to conduct an investigation. He felt there were severe limitations to Olympus's own internal investigation.[68] On October 10, Woodford received the interim report from PwC. The report claimed that US$1,287.0 million worth of shareholder value had evaporated on back of a series of investments.[69] The next day, on October 11, Woodford sent the PwC report and a 13-page letter to Kikukawa and Mori, asking for their resignations.[70]

DECISION POINT

Woodford was then called to an emergency board meeting in Japan on October 14. The purported topic of the meeting was governance issues regarding corporate M&A.[71] From his office in London, he sat and pondered. How should he plan for the meeting? What could he expect? What position should he take? How should he influence decisions regarding the company's immediate problems and its longer-term corporate governance?

Exhibit 1

SALES BREAKDOWN OF OLYMPUS CORPoration, MARch 2011

Olympus Crop Sales Breakdown: March 2011 (yen millions, %)		
Divisions	Mar 2011	% of Total
Medical	350,716	40
Life/Industrial	114,095	13
Imaging	174,924	20
Information/Telecommunications	189,354	21
Others	53,997	6
TOTAL	883,086	100

Source: "オリンパス株式会社　2011年3月期　決算参考資料　セグメント別売上高・営業利益 2011"

["Segmented Sales and Operating Profit Breakdown 2011, Reference to March 2011 Earnings Statement, Olympus Corp."]

Exhibit 2

OLYMPUS CORPORATION'S OPERATING PROFIT BREAKDOWN, MARCH 2010
AND MARCH 2011 (IN YEN MILLIONS)

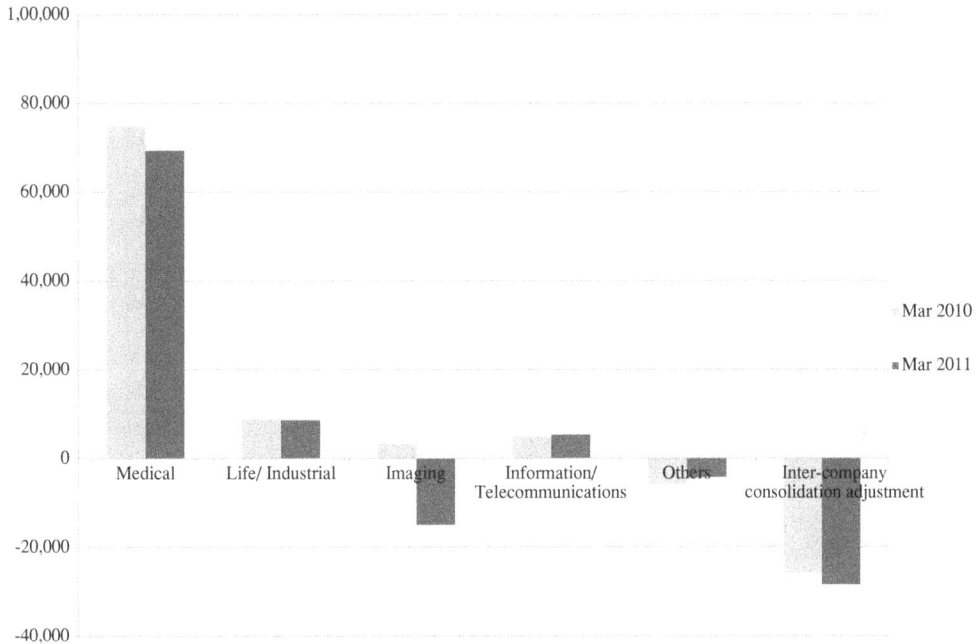

Source: "オリンパス株式会社　2011年3月期　決算参考資料　セグメント別売上高・営業利益 2011" ["Segmented Sales and Operating Profit Breakdown 2011, Reference to March 2011 Earnings Statement, Olympus Corp."]

Exhibit 3

BOARD MEMBER COMPOSITION (JUNE 2011)

Position	Name	Career start	Birthdate	Age
Board of Directors & Chairman of the Board	Tsuyoshi Kikukawa	Olympus Corp	February 27, 1941	70
Board of Directors & President	Michael Woodford	KeyMed	June 12, 1960	51
Board of Directors & Executive Vice President	Haruhito Morishima	Olympus Corp	November 20, 1947	63
Board of Directors & Executive Vice President	Hisashi Mori	Olympus Corp	May 10, 1957	54
Board of Directors & Senior Executive Managing Officer	Masataka Suzuki	Olympus Corp	February 19, 1951	60
Board of Directors & Senior Executive Managing Officer	Kazuhisa Yanagisawa	Olympus Corp	March 20, 1949	63
Board of Directors & Senior Managing Director	Shuichi Takayama	Olympus Corp	January 13, 1950	61
Board of Directors & Executive Managing Officer	Takashi Tsukaya	Olympus Corp	July 30, 1951	59
Board of Directors & Executive Managing Officer	Kazuhiro Watanabe	Olympus Corp	July 1, 1952	58
Board of Directors & Executive Managing Officer	Makoto Nakatsuka	Olympus Corp	September 9, 1957	59
Board of Directors & Executive Officer	Shinichi Nichigaki	Olympus Corp	December 4, 1954	56
Board of Directors & Executive Officer	Hironobu Kawamata	Olympus Corp	January 7, 1959	53
External Director	Yasuo Hayashida	Juntendo University Hospital	January 22, 1943	67
External Director	Hiroshi Kuruma	Nihon Keizai Shinbun	January 15, 1945	66
External Director	Junichi Hayashi	Nomura Securities	December 4, 1950	59
Full-time Auditor	Hideto Yamada	Olympus Corp	December 25, 1944	64
Full-time Auditor	Tadao Imai	Olympus Corp	August 7, 1943	65
Auditor	Makoto Shimada	Copal (currently NIDEC Copal)	April 3, 1941	68
Auditor	Yasuo Nakamura	Mitsubishi Rayon	March 21, 1941	68

Source: "オリンパス株式会社　有価証券報告書　平成23年" ["Financial Statement, Olympus, FY 2011"]

Exhibit 4

CORPORATE GOVERNANCE STRUCTURE (2011)

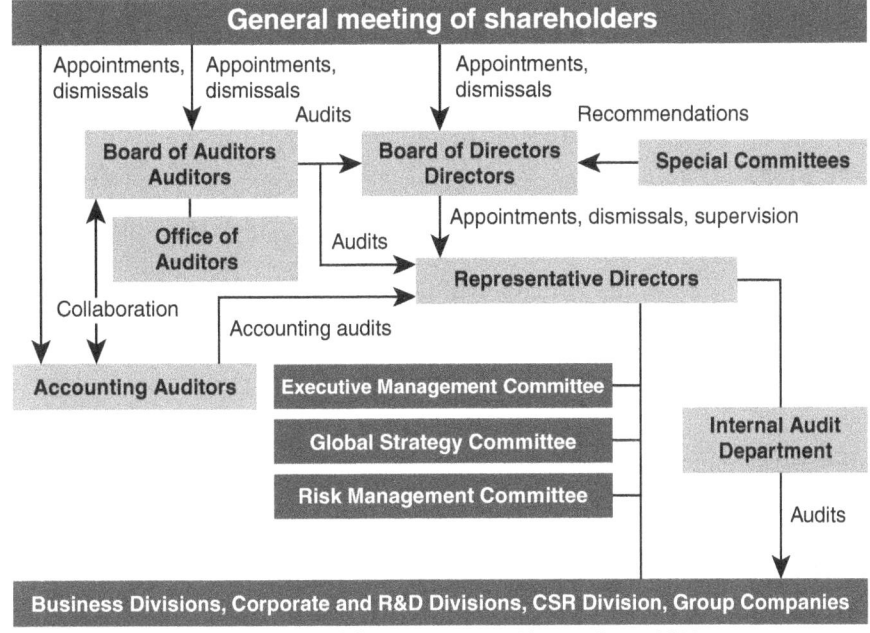

Source: Olympus Corporate Social Responsibility Report Digest, Olympus Corp., 2011

Exhibit 5

OLYMPUS CORP GROUP ORGANIZATIONAL CHART

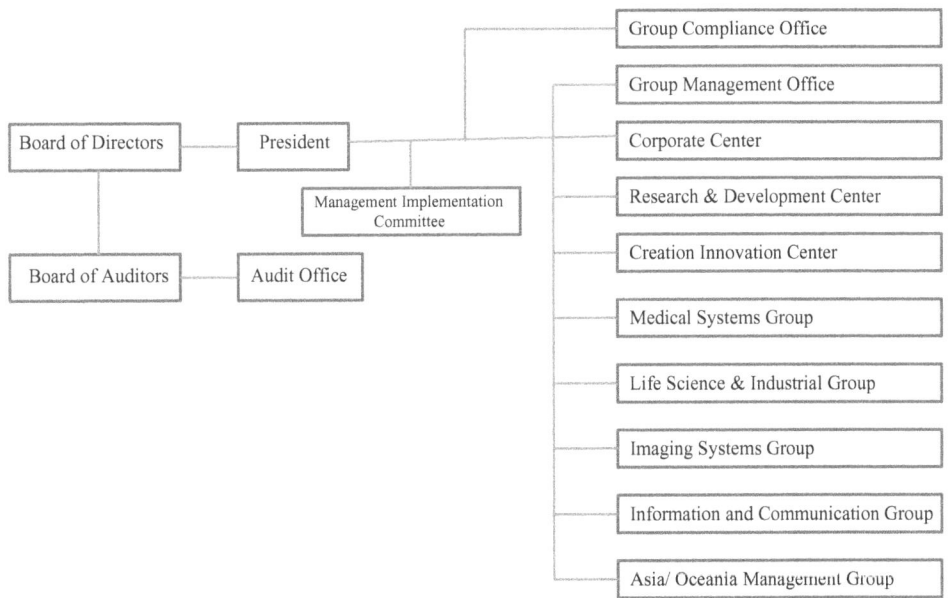

Source: "Organizational Chart," http://www.olympus.co.jp/jp/corc/profile/org_chrt/, accessed January 10, 2012.

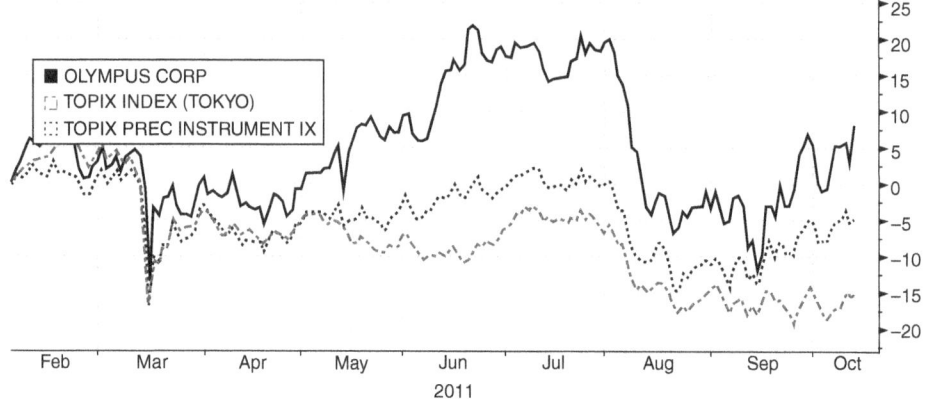

Source: Bloomberg

ANALYSIS OF THE OLYMPUS CASE USING A HYBRID APPROACH

There are several interrelated issues in this case. Firstly, we have the immediate issue of how Woodford should prepare for the forthcoming board meeting in Tokyo. What should he try to achieve? What outcomes are likely? How should he prepare for those outcomes? Examining this necessitates a focus at individual level, on Woodford and what he needs to do next. Secondly, we have the issue of broader corporate governance, and more precisely, of corporate governance in Olympus and within the specific context of Japan. Many of the issues that Woodford has encountered in the case are rooted in the very distinctive corporate governance system in Japan, and the close-knit strategic apex that he has confronted and come into conflict with. A key theme here is the issue of Woodford as an 'outsider'. Indeed, we see from case Exhibit 3 (members of the board as of June 2011) that the rest of the board are all Japanese, mostly male, and somewhat older. We also see evidence of the rather complex (and possibly opaque) nature of the corporate governance system (case Exhibit 4). Thirdly, we have the issue of Olympus Corporation's overall performance. Here we can think of both financial performance (revenues, profitability, (case Exhibits 1 and 2), debt levels (mentioned in the text), and share price (case Exhibit 6)) as well as non-financial performance, such as reputation. For the latter, big question marks have been placed on the corporation's reputation following a series of revelations about possible corporate fraud. There were increasing doubts in the financial markets, revelations of suspicious relationships with consultants, and mysterious transactions. These were exposed through the work of independent journalists (the FACTA magazine).

As we try and position our analysis of this case on the Case Analysis Spectrum, we must be clear about which of these issues we are focusing on. While it is possible to focus in on any one of them in isolation, we choose here to treat them as interrelated and interdependent. A reductionist stance would not do these interdependencies justice. A holistic stance is possible; we could treat the multilevel nature of the issue using a systems technique. However, we opt for a hybrid stance as we consider that we will achieve more optimal insights using a mix of reductionist and holistic logics. The following points support this stance, drawing on Table 5.1.

Firstly, we do not consider the problem to be a wicked problem (Grewatsch et al., 2021). If we did, we would be more encouraged to adopt a holistic stance. There certainly is complexity, but it is moderate to high, rather than extremely high. Secondly, we consider that there are multiple aspects to the case and that these can be thematically grouped (Verschuren, 2001). As noted above, these relate to Woodford and his personal entrance at board level, the whole issue of corporate governance in Olympus and in Japan, and the performance outcomes in both financial and non-financial terms. Thirdly, we can use both simple (reductionist) and more complex (holistic) diagrams at different stages in the analysis (Jennings, 1997). These diagrams will help us make sense of the complexity that is in the case. Overall, we have sufficient support for treating this case using a hybrid stance.

As in the previous two cases, the case is not limited to a single dominant context. There are several dominant contexts at play in the Olympus case. There is a clear geographic and cultural context in the form of the country setting: Japan. This has played a pivotal role in the previous success and growth of the case company. Japan's so-called 'miracle' economy (Johnson, 1982), based on innovation and efficiency, helped grow the country from the ruins of World War II into the world's leading innovator and a major industrial powerhouse. This success had occurred over a range of industries, including electronics, optics, and photography; segments in which Olympus had become a world leader. The country context also sets the scene for the corporate governance issues that the company was facing in the case. Woodford had encountered a board that coalesced around its former leaders (Kikukawa and Mori), especially once the news of the scandal had come to light. The unique and distinct national business system of Japan is a central feature in the case, as is the apparent clash between Woodford with this system. In other words, if Woodford had not accepted the CEO position and been promoted to the board, but another Japanese board member had, it is arguably more likely that the status quo would have been maintained. A perhaps more subtle dominant context in the case is the context for corporate responsibility and accountability. Large international companies of all countries of origin have increasingly been scrutinised by international stakeholders, including the investment community and the public. The pressures on firms to be accountable for their actions have increased. Distinctions have increasingly been made between corporate social responsibility (CSR) and corporate social irresponsibility (CSIR) (Kotchen & Moon, 2012). We see a context for accountability and responsibility in the way in which the scandal had come to light, and the perceived shock of Woodford – amongst others – at the revelations. There is also a strategy context for corporate growth and acquisition in the case. Although these investments were later revealed to be potentially fraudulent, what is clear is that the previous strategy of the company was to expand using corporate acquisition in addition to any internal R&D that was common at the time in Japanese corporations.

We analyse the Olympus case using the fuzzy cognitive mapping (FCM) technique. FCM can be used in a wide range of analytical situations to capture the interrelationships between multiple variables within a qualitative model. And it can be used to synthesise and reduce many variables into a condensed form in data poor situations (Özesmi & Özesmi, 2004). It can be used on primary data to study small companies and large companies alike, including how they deal with pressures within their stakeholder environment (Williams et al., 2020; You & Williams, 2023). We use it here on secondary case data. Ideally, we would have interviewed Woodford, Mori, and Kikukawa as well as other stakeholders involved at the time, and produced a social cognitive map based on individual cognitive maps created through those interviews. Clearly, this would have been impossible! In contrast to substantial interview data, summary case data of the type that one sees in the Olympus case is inevitably data-poor. Nevertheless, it can still be used to capture and articulate the main variables and their associations. As Özesmi and Özesmi (2004) state: cognitive maps can be extracted from written texts (p. 47), they do not necessarily have to be created directly through primary interviews.

We proceed in four steps, broadly following the process documented by Özesmi and Özesmi (2004). This uses elements of both holism and reductionism as we proceed from an initial capturing of as many salient variables as possible, through to an ordering and grouping of themes and an articulation of the vectors between variables.

Step 1: Creating an initial social cognitive map. In this first step we identify the most important variables in the case and represent them as bubbles in a diagram. If we were doing this through interviews, we could use a large piece of paper or whiteboard directly with each interviewee. As we are working directly from the published case, we do this using MS-Word and work directly from our reading of the case. The initial social cognitive map is shown in Figure 7.4. We then identify the relationships between the variables and draw these using simple arrows. These arrows denote a relationship in the form of X⇨Y, although at this stage they do not indicate the strength of the relationship or whether it is a positive or negative one. This results in 34 discrete variables and 54 connecting lines between the variables. This high number of variables and lines shows just how complex strategic business cases can be. In this case, it underscores the use of a more holistic stance in the first part of the analysis. But it is also suggestive of the need to take steps to reduce the complexity to make sense of the case as the analysis proceeds. The variables captured in this initial map in Figure 7.4 are a mix of broad characteristics of the case that are binary (present/non-present) or continuous in nature (e.g., diversity of board, debt, promotion), events that happened in the case with a specific actor (e.g., PwC investigation, FACTA article), and social dynamics linked to people (e.g., blame, loyalty, frustration). One of the benefits of the FCM approach is that it allows the capture of variables of different types. Some of the variables are external to the case organisation (e.g., competitor threats, Tokyo Stock Exchange (TSE) disclosure rules), while others occur in the internal environment (e.g., call for board changes, demanding resignations). The initial social cognitive map serves to capture all the main variables perceived to be material to the situation described in the case, along with an initial take on how those variables are interlinked.

Step 2: Assigning strengths and signs to the map. In Özesmi and Özesmi (2004), the strengths and signs of relationships between variables are captured during interviews with participants (see also Williams et al., 2020; You & Williams, 2023). As we are not using primary interviews here, we assign strengths and signs based on our interpretation of the written case document. This is shown in Figure 7.5. We take the initial social cognitive map and consider each path in turn. Different ways of denoting strengths and signs are possible. Özesmi and Özesmi (2004) recommend a range from −1 to +1. In the current analysis, we show negative relationships as dotted arrows, positive ones as solid arrows. And we denote differences in strengths by making some lines thicker (interpretation of a stronger relationship) and some thinner (interpreting a weaker relationship). The result in Figure 7.5 shows an emerging social cognitive map that captures our view of the system of many variables at play in this case. In essence, this would have been the type of mental model – although likely not the exact one because of additional insider case knowledge that he would have had – going through Woodford's mind at the decision point in the case. In this analysis, we see most relationships are positive, some negative. This is also a reflection of how the variable was worded (e.g., blame vs. lack of blame).

Step 3: Initial condensed map. The condensing of social cognitive maps into higher level aggregate dimensions is a core feature of the FCM process (Williams et al., 2020; You & Williams, 2023). It is usually done by grouping the variables identified in the initial social cognitive map together. This is done based on their interconnectivity on the map, as well as by their logical fit. This condensing step is important because, as Özesmi and Özesmi (2004) state: "It is difficult to look at a complex cognitive map with many variables and connections and make sense of how the map operates" (p. 53). Condensing is a simplifying process and therefore reductionist in nature. This first activity we do here is to group variables into larger groups, where all variables have something in common. This allows the sub-graphs of the initial map to be replaced by more abstract single units. Figure 7.6 shows the grouping process in the current analysis of the Olympus case. We derive five high level groups: (1) the Japanese system: 8 variables related to the distinctive nature of corporate governance in Japan as illustrated in the case; (2) Performance: 5 variables capturing financial and non-financial outcomes; (3) Awareness of fraud: 7 variables capturing the precursors to the FACTA article and the investigations; (4) Board conflict: 8 variables depicting the clash between Woodford and the board; and (5) Woodford as leader: 5 variables relating to Woodford's status as a new leader within the organisation. One additional variable – competitor threats – stays isolated and forms its own group containing only the one variable.

Step 4: Final condensed map. In the final condensed map, we show these six higher-level factors along with the relationships between them. We calculate these relationships using the sum of the {−1 to +1} scores on each of the individual relationships (Williams et al., 2020; You & Williams, 2023). For illustration purposes, we use dotted and solid arrows of differing widths. The result is shown in Figure 7.7. This reveals different positive and negative influences. It also suggests how the Japanese business system influenced performance both positively and negatively. The positive influence was through the traditional strategic focus on excellence in technology. The negative influence was due to the behaviours that led to debt through suspicious transactions. The analysis also shows emerging board conflict to be a prominent feature of the case. This came about through three interacting forces: the Japanese corporate governance system, Woodford assuming a board position in the corporation, and the discovery of – and investigation into – potentially fraudulent transactions.

Having gone through this hybrid process using FCM and moving from a more holistic assessment to a more reductionist one (i.e., moving progressively towards a final condensed map), we now need to interpret the case to generate implications and recommendations for Woodford. The mapping process only goes part way to producing the full interpretation. Care must be taken when proceeding from the mapping to the recommendations and next steps. We argue there are three elements to the interpretation step, emanating from the final condensed map in Figure 7.7.

Firstly, from a corporate performance perspective, events revealed a negative association between the Japanese corporate governance system and performance. This is highly concerning for all stakeholders, including shareholders. In an environment of competitive threats, this is worrisome for any strategic leader. Secondly, the analysis does not depict a harmonious and well-functioning strategic apex for a major international corporation. What it shows is the presence of emerging board conflict between the Japanese side and outsiders – and this emergence of internal board conflict is made worse by the growing awareness of fraud, including multiple investigations. In many ways, this is overshadowing strategic considerations relating to performance of the corporation. Thirdly, the model indicates an entrenchment of positions either side of the board conflict. Here it is important to consider what is absent from the map, what is not captured. Is there any indication of how the board conflict might be resolved? Are there any variables or groupings that may suggest a direction towards resolution of the board conflict? This would be useful for Woodford as he plans his next steps. No such variables are forthcoming in the analysis.

We do see that Woodford is armed with data, including the PwC investigation and FACTA article. But it seems he is alone against a large, homogeneous, and resolute Japanese board that are loyal the Kikukawa and Mori. This absence of variables that would help to predict outcomes and resolution is important because it suggests that a moment of 'reckoning' is inevitable, and that Woodford's odds of surviving as a board member are stacked against him. The emerging board conflict is not a small or peripheral grouping. It is central to the map, indicated by the high level of 'in-degree' arrows going into it, which suggest the conflict continues to be fuelled.

In conclusion, we can say the following: emerging board conflict internal to the strategic apex of the corporation has increasingly taken the attention of the strategic leaders of Olympus. Emerging board conflict is a stronger theme than it should be, and it appears to be distracting the attention of the leaders away from the issues that should drive the competitiveness and performance of the firm. This is not a healthy situation and a moment of 'reckoning' is very likely. As he prepares for the meeting in Tokyo, it is important that his plans include an exit scenario. Should he find himself in a position that the Japanese side of the board is unwilling to relent and that its loyalty to Kikukawa and Mori is unshaken, then he must prepare for being ousted or resigning. This might entail his preparedness to become a whistleblower to the events, and to inform the international press. This is perhaps the last weapon left to deploy.

Action box

- Reflect on the three cases and the three associated illustrative analyses above
- Would you adopt a different stance for any of the cases? If so, which stance would you adopt and why?
- How would you approach the analysis differently? Why?

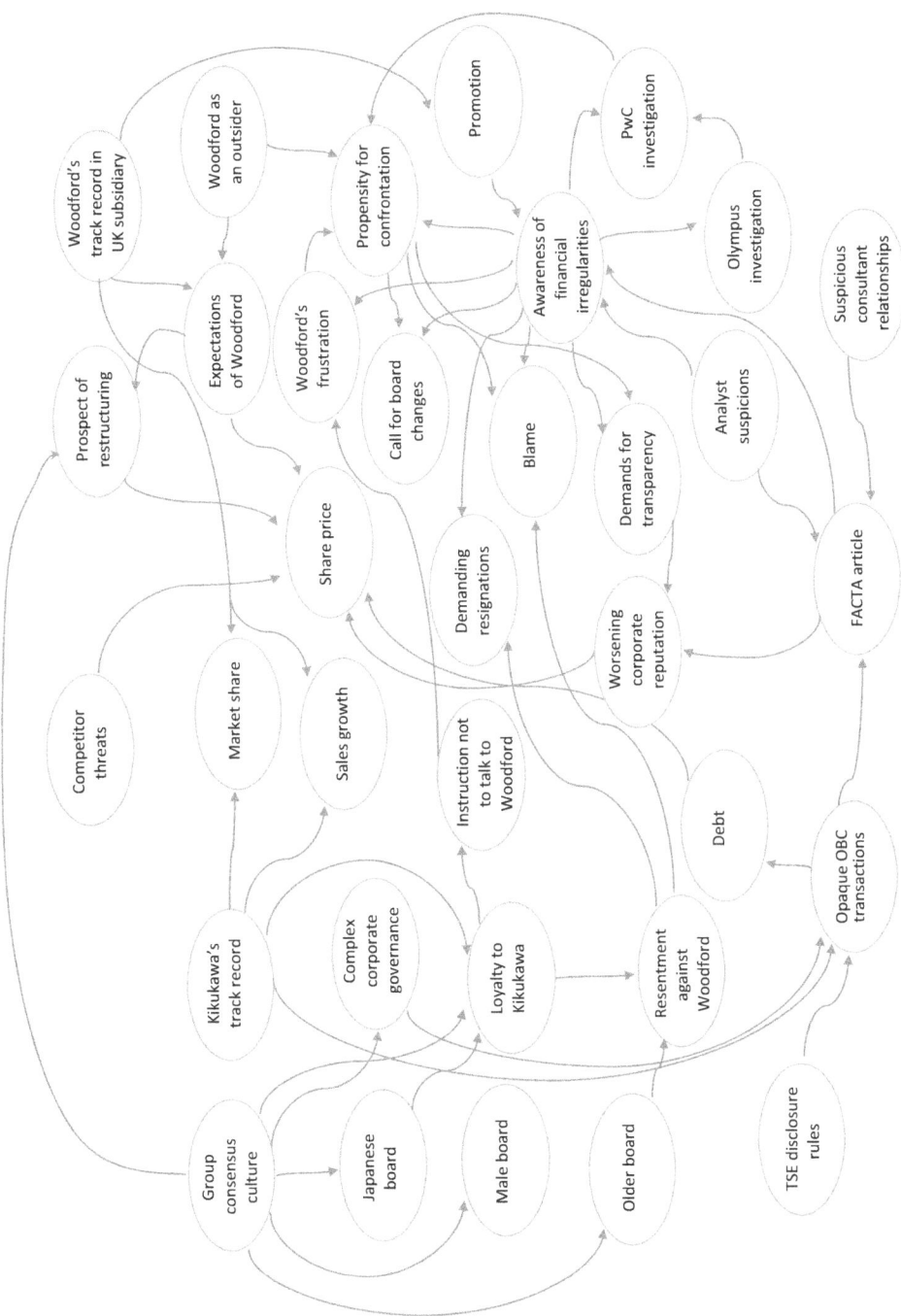

FIGURE 7.4 Initial social cognitive map – Olympus case

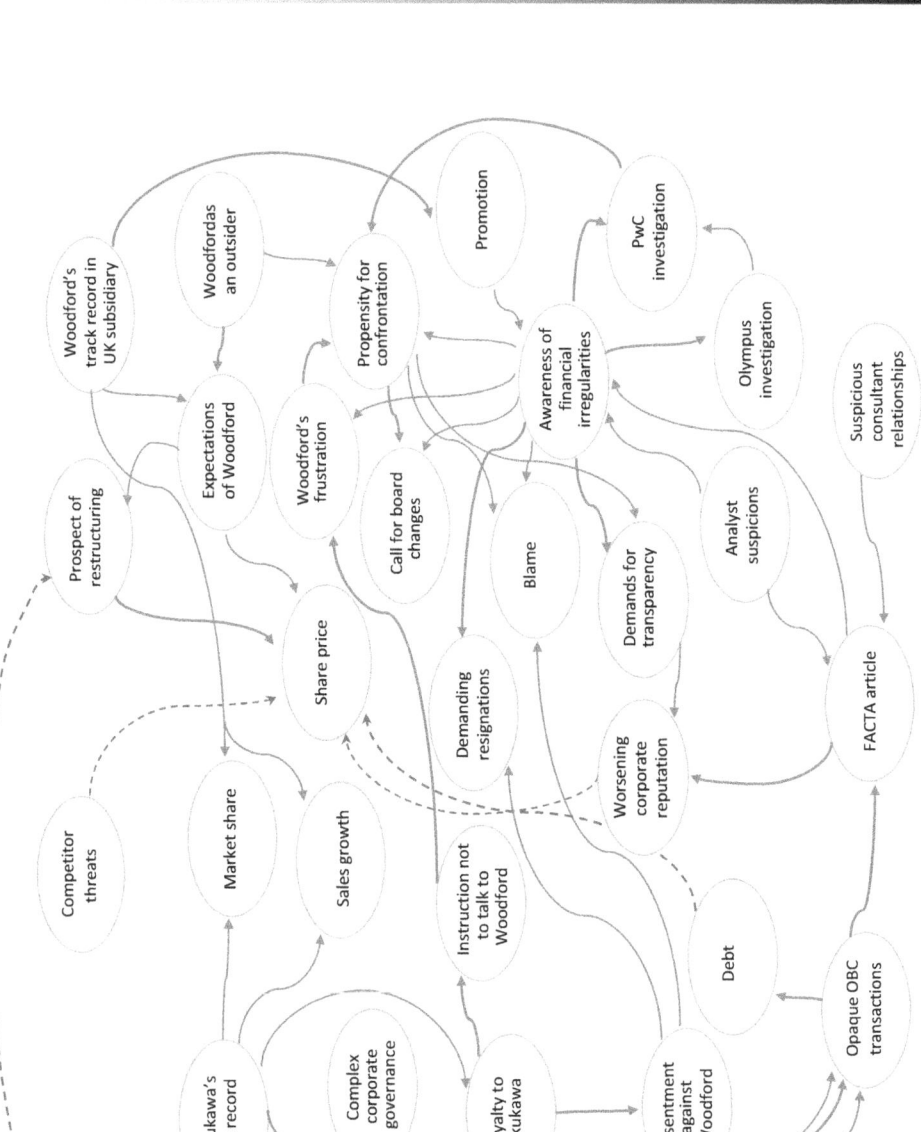

FIGURE 7.5 Social cognitive map with signed paths – Olympus case

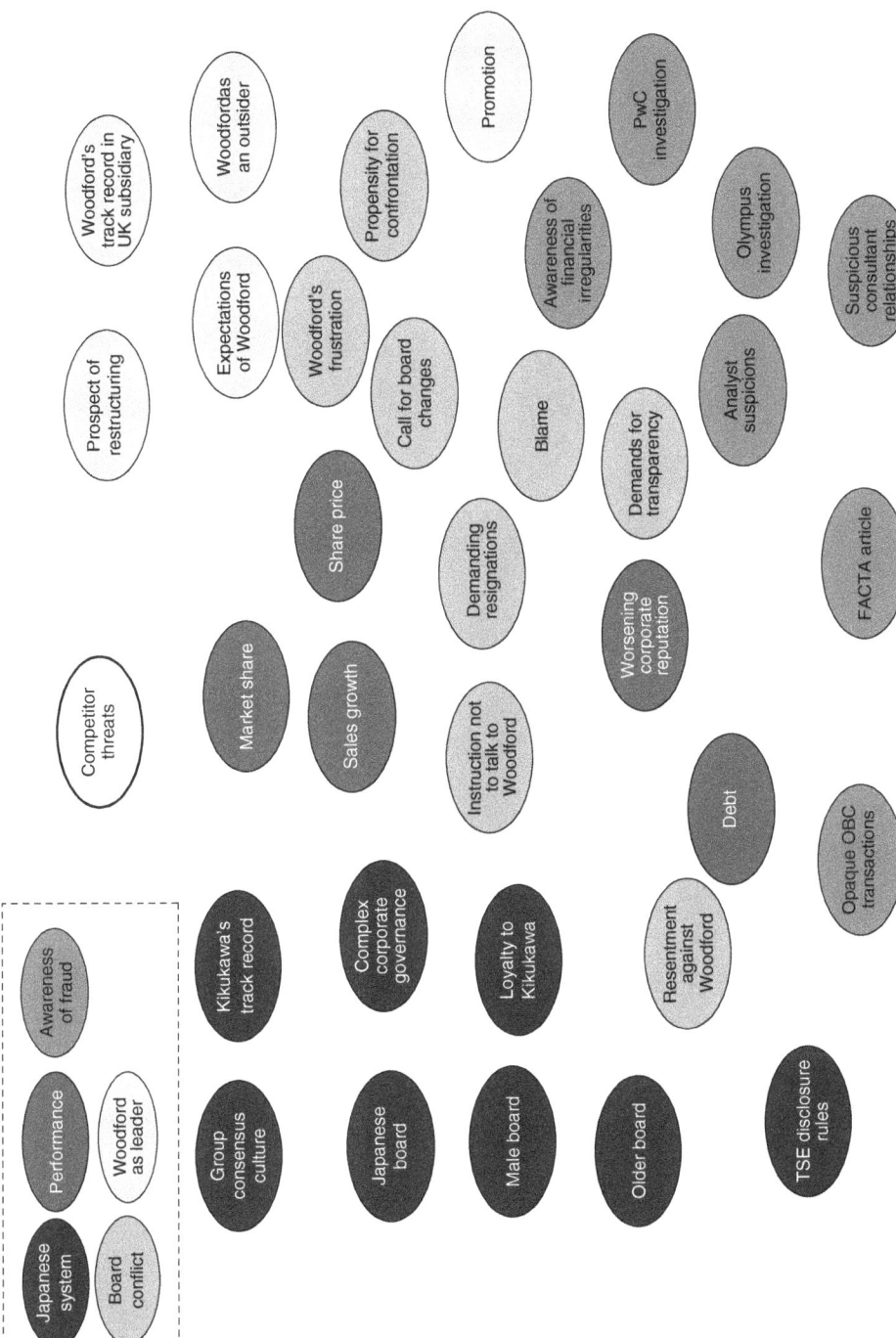

FIGURE 7.6 Condensed social cognitive map – Olympus case

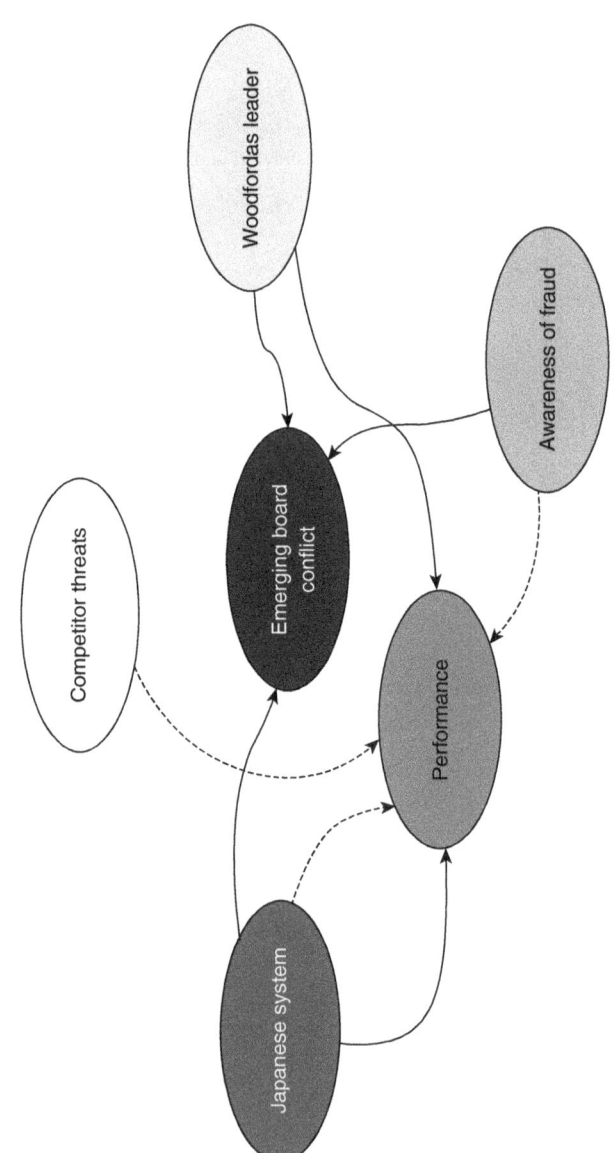

FIGURE 7.7 Final condensed map – Olympus case

OTHER SUGGESTED CASES

Table 7.3 shows a selection of other cases, the primary issue in the case, and potential stances and approaches that could be adopted.

TABLE 7.3 Selection of alternative cases and analytical approaches

Case title	Author(s) (year)	Publisher	Primary issue	Suggested stance and analytical approach
Arcadia Medical Center: Emergency Department Crowding (A + B)	Raul O. Chao; Courtney Terry (2012)	Darden	Performance of an emergency room of a large public hospital – the main indicator of the problem is patient overcrowding and high lengths of patient stay	*Reductionist:* (1) process behaviour analysis to determine out-of-control phase of day; (2) use of tools such as scatter diagrams and root cause analysis based on a finite set of factors; (3) qualitative data in part B of the case is thematically grouped
Collision Course: Selling European High Performance Motorcycles in Japan	Jeff Hicks; Derek Lehmberg (2012)	Ivey Publishing	Underperformance of a Japanese subsidiary of high-end Italian motorcycle manufacturer are linked to internal communication problems, cultural awareness issues, diverging interests, and priorities of expat managers	*Holistic:* Given the soft nature of the underlying cultural problem, the multitude of actors, complex internal – external interfaces, and the qualitative nature of the data in the case (which is mostly written as conversations), an organisational complexity approach such as organisational cybernetics would be suitable
Campbell Management Consulting	James A. Erskine; Colin Cruji (1999)	Ivey Publishing	Operational issues in a car manufacturing plant with inefficiency in waste management processes; at the same time a unionised environment with hostility towards the consultant at the centre of the case	*Hybrid:* Two problem areas running through the case: (1) the need for a quantitative calculation based on a limited range of variables to optimise tug operations usage across shifts, and (2) an issue within the social system of the organisation involving tense relationships between workers, management, and the consultant. A part-reductionist (quantitative) and part-holistic (broader internal relations) can be adopted.

KEY TAKEAWAYS

The following are key learning points from this chapter:

- Three worked examples illustrate different stances that can be taken along the Case Analysis Spectrum to complex strategic business cases
- The Time Out case illustrates a reductionist stance, the use of a question tree and a Matrix of Principles for bringing the sub-analyses together
- The Brightwater case illustrates a holistic stance, and the use of a socio-technical systems approach to a complex problem involving interactions between human and non-component parts
- The Olympus case illustrates a hybrid stance, combining holistic and reductionist elements using a version of fuzzy cognitive mapping (FCM)
- In each analysis, the use of diagrams and figures at the centre of the analysis aids in critical reflection and development of a solution to the central case issue.

REFLECTIVE PRACTICE TASK

Reflect on the different analyses conducted in this chapter and consider their merits and drawbacks. Reflect further on the following questions:

1. What?

   Select one of the approaches or tools you identified in the previous chapter and apply it to your case data. Do you need to do additional reading or training on how to apply the tool? What new insights do you generate from applying the tool? Are you comfortable with the stance you are adopting and the tool selection?

2. So what?

   It is important not only to justify the selection of a tool for analysing case data, but also to allow time to get familiar with it and how to use it. Reflect on how much time and what resources you needed to draw on to become familiar enough with your tool selection to apply it to your case data in a useful way.

3. Now what?

   As you approach the closure of the analysis phase, you should have clear recommendations for how the focal organisation should solve the central issue at the heart of the case. Think now about how you will be able to build on these to generate impact from the process of strategic business case analysis in the future.

ADDITIONAL READINGS AND RESOURCES

Time Out:

www.timeout.com/about/history
www.theguardian.com/media/gallery/2008/aug/11/timeout

Clean water in the developing world

Sodhi, M. S., & Tang, C. S. (2011). Social enterprises as supply-chain enablers for the poor. *Socio-Economic Planning Sciences*, *45*(4), 146–153.

Tumwine, J. K. (2005). Clean drinking water for homes in Africa and other less developed countries. *British Medical Journal*, *331*(7515), 468–469.

Woodford's account of events at Olympus

Woodford, M. (2012). Exposure: From president to whistleblower at Olympus. Penguin UK.

CASE 1 NOTES

1 £ = GBP = British pound sterling; all currency amounts are in £ unless otherwise specified; £1 = US$1.33 on June 30, 2016.

2 "Oakley Capital Takes 50% Stake in Time Out," *The Financial Times*, accessed November 18, 2016, https://www.ft.com/content/24cd8294-f8c7-11df-b550-00144feab49a.

3 Ibid.

4 "Swinging 60s—Capital of Cool," History, accessed November 18, 2016, www.history.co.uk/topics/history-of-london/swinging-60s-capital-cool; "Worldwide Brand of the Year . . . Again!," TimeOut, July 15, 2014, accessed November 18, 2016, www.timeout.com/about/time-out-group/latest-news/worldwide-brand-of-the-year-again.

5 Ibid.

6 Time Out Group came into being with the company's investment in Time Out Market. Initially, this was a 10 per cent stake, with Oakley Capital having a majority stake. Just prior to the IPO in June 2016, Time Out acquired the remaining equity.

7 Graeme Davies, "Boardroom Talk: Time Out's Growth Quest," Investors Chronicle, December 16, 2016, accessed January 5, 2017, www.investorschronicle.co.uk/2016/12/16/shares/news-and-analysis/boardroom-talk-time-out-s-growth-quest-A6G831XbmtFZpibEv1bGmJ/article.html.

8 "Time Out* - Buy a Ticket," accessed April 3, 2017, 1, http://oakleycapital.com/media/170328-Time_Out_BUY_TP_195p_Buy_a_ticket_22_pgs.pdf.

9 Click-throughs occurred when web users clicked on advertisements to open up advertisers' websites to make purchases electronically.

10 "Muitos Mas Bons," TimeOut Market Lisboa, accessed November 18, 2016, www.timeoutmarket.com/en/highlights/muitos-mas-bons/.

11 "Academia Time Out," accessed November 18, 2016, www.timeoutmarket.com/en/academy/.

12 "FY16 Interim Results Presentation," Time Out Group plc, October 2016; Jillian Ambrose, "Time Out Market to Open in Shoreditch in 2017," *The Telegraph*, October 12, 2016, accessed November 17, 2016, www.telegraph.co.uk/business/2016/10/12/time-out-market-to-open-in-shoreditch-in-2017/.

13 "About TripAdvisor," TripAdvisor, accessed January 10, 2017, https://www.tripadvisor.co.uk/PressCenter-c6-About_Us.html; "About Us," Yelp, accessed January 10, 2017, https://www.yelp.co.uk/about.

14 Mechanisms that encouraged firms to simultaneously cooperate and compete; see Adam M. Brandenburger and Barry J. Nalebuff, *Co-Opetition*, (New York: Crown Publishing Group, 2011).

15 Simon Das, "Magazine Publishing Innovation: Two Case Studies on Managing Creativity," *Publications* 4, no. 2 (2016): 15. doi:10.3390/publications4020015.

16 "Top 5 Customer Experience Trends for 2016," iperceptions, January 13, 2016, accessed April 3, 2017, https://www.iperceptions.com/blog/customer-experience-trends-2016.

17 "Time Out Group Appoints Julio Bruno as Executive Chairman and Noel Penzer as CEO," TimeOut, October 1, 2015, accessed November 18, 2016, www.timeout.com/about/time-out-group/latest-news/time-out-group-appoints-julio-bruno-as-executive-chairman-and-noel-penzer-as-ceo.

18 Angela Monaghan, "Sterling Hits New 31-Year Low against the Dollar," *The Guardian*, July 6, 2016, accessed August 17, 2016, https://www.theguardian.com/business/2016/jul/06/brexit-pound-plunges-to-30-year-lows-as-eu-fears-bite-into-global-markets-again; Tara Cunningham, "FTSE 100 Loses £100bn in Four Days as Brexit Paralyses Markets and Pound Crumbles," *The Telegraph*, June 15, 2016, accessed November 18, 2016, www.telegraph.co.uk/business/2016/06/14/ftse-100-slides-towards-6000-and-pound-falls-as-brexit-fears-dri/.

19 "FY16 Interim Results Presentation," Time Out Group plc, October 2016.

CASE 2 NOTES

1 Mandefro Chala Debela and Habtamu Kassa Muhye, "Water Supply and Demand Scenario of Dilla Town, Southern Ethiopia," *International Journal of Water Resources and Environmental Engineering* 9, no. 12 (December 2017): 270–76, https://doi.org/10.5897/IJWREE2017.0748.

2 We Are Water Foundation, "Drinking Water, Sanitation and Hygiene in Ethiopia," 2011, accessed August 26, 2022, https://www.wearewater.org/en/drinking-water-sanitation-and-hygiene-in-ethiopia_253215.

3 Debela and Muhye, "Water Supply and Demand."

4 WHO/UNICEF Joint Monitoring Programme for Water Supply and Sanitation, "Progress on Drinking Water and Sanitation: 2012 Update," World Health Organization, 2012, https://apps.who.int/iris/handle/10665/44842.

5 All dollar amounts are in US dollars.

6 Debela and Muhye, "Water Supply and Demand."

7 UN-Water Decade Programme on Advocacy and Communication and Water Supply and Sanitation Collaborative Council, "The Human Right to Water and Sanitation," accessed December 10, 2021, https://www.un.org/waterforlifedecade/pdf/

8 Debela and Muhye, "Water Supply and Demand."

9 Debela and Muhye, "Water Supply and Demand."

10 Debela and Muhye, "Water Supply and Demand."

11 ETB = Ethiopian birr; USD 1 = ETB 51.3850 on May 1, 2022.

OTHER NOTES

1 "The Human Right to Water and Sanitation", accessed 21st March 2023, www.un.org/waterforlifedecade/pdf/human_right_to_water_and_sanitation_media_brief.pdf

CASE 3 NOTES

1 This case has been written on the basis of published sources only. Consequently, the interpretation and perspectives presented in this case are not necessarily those of Olympus Corporation or any of its employees.
2 "先進企業、のはずが" ["The Firm Should Have Been a Blue Chip"], Asahi Newspaper, November 9, 2011, p.9.
3 "先進企業、のはずが" ["The Firm Should Have Been a Blue Chip"], Asahi Newspaper, November 9, 2011, p.9.
4 "内視鏡が拓く新しい未来　オリンパスの医療事業 2011" ["Endoscope that Creates a New Future — Olympus's Medical Business, 2011"], Olympus Corporation, 2011.
5 会社四季報2011年秋号 [Company Handbook 2011, autumn version], Toyo Keizai, 2011.
6 "日経会社情報2011年秋号" ["Nikkei Corporate Information 2011, autumn version"], Nikkei, 2011.
7 Japan Company Handbook, winter 2011, Toyo Keizai, 2011.
8 "オリンパス社長辞任" ["Resignation of Olympus's President"], Sankei Newspaper, October 27, 2011, p. 3.
9 "Corporate Profile, 2011," Olympus Corporation, 2011.
10 "Olympus Company Outline, 2011," Olympus Corporation, 2011.
11 Hidekatsu Watanabe, "新社長が何を打ち出すかは注目されるものの、映像事業は依然として厳しい" ["Expectation for New President to Come Up with a New Plan, but Imaging Business Still Tough"], Mizuho Securities Co., Ltd., Feb 21, 2011.
12 "オリンパスの内視鏡神話に揺らぎ" ["Weakness Cited on Olympus's Unbreakable Endoscope Business"], Reuters, November 25, 2011.
13 "オリンパス株式会社2011年3月期決算参考資料" ["March 2011 Term Olympus Corp. Financial Account – Reference"], Olympus Corporation, 2011.
14 会社四季報2011年秋号 [Company Handbook 2011, autumn version], Toyo Keizai, 2011.
15 "デジカメ、1000万台で明暗" ["Digital Camera, 10 Million Units Deciding the Fate of Success"], Nihon Keizai Shinbun, May 31, 2011, p. 9.
16 Ibid.
17 "デジカメ再編加速" ["Reorganization of Digital Camera Market Accelerating"], Nihon Keizai Shinbun, July 2, 2011, p. 9.
18 Hidekatsu Watanabe,"会社側が12/3期計画を公表したが、楽観的な予想と思われる" ["Company's March 12 Earnings Estimate Seems Optimistic"], Mizuho Securities. Co., Ltd., June 20, 2011.

19 Total Shipments of Digital Cameras 2011, CIPA, Camera & Imaging Products Association, 2011.

20 "オリンパスが新社長に50歳の英国人を抜擢、グローバル化加速へ" ["Olympus Appoints a 50-Year-Old Foreigner as the New President, Globalization to Accelerate"], Toyo Keizai Shikiho, prompt version, February 14, 2011.

21 "躍進するミラーレス一眼カメラ、ニコン参入はあるか" ["Will Nikon enter into Rapidly Growing Mirror-less SLR?"], Nihon Keizai Shinbun, electronic version, January 10, 2011, http://www.nikkei.com/, accessed on December 7, 2011.

22 Hidekatsu Watanabe, "新社長が何を打ち出すかは注目されるものの、映像事業は依然として厳しい" ["Expectation for New President to Come Up with a New Plan, but Imaging Business Still Tough"], Mizuho Securities Co., Ltd. February 21, 2011.

23 "老舗企業はどこで躓いたのか" ["Where Did the Time-honored Firm Go Wrong?"], Nikkei Business, October 31, 2011, p.13.

24 "オリンパス、内視鏡好調の陰で" ["Olympus, Behind Its Success of Endoscopes"], Nihon Keizai Shinbun, November 12, 2011, p. 9.

25 "老老舗企業はどこで躓いたのか" ["Where Did the Time-honored Firm Go Wrong?"], Nikkei Business, October 31, 2011, p. 14.

26 "オリンパス、内視鏡好調の陰で" ["Olympus, Behind Its Success of Endoscopes"], Nihon Keizai Shinbun, November 12, 2011, p. 9.

27 Ibid.

28 Ibid.

29 "老老舗企業はどこで躓いたのか" ["Where Did the Time-honored Firm Go Wrong?"], Nikkei Business, October 31, 2011, p. 14

30 "オリンパス社長辞任" ["Olympus's President Resigns"], Sankei Newspaper, October 27, 2011, p. 3.

31 Calculated from Bloomberg data: Nikkei 225 Debt-Equity Ratio, Bloomberg, December 12, 2011.

32 "オリンパス：社長、初の外人起用" ["Olympus, Foreign President to Be Appointed for the First Time"], Mainichi Newspaper, February 11, 2011, p. 7.

33 "オリンパス、グローバル戦略推進" ["Olympus Accelerating on Global Strategy"], Sankei Newspaper, February 11, 2011, p. 11.

34 Ibid.

35 "M&A果断、改革に挑む英国人"["British Challenging on Reform, Drastic Measures to Be Taken on M&A"], Nihon Keizai Shinbun, electronic version, February 10, 2011, http://www.nikkei.com/, accessed on December 8, 2011.

36 "有価証券報告書" ["Financial Statement," Olympus Corporation June 29, 2011.

37 2011 KeyMed Ltd. Company Website, Olympus KeyMed, 2011, http://www.keymed.co.uk/, accessed on December 10, 2011

38 "解任劇の真相を話そう" ["Let's Talk about the Truth of the Dismissal Incident"], Nikkei Business, October 31, 2011, p. 12.

39 "販管費削減、一年で黒字に" ["Cut in SGA, Turning to Black in a Year'], Nihon Keizai Shinbun, May 22, 2011, p. 7.

40 "解任劇の真相を話そう" ["Let's Talk about the Truth of the Dismissal Incident"], Nikkei Business, October 31, 2011, p. 11.

41 "オリンパス、英国人社長誕生が意味するもの" ["What the Birth of a New British President Means for Olympus"], Nihon Keizai Shinbun, electronic version, March 7, 2011, http://www.nikkei.com/, accessed on January 10, 2012.

42 Ibid.

43 "販管費削減、一年で黒字に" ["Cut in SGA, Turning to Black in a Year"], Nihon Keizai Shinbun, May 22, 2011, p. 7.

44 "オリンパス社長解任" ["Olympus President Dismissed"], Tokyo Yomiuri Shinbun, October 15, 2011, p. 8.

45 "オリンパス、新社長による合理化期待で株価上昇" ["Olympus: Share Price Rising Thanks to Expectation of Rationalization by the New President"], Nihon Keizai Shinbun, electronic version, May 16, 2011, http://www.nikkei.com/, accessed on January 10, 2012.

46 "オリンパス株反発、新製品効果で中期高成長期待" ["Olympus Share Rebounds, Expectation of Mid- Long-Term Growth Backed by New Products"], Bloomberg, June 17, 2011.

47 "オリンパス株が続伸、下期回復とコスト削減で今期純利益2.4倍へ" ["Olympus Share Continues to Rise, Net Profit Jump 2.4 Fold Thanks to Second Half Revival and Cost Reduction"], Bloomberg, June 20, 2011.

48 "解任劇の真相を話そう" ["Let's Talk about the Truth of the Dismissal Incident"], Nikkei Business, October 31, 2011, p. 9.

49 "オリンパス「無謀M&A」巨額損失の怪" ["Mystery of Huge Loss – Olympus's Reckless M&A"], FACTA, August 2011, pp. 7–10.

50 Ibid.

51 "オリンパス「無謀M&A」巨額損失の怪" ["Mystery of Huge Loss – Olympus's Reckless M&A"], FACTA, August 2011, pp. 7–10.

52 "オリンパス上場維持4つの関門" ["Olympus: Four Obstacles over Maintaining Its Listings,"] Nikkei Veritas, November 27, 2011, p. 14.

53 "オリンパス損失隠し" ["Olympus Hiding Losses,"] Sankei Newspaper, November 9, 2011, p. 3.

54 "解任劇の真相を話そう" ["Let's Talk about the Truth of the Dismissal Incident,"] Nikkei Business, October 31, 2011, p. 9.

55 "解任劇の真相を話そう" ["Let's Talk about the Truth of the Dismissal Incident,"] Nikkei Business, October 31, 2011, p. 9.

56 "オリンパス前社長「これは組織的犯罪" ["Olympus's Previous President: 'This Is an Organized Crime,'"] Sankei Newspaper, October 22, 2011, p. 10.

57 "解任劇の真相を話そう" ["Let's Talk about the Truth of the Dismissal Incident,"] Nikkei Business, October 31, 2011, p. 9.

58 Ibid.

59 Ibid.

60 Ibid.

61 Ibid.

62 Ibid.

63 Ibid.

64 Ibid.

65 Ibid.
66 "オリンパス前社長、ＣＥＯ就任➔会長らに時に辞任要求➔２週間で解任" ["Olympus's Ex-president, Assigned as a CEO➔Asking Chairman to Leave➔Dismissed in 2 Weeks,"] Nihon Keizai Shinbun, October 18, 2011, p. 9.
67 "解任劇の真相を話そう" ["Let's Talk about the Truth of the Dismissal Incident,'] Nikkei Business, October 31, 2011, p. 10.
68 "解任劇の真相を話そう" ["Let's Talk about the Truth of the Dismissal Incident,'] Nikkei Business, October 31, 2011, p. 11.
69 Ibid.
70 "巨額の投資損失の追及が理由　解職―オリンパス前社長の反撃" ["Counterattack by the Olympus's Ex-president: Dismissal Due to Pursuit of Large Investment Loss,"] Shukan Diamond, October 29, 2011, pp. 12–13.
71 解任劇の真相を話そう" ["Let's Talk about the Truth of the Dismissal Incident,"] Nikkei Business, October 31, 2011, p. 11.

PART III

Maximising impact from a strategic business case analysis

CHAPTER 8

Externalising the impact of a strategic business case analysis

DOMAINS FOR IMPACT

Even though academics and practitioners have operated in different paradigms for many decades (Carton & Mouricou, 2017), bridging the persisting 'research–practice gap' is important because it can result in an improvement to peoples' lives (Sharma & Bansal, 2020). With a strategic business case analysis, the research–practice gap is not as large as is commonly the case in mainstream academic research. A strategic business case analysis is naturally more applied in nature.

On the holistic end of the Case Analysis Spectrum, scholars emphasise a tight connection and interaction between the analyst and the phenomenon under scrutiny (Verschuren, 2001). Indeed, writing in the context of systems thinking and action research, Jackson (2019) notes: "Systems practitioners tend to see themselves as fully involved, with other participants, in a social process that will change the problem situation they are engaging in" (p. 149). This idea that analysis of complex situations should not end as an academic exercise but that it should somehow influence positive outcomes *for* the phenomenon is not limited to systems thinking and holism. It is central to the ethos of a meaningful strategic business case analysis in management or executive education. You might well be involved in the problem situation that you are analysing to the extent that you can provide a resolution to it, regardless of the stance taken on the Case Analysis Spectrum.

It is important to consider how your analysis can be used by external agents and beneficiaries as part of their drive for improvement and resolution to strategic issues. Many scholars have written about the need for relevant and impactful research. Cunliffe and Scaratti (2017) see this as a process of generating socially useful knowledge. At the heart of this are researcher–practitioner conversations. This requires analysts to directly interact with practitioners who may be positively impacted by the results of analysis, involving their situated knowledge and a process of dialogical sensemaking. The latter refers to shared conversations that generate "situated and impactful knowledge" (Cunliffe and Scaratti, 2017, p. 32). According to the authors, there are five conversational resources needed for this: (1) being attuned to relationally responsive dialogue (involving openness to exploring of meanings), (2) engaging in shared reflexivity (to explore opacity and avoid overcommitment), (3) recognising and building on arresting moments (being sensitive to moments in conversations that 'strike' us), (4) surfacing the play of tensions,

DOI: 10.4324/9781003288916-11

contradictions, binaries, and boundaries (which helps in the process of reseeing, reviewing and reimagining), and (5) creating action guiding anticipatory understandings (using practical theory to sensitise practitioners to their situation). The stress here is on the role of the analyst in holding dialogue directly with those who may be impacted by the results of a strategic business case analysis.

There are many ways of looking at impact from academic research. Hunt (2021) examines impact in marketing research. The emphasis here is making an impact in the academic community. There are many others in the academic community treating impact in this way. Tellis (2017), for instance, treats impact as academic research that "runs counter to what is currently assumed as true" (p. 1) by a scholarly audience.

Others have been frustrated by this tendency for academic work to only be useful by other academics (Vermeulen, 2005). For instance, Bartlett and Ghoshal (1991) were amongst the first in the strategy field calling for academics' work to have more relevance to practising managers and strategists: "We now need to spend more time understanding the impact of our findings on the manager's job" (p. 14). They take a critical tone, noting how: "Scholarly researchers may fleetingly acknowledge the importance of [environmental] change in the obligatory 'implications for managers' paragraph near the end of the paper" (p. 14). The academic domain is clearly one area for making impact with academic analysis, but it is a rather narrow one.

Scholars do note the importance for academic analysis of problems to be impactful in practice, i.e., useful for those dealing with organisational and managerial situations in the real world. Wickert, Post, Doh, Prescott and Prencipe (2021) discuss the challenge of 'making a difference' in management research in this wider sense. They describe five areas for making a difference: (1) scholarly – providing a "clear, compelling, and meaningful theoretical contribution" (p. 299), (2) practical – research that is "used for actually doing (rather than just theorizing or abstracting about) something" (p. 304), (3) societal – analysis

TABLE 8.1 Domains and areas for impact

Actors with an interest in new case knowledge	Imperative	Mapping to area(s) in Wickert et al. (2021)
Practitioners	Solving the problem in specific situations as well as in general terms	Practical, Societal, Policy
Academic system, scholars, and theorists	Delivering up to date and current knowledge concerning theory and pedagogy	Scholarly, Educational
Case writers	Creating fresh insights into how cases can benefit a wide spectrum of stakeholders in business and management education	Educational
Students	Developing skills and knowledge in how to solve similar strategic problems in the future	Educational

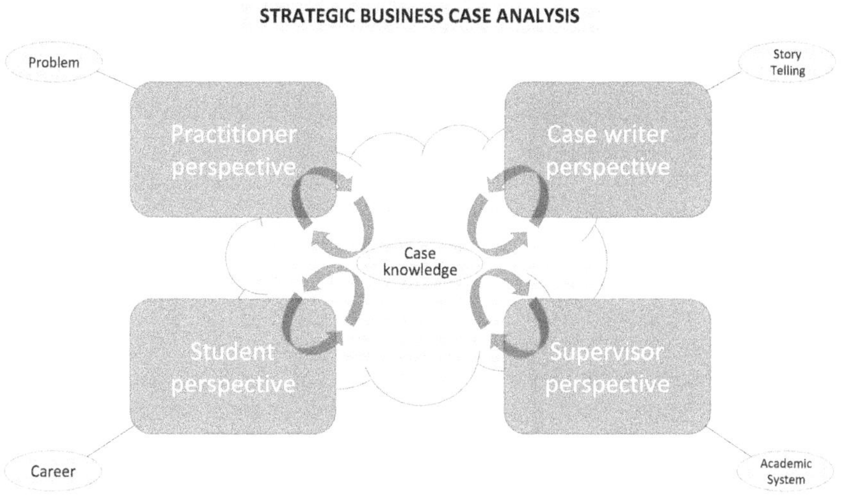

Figure 8.1 Case knowledge and domains for impact

that contributes "more substantially to broader societal concerns" (p. 307), (4), policy – work that provides a deeper understanding of "important policy issues among political decision-makers" (p. 310), and (5) educational – where good education is "fundamentally based on state-of-the-art research" (p. 314). It is possible for a strategic business case analysis to make an impact in all these areas. Consequently, it is worth considering how you can take responsibility for outcomes and provide a basis for change in any or all these areas.

In Chapter 1 we referred to four stakeholder domains for a strategic business case analysis. We stated that case knowledge generated through work on a strategic business case analysis can diffuse into any of four stakeholder domains (shown again in Figure 8.1). These are: (1) the practitioner audience directly affected by the problem analysed in the case; (2) scholars and theorists within the academic system, where existing theory may be challenged by the case analysis; (3) the case writing and case publishing world; (4) students and learners. These four stakeholder domains for case work map onto the five areas for making a difference noted by Wickert et al. (2021), as shown in Table 8.1.

OVERLAPPING DOMAINS FOR CREATING IMPACT

New case knowledge created as part of a strategic business case analysis can be of interest to the different domains in Figure 8.1. These domains can have interest in both the case story and the case analysis. New case knowledge has developed because of the strategic business case analysis project. Case knowledge is no longer simply the articulation of a storyline (such as in a published case document or documents), or the enormous (arguably, unending) volume of untapped tacit knowledge surrounding the case that is not written down. Case knowledge now includes a new piece of work (namely, a strategic business case analysis) that looks at the case in a unique way. It augments the case storyline and represents a new articulation of structured thinking about the issues in the case. Without the analysis, case knowledge could remain messy and tacitly stored in the heads of many people. Case knowledge now includes a distinct, standalone unit of explicit knowledge that helps make sense of a complex situation and the messy knowledge associated with it. And the analysis has a specific purpose, namely, to provide answers to challenging questions surrounding the strategic issue at the heart of the case. This makes it potentially valuable to stakeholders in any of the four domains.

These different domains for impact overlap in terms of their interest and involvement with case knowledge. These overlaps are important to understand as you seek to drive external impact with your case analysis. As shown in Table 8.1, one way for impact to be expressed is on the educational and scholarly side of the coin. Students who have conducted a strategic business case analysis can use their new insights, skills, and knowledge to bolster their own impact in their careers going forward. The strategic business case analysis process has become a meaningful part of their management or executive education. We will discuss this in greater depth in the next chapter on 'internalising the impact of a strategic business case analysis'. Case writers can benefit by understanding how their cases have been used in detailed analytical conditions and how value has been created from the original articulation of the case. This can help case writers develop and hone their skills in researching and writing future cases. And the academic system can use strategic business case analysis output both in teaching and in theory development. When presented in an appropriate way (see next section), the analysis can complement the original case and can be used in class teaching environments for the benefit of many students. Academics can also use the analysis to sharpen their critical thinking as it pertains to theory: what theory is supported/partially supported/refuted because of the analysis? We can see that on this educational and scholarly side how the domains are very much overlapping (academic system, case writing community, students) and how they may all benefit from the production and dissemination of new case knowledge as embodied in a strategic business case analysis.

In the case of Time Out in Chapter 7, a reductionist approach was applied to analyse the problems facing the company. These related to its quest for profitability in a very competitive environment where there were many alternatives and substitutes for information about entertainment options in cities. The Matrix of Principles summary for profitability in Table 7.2 suggested strong support for theory on subsidiary initiatives (Birkinshaw & Hood, 1998) and the links between subsidiary initiatives and global competitive advantage. The lack of evidence and support for principles related to value creation in e-business on the other hand (Amit & Zott, 2001), suggests that the novelty–lock-in–complementarities–efficiency (NICE) framework is useful for students and educators in learning and teaching in the field of e-business.

On the practitioner side of the coin, there are opportunities for practical, societal, and policy impact (Wickert et al., 2021) through a strategic business case analysis. This concerns the real world, not the academic one. There are important differences between practical, societal, and policy areas for impact as noted above. However, if impact can be created in one of them, there is a high chance it can be created in one or more of the others as well. As Wickert et al. (2021) point out, there are important differences between practical, societal, and policy areas for impact. Where they do converge is in the fundamental desire to make a difference to a problem space in practice, and to be relevant beyond the academic domain. Vermeulen (2005) argues that relevant work will come about when researchers focus on issues that are of a practical – rather than a theoretical – nature at the outset. According to Vermeulen, the academic system does not value relevance and is even described as an "incestuous circle of academic producers and consumers only" (p. 980). He argues that the system should value relevance and that each researcher can work out how to do this. By engaging with a strategic business case analysis project, you are engaging with relevance. If your findings mean something to managers in an organisation, they are also likely to be relevant to policy and societal environments surrounding that organisation. If your findings have a direct bearing on actors in society – the disadvantaged, or minorities, let's say – then they have relevance to the policy domain relating to those groups as well as to managers in NGOs and the public space dealing with those groups on a day-to-day basis.

In the case of Brightwater in Chapter 7, a holistic approach allowed us to view the case as a socio-technical system, with human and non-human aspects. There were clear achievements of the social enterprise up to the decision point. But there were now potential implications of the idea proposed by the main protagonist in the case to start to produce and distribute clean water in plastic bottles. For the former, implications for the organisation included the need to shift strategic focus during the Covid-19 pandemic (to include provision of showers), as well as the role of the foreign NGO (Wuhu Sira) in providing grant money and expertise to allow water pumps to be upgraded using solar power technology. For the latter, there were implications related to potential investment in a new plastic bottling plant, as well as how to deal with concerns relating to plastics in a context where there is little recycling infrastructure. In both areas of relevance for the organisation, we see overlaps with societal and policy areas. Up to the decision point, people in Dilla have undoubtedly benefited both in terms of clean water access and support for girls' education (addressing two UN SDGs). Decisions going forward should not threaten these impacts. In terms of policy, the implications of the analysis also speak to regional and national policy for foreign NGO involvement in local social enterprises. Encouraging this involvement in situations where multiple UN SDGs are addressed in specific localities can be framed as a policy intervention for other locations around Ethiopia, and perhaps the Global South in general. In sum, we need to be cognisant of how implications from a strategic business case analysis can be applied in multiple sub-areas of the real-world domain of relevance, and not restrict ourselves just to one area.

CREATING IMPACT THROUGH A STRATEGIC BUSINESS CASE ANALYSIS: DISCOVERY AND ACTION

Creating impact from a strategic business case analysis is not a single, one-off activity. There are many options available to you to influence different stakeholders in a meaningful way. The options that you choose may be different to those of another analyst, and they may be different next time you conduct such an in-depth piece of work. We divide these routes to impact into two broad camps. The first is general: they can be applied to all domains in Figure 8.1. They represent core options and channels for influence. The second camp is more tailored and specific to a stakeholder group.

In both general and specific camps, impact cannot be created without a beneficiary being aware of the analysis work. The beneficiary needs to 'discover' that the analysis has taken place, that it is available to be read and understood. It is therefore important for case analysts wishing to make an impact to find ways of allowing stakeholders from any of the domains to have access to the insights from the analysis. Carton and Mouricou (2017) describe this in terms of gatekeeper's orthodoxy: without dissemination by academic analysts there can be no relevance. Analysts can see themselves as gatekeepers, having a responsibility to make others aware of the existence of their work and allowing access to their work. Secondly, key decision-makers within a beneficiary organisation must be convinced to take new action based on the findings of the analysis, potentially in combination with other contextual knowledge. This step is an 'action' step. It will require fresh decision-making and re-allocating of resources. Decision-making in beneficiary organisations on strategic issues will not be taken lightly; solid evidence and persuasion will matter. While discovery and action steps are interlinked (you cannot have action without the knowledge to underpin the action), it will be easier to create opportunities for awareness than it will be to convince decision-makers in beneficiary organisations to change the way they do things. There are many impediments to change, including structural, cultural, and political barriers within organisations. Rosenberg and Mosca (2011) identify no fewer than 20 barriers to organisational change, ranging from employees' disposition towards change and fear of the unknown to internal conflict for resources and poor implementation planning. Discovery, then, is important. It can be used to help lower (although not eliminate) barriers to change, making subsequent action easier.

General routes for discovery and action within an impact activity include the following, not mutually exclusive options. This is schematised in Figure 8.2.

1. *Conversations*: Conversations about the results of a strategic business case analysis can be the backbone of effective impact. Cunliffe and Scaratti (2017) note the importance of active participation of those with direct experience of the phenomenon in socially relevant research. Conversations form the basis by which researchers (in our case, the case analyst) are "open to moment-by-moment interpretations and possibilities" (Cunliffe & Scaratti, 2017: 41). In knowledge transfer theory, socialisation (through conversations) allows the transfer of knowledge in tacit form from one individual to another (Nonaka & Takeuchi, 1995). This tacit knowledge is often difficult to articulate and capture in explicit form and allows awareness to develop in a beneficiary organisation about the intricacies of insights and solutions proposed in a strategic business case analysis. While the final report is captured in an explicit form, conversations will allow its process and relevance to be conveyed in a way that is in tune with the concerns of the beneficiary organisation. Conversations can be held in many ways, including formal meetings and workshops, and as well as informal opportunities to interact. They can be face-to-face, or computer-mediated. Heracleous (2022) places a strong emphasis on conversations in his work on process consultation (Schein, 1969) at NASA. His guidelines for conducting impactful research include various mechanisms that have conversations at the centre. These include conducting engagement workshops, assuming the role of a 'doctor' or 'expert' *when requested*, grappling with dilemmas through conversations, and maintaining ongoing coordination with a sponsor. Conversations allow beneficiary

organisations (including the one at the heart of the case) to discover both the existence and the value of the strategic business case analysis conducted by the analyst.

2. *Direct (point-to-point) transmission*: Direct transmission of the results of a strategic busi-ness case analysis can be used to create discovery and guide action. Direct transmis-sion is a point-to-point communication of content for a named person's attention only (i.e., case analyst to specific individual in a specific beneficiary organisation). What is transferred is the case analysis report, or more likely, an edited summary of the anal-ysis tailored to the specific organisation. A report that has been generated as part of the student's management studies will be initially packaged for their higher education institution. This packaging will likely need to be removed before wider dissemination beyond the academic institution. It will make sense to have conversations with the target individual in advance to lay the path for the dissemination of the work and to establish whether the whole report is needed or a part or summary of it. In a discovery mode, direct transmission can be used to ensure the potential beneficiary organisation has access to outputs. This is one of the guidelines given by Heracleous (2022). In an action mode, direct transmission can be used as part of ongoing coordination with the beneficiary during an intervention as well as to influence subsequent interventions (both guidelines in Heracleous, 2022). It is not advisable to undertake direct transmission of strategic business case analysis output in the absence of conversations. As shown in Fig-ure 8.2, ongoing conversations can run in parallel with all other impact activities. Going in 'blind', without pre-warning and prior establishment of social capital and trust with a potential beneficiary organisation will appear somewhat cold, uncontextualized, and possibly even rude! There is a high chance the transmitted file (most likely over email) will end up in a spam or trash folder.

3. *Publication to broad audiences*: Publication of a strategic business case analysis – or parts thereof – in business and management outlets will allow discovery across a broad audience base and a multitude of potential beneficiary organisations. Her-acleous (2022) recommends this in terms of developing joint applied and scholarly publications. Applied publications are more likely to reach practitioner audiences to enable discovery. In similarity with the previous point about direct transmission, the strategic case analysis document will need to be re-worked and edited before being publication-ready for these types of outlets. Some journals – such as *Business Horizons* and *California Management Review* – have been connecting academic and manage-ment domains for many decades. They are broad in remit and accomplished academic scholars tend to publish in them. Publication will be competitive and may take many months, given the time for review and multiple rounds of revision. Rejection is always possible. Other narrower outlets – such as *FDi Intelligence* (trade and investment) and *IT NOW* (British Computer Society magazine for IT Professionals) – are more focussed in scope and have a higher proportion of practitioners and subject experts writing in them. White papers also provide information and proposals for a specific issue in the policy domain and – depending on the strategic issue in the case – could be one type of publication emanating from a strategic business case analysis. White papers can be highly influential, sparking debate and innovation. One famous example is Nakamoto's

(2008) white paper on bitcoin that spearheaded the whole blockchain phenomenon. This is not to say that a strategic business case analysis will be as ground-breaking and influential as the invention of blockchain. But when presented as a white paper, it can be used to guide policy debate and discourse. It allows the author (the case analyst) to create a platform to discuss and influence policy based on the findings from the analysis of the single case in context. Relatedly, publishing the analysis as a book chapter or as part of a book may also serve to aid discovery in multiple audiences. If any of these options are pursued, the publication can serve as a basis for conversations about intervention and action in any potential beneficiary organisation. Action will likely need to involve further careful engagement and planning within the organisation (see items 5–7 below).

4. *Social media and social networking*: There are many ways in which a strategic business case analysis can be shared on social media and social networking sites (SNS) to reach broad audiences. Firstly, in terms of social media, packaging the analysis using a single (or set of) videos, blogs, or podcasts can enable the work to be visible to a global audience and viewed on handheld devices such as phones, tablets, and laptops. The question is whether global audiences will be interested in listening to or viewing an analysis in this way. Why would it appeal? How can it contribute to broader discussions and debates? Some additional work will be needed to answer these questions. It is probable that the analysis will need to be presented as part of a bigger picture to achieve mass appeal on social media. This will require careful thinking about the overall purpose of the post and the content. Should it be a one-off post? Should it be a part of a series of posts and content related to an issue of broader concern? For example, the analysis of the Olympus case in the previous chapter could be used in summary form to discuss issues surrounding corporate governance, Japan, and board-level cultures. The analysis of the Brightwater case could be used to support a more generalised set of content on the issues of clean water and gender equality in developing countries and the Global South. There is much to be gained in terms of developing your own reputation as an expert in a space (see next chapter), by going beyond a simple post on LinkedIn announcing the completion of your strategic business case analysis project, to a coordinated and joined-up sequence of content on the broader issues at play. Secondly, SNS can be used to engage in follow-on discussions after content has been posted containing reference to a strategic business case analysis. Follow-on discussions on SNS are important for various reasons. Chai and Kim (2012) examine determinants of knowledge contribution behaviour amongst SNS users. Knowledge contribution behaviour was captured as a multi-item scale amongst SNS users: "I frequently leave my feedback/comments on the SNSs, I spend time on my SNSs to update new information and knowledge, I update my SNSs regularly, I frequently share my experience or know-how with other SNS users, I share my educational knowledge with other SNS users, I post useful documents or files on my SNSs to share with other SNS users" (Chai & Kim, 2012, p. 122). The authors find ethical culture (ethical behaviour in cyberspace and looking out for the good of other users), a sense of belonging to SNS (including commitment to and enjoyment of SNS), and social ties (spending time on SNS, having frequent communications with others, and even knowing others on a personal basis), to

all have positive effects on knowledge contribution behaviour. Nurturing these factors will be important to have a sustained impact through SNS from the output of a strategic business case analysis.

5. *Consultancy*: A potentially impactful option following the competition of a strategic business case analysis is to build consultancy or training offerings for beneficiary organisations based on the analysis. In similarity to the previous point concerning social media platforms, a consultancy or training offering will very likely need to be established as a broader service, with the analytical work positioned as one component within this. Indeed, it may not be the only piece of evidence used. It may need to be packaged and combined with other sources of evidence, depending on the nature of the client needs. This needs to be established in preparation and negotiation with the client. The existence of a strategic business case analysis can be used in the pre-sales and selling process in advance of signing a contract to deliver consultancy. Credibility is of utmost importance to build trust with new clients (Maister, Galford & Green, 2021), and the evidence gained as part of a strategic business case analysis can be used in support of this, even if it is not used in the consultancy or training per se. Where this option differs from the aforementioned options of conversations, direct transmission, publication to broad audiences, and social media dissemination, is the fact that consultancy and training are more likely than not to be income-generating services for the provider. Of course, they can be offered on a pro bono basis. This can be done for certain types of clients (e.g., NGOs and charities) as a way of 'giving back'. But in many cases the analyst will seek revenue income from consultancy and training. To win and successfully deliver the contract, the needs of the client will need to be listened to very carefully. This mode of interacting for impact will be more client-centric than analyst-centric. Care will also need to be exercised with respect to any conflicts of interest and the terms of non-disclosure agreements as they pertain to the case organisation if it is a different organisation to the beneficiary or client.

6. *Direct involvement*: Discovery and action are underpinned by direct embedment of the analyst in a beneficiary organisation. This involves the analyst engaging in intricate conversations with organisations – as noted above – and managing this process thoughtfully and carefully (Cunliffe & Scaratti, 2017). But it also involves being aware of the need to combine academic rigour with practical relevance. This can be achieved with the researcher and organisation involved in a continuous process of co-creation over time (Sharma & Bansal, 2020). Direct involvement of a strategic business case analyst within an organisation looking to solve a strategic issue can be brought about in various ways. One way is when the analyst is employed by the organisation. Oftentimes, executive and management students conduct their case work while being sponsored by their employer, researching and addressing a strategic issue for the employer. In other situations, the student can become involved in the case organisation or other organisation with a similar strategic issue on a consultancy basis (see previous points). Both require a direct involvement of the student, now acting as an active advisor, within a beneficiary organisation. Sharma and Bansal (2020) develop a helpful model of cocreation between researchers and managers. The model sees co-creation as the key to creating value and impact of research activity. This process involves a series of joint

activities in time, with temporal connections between and across events. Some of these joint events do not involve co-creation, these being characterised by researchers being inflexible, not building ideas with managers but defending the results of their research work. Other joint events come with co-creation; they have dialogue. According to the authors, in joint events with co-creation: "The researchers indicated that they did not have all the answers, inviting the managers to contribute. The researchers asked the managers questions, to which the managers responded with their inputs. The managers also asked other managers questions, instead of looking to the researchers for the answers" (p. 394). Researchers expressed uncertainty in these types of events, looking to managers to fill in knowledge gaps. What is interesting in Sharma and Bansal's (2020) model is how manager knowledge (practice) and researcher knowledge (academic) merge together through this process and how it becomes increasingly blurry over time. Through direct involvement following the completion of a strategic business case analysis one should not expect every interaction with an organisation to yield meaningful co-creation. Those interactions that do should recognise that the analyst may not have all the answers and that there is a temporal process at play consisting of a joined-up sequence of events where sharing knowledge across events is just as important as sharing knowledge within any specific event.

7. *Monitoring and learning*: Discovery and action can be supported by ongoing monitoring of a strategic issue in the context of a focal organisation. This serves as a way of continuously learning about a given organisation and its strategic context. Monitoring allows the analyst to sharpen and refine the results of their strategic business case analysis during the months and years after its completion, to facilitate impact in the longer term. Ongoing monitoring can happen informally through conversations, consultancy work, and direct involvement with a beneficiary organisation, mechanisms described above. It will not happen easily through direct transmission, publication, or social media posts of knowledge connected to a strategic business case analysis. These imply an outward dissemination from the analyst to an external party or multiple parties. However, following direct transmission, publication, or social media posts, new information may come to light, either from the focal case organisation or other sources familiar with the organisation. Such new information can assist the analyst in their continuous improvement and can feed into the analyst's ongoing monitoring activity. According to agency theory, monitoring is a problem that makes it difficult for principals (such as CEOs) to assess performance of agents (such as lower-level workers closer to the operational tasks of the organisation) (Bourgeois & Brodwin, 1984). This problem translates to analysts attempting to create impact from a strategic business case analysis. The extent to which an analyst in a strategic business case analysis project can effectively monitor implementation of recommendations is uncertain. Analysts – especially those external to a beneficiary organisation – will also suffer from information asymmetry and moral hazard problems (Bourgeois & Brodwin, 1984). Nevertheless, there are ways in which monitoring can be performed effectively, including through informal conversations (Cunliffe & Scaratti, 2017). Large-scale transformational change can be monitored by large numbers of individuals organised in learning communities (Senge & Scharmer, 2008).

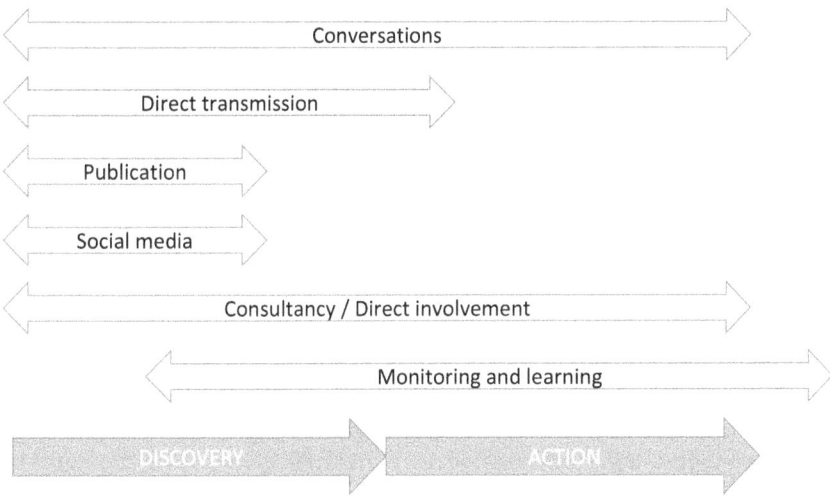

Figure 8.2 From discovery to action in delivering impact from a strategic business case
analysis

In addition to these general options, stakeholder-specific routes to impact are possible.
These include the following.

1. *Practitioners*: Forums and spaces for knowledge exchange centred around the strategic
   issue at the heart of the case provide an opportunity for discovery of a strategic business
   case analysis and a basis for subsequent action. Examples include: a conference of the
   parties (COP) conference, [1] a digital trade fair such as CeBIT in Hannover, or a company
   specific event such as an annual general meeting (AGM). Universities and incubators that
   bring together a multitude of entrepreneurs and small businesses are central players in
   practice networks. These forums can also be targeted if the strategic issue aligns with them.
   Any organised gathering involving managers and stakeholders from the case organisation
   itself, or from other organisations facing the same or similar strategic issues, are potential
   beneficiaries and targets to create discovery and action within a practice community.
   Practitioners will gather with concerns for the same strategic issue (e.g., climate change,
   digital transformation, strategic turnaround, regional development, growth). The analyst
   can seek out such opportunities proactively and participate in them to allow the discovery
   of the analysis and find potential beneficiary organisations for subsequent action.

2. *Academic system*: Academia is a large and complex international institutional system.
   It may seem daunting for a former student, now turned case analyst, to penetrate the
   academic system to create impact with a strategic business case analysis. But there are
   ways, and the best ones will be those that are realistic and feasible. Where possible,
   interacting with the academic system should be based on human interaction rather than
   cold calling through emails and electronic messaging – academics won't respond to
   these. The analyst can seek opportunities to present the results of the analysis at academic conferences, particularly those that emphasise practice-oriented work. Analysts

can reach out to local universities and business schools to seek opportunities for presenting and discussing the strategic business case analysis with local academics. This could lead to invitations to give presentations, contribute to student learning (see point below) in the immediate locale, as well as opening the gate to connections with other academics internationally. Further afield, academics based in distant places can be contacted and engaged using video communications. These efforts can facilitate discovery as well as probing the possibilities for action within the academic system based on the analysis. Academics may be inspired by the analysis to craft a particular study in a different way, to embark on a new study, to use the evidence of a strategic business case analysis as part of a funding bid, or to join in efforts for impact through its results.

3. *Case writers*: Accessing and influencing the case writing community using the results of a strategic business case analysis may not seem so straightforward. There is no one single guild of case writers, no one global institution or network to contact. Case writers come in all shapes and sizes and from all parts of the globe. Some are students, some are academics, some are independent researchers and writers, often with different jobs. Oftentimes, these different types of individuals come together to research and publish cases, working in teams. One way of accessing and influencing the case writing community is through the organisations that operate in the case publishing and distribution industry. Organisations such as the Case Centre (thecasecentre.org) offer a variety of ways to get involved. These include discussion groups, newsletters, and being involved in events such as the #WorldCaseTeachingDay. They also offer webinars and training on case use. A case analyst can seek to engage in various activities across different case publishing and distributing organisations to influence the case writing community. Perhaps there were learnings about the methods used in the strategic business case analysis that can be fed back into the case writing community. Perhaps there are new insights into what makes a suitable case for a larger strategic level analysis and longer-term impact. Perhaps there are substantive insights based on the topic and strategic issue at the heart of the case – new and emerging topics in AI, CSR, grand challenges, and leadership that require new cases to be developed. These types of messages are ones that an analyst can feed back into the case writing community.

4. *Students*: Impacting student learning by making a strategic business case analysis available to them is possible by working through the academic system. Faculty members and educational content designers will be the gatekeepers to decide whether the analysis can be used as a component on one or more courses. Contacting – and working through – the academic system will be necessary. In terms of substance for learning, making sense of the strategic issue at the heart of the case, with its resolution or outcome, is an obvious area of knowledge that can be imparted to students for their benefit over the longer term. But it is not the only way a strategic business case analysis can impact students. Another way is for the analyst to share their experiences with other management and executive students of conducting a strategic business case analysis. Nick Waters and Katherine Neufield have done exactly that with their contributions in this book! Giving talks and joining discussion on case work in different contexts is useful for future generations of students. Note that this does not have to be only about a particular method or approach in the actual analysis of the case data. As we have covered in this book, learning can also be shared with students of case problems on aspects such

as how to choose a case, how to decide the questions for analysis, how to reach an analytical stance, and how to plan for subsequent impact.

ADDRESSING GRAND CHALLENGES THROUGH A STRATEGIC BUSINESS CASE ANALYSIS

The four domains in Figure 8.1 can be impacted by a strategic business case analysis in the areas of grand challenge and societal issues on our planet. Grand challenges – such as addressing climate change and solving inequality and poverty – are complex problems facing society globally. They lack a solution, and require interdisciplinary and international collaboration to be addressed. Some grand challenges, such as sending a man to the moon, are well defined; others are much broader (Grodal & O'Mahony, 2017). They have been described as: "… open-ended missions, concerning the socio-economic system as a whole, even inducing (or requiring) system transformation" (Kuhlmann & Rip, 2014, p. 3). Often represented by the 17 UN SDGs, they are problems facing humanity at large. They are much broader and more complex than a single strategic issue facing a single organisation at a single moment in time. However, even organisations whose purpose is not explicitly concerned with addressing one or more UN SDGs need to be savvy when it comes to grand challenge. Greater awareness of corporate social responsibility (CSR) and inclusion of CSR in corporate strategy has become more prominent in the minds of C-suite executives (Kakabadse, 2007). More recently this awareness and strategic concern amongst organisational leaders have taken a new focus with the emerging demands related to environment social governance (ESG) reporting (Arvidsson & Dumay, 2022). Organisations in all industries and locations, and of all sizes, will be concerned with the strategic implications of grand challenges at some point.

If this is a strong theme in a strategic business case, the analyst can seek to influence any or all of the four domains for impact in a substantive way, engaging in the theme of responsibility head on. This clearly is a theme in the Brightwater case, a social enterprise seeking to provide clean water in Dilla, Ethiopia, while providing career prospects for girls. It is not so conspicuous in the Olympus or Time Out cases. However, we do see corporate governance and the theme of ethical behaviour of corporate leaders as a prominent theme in the Olympus case. In the practitioner community, the analyst can seek to influence norms of corporate behaviour, how executives and leaders think and approach grand challenges, and how they incorporate CSR into their strategic investments. In the academic system, the analyst can seek to influence the design of new research agendas, contribute to, or challenge theory, and support academic work on specific areas of grand challenge. In the case writing community, the analyst can seek to inspire and encourage new cases in untapped areas of organisational interaction with grand challenges for the ultimate benefit of learners from cases, notably students who will become leaders in the future. And in the student community itself, the analyst can seek to provide direct learning and insights that will guide and shape the thinking of future leaders of organisations and their future roles as good global citizens. All these domains can be influenced using the results of a strategic business case analysis.

There are many ways in which a strategic business case analysis will stand out from the crowd in the grand challenge space. The success of discovery and action based on its findings and conclusions will depend on whether these types of substantive features are present in the case analysis:

1. *How does the analysis help with understanding best practice in environmental sustainability?* Environmental sustainability is a grand challenge that has received an enormous amount of attention. Organisations in all industries have had to deal with the pressures to become more environmentally sustainable and have adopted practices that are geared towards achieving this goal. In tourism, social innovation has been seen as an area of focus (Batle, Orfila-Sintes & Moon, 2018). Best practices identified by Batle et al. (2018) include alternative energy saving systems, symbiotic relations with local farms, collaborations with ecological and slow food associations, and alternative agricultural methods. Scholars also note how information systems underpin efforts to be sustainable and conserve, deploy, and re-use resources in responsible ways (Malhotra, Melville & Watson, 2013). Best practices in this field include deployment of enterprise-wide software that is used strategically to manage an organisation's carbon footprint. The identification and critical appraisal of best practices in environmental sustainability can be undertaken in a strategic business case analysis. If the analysis helps to identify 'good' vs. 'bad' practices, revealing interesting results while challenging assumptions on what makes a practice environmentally sustainable, the work will be eye-catching – i.e., discoverable – to stakeholders in the various domains. This will increase the chances for action based on the results of the analysis.

2. *Does the analysis provide insight into how organisations can transform to become greener?* To develop these best practices, organisations worldwide have needed to adapt their business operations to become more sustainable and respond to environmental concerns. They have needed to transform. How this process unfolds is a topic of immense interest, and case analysis can play a key role in creating knowledge on determinants of success and failure with respect to green transformations. An example from the academic literature is the use of information systems in a sustainability transformation within a global software solutions provider (Seidel, Recker & vom Brocke, 2013). As noted by the authors, the case organisation was under pressure from other actors in its value chain – as well as regulatory pressures – to focus on ESG concerns. Their approach was a *revelatory* one; a good example of a successful sustainability transition. Information systems were found to play a key role in the realisation of green transition, including reflective disclosure (information systems allowing individuals to communicate and alter their belief systems), information democratisation (allowing dissemination of sustainability-related information), output management (monitoring output that can be harmful to the environment), and delocalisation (reducing resource movement through the use of information systems) (Seidel et al., 2013). If a strategic business case analysis reveals how an organisation successfully negotiated a green transition, both practitioners and non-practitioner audiences with an interest in sustainability will be open to discovery, and possibly, action, based on the analysis.

3. *Does the analysis shed light on how businesses can contribute to peace in fragile states?* Experts in the field of Business and Peace have debated the role of private sector organisations in contributing to recovery and peacebuilding in countries beset

by armed conflict. This is a contested and debated space because, while companies can contribute to peace, for instance through social investments (Williams & Steriu, 2022), they can also be complicit in conflict, contributing to enduring violence (Miklian & Schouten, 2014). Scholars note the importance of ethical leadership, helping to settle disputes and working in the community's interests (Katsos & Fort, 2016). Much case work has been conducted in this field, with researchers personally visiting conflict zones to collect primary data and evidence. A strategic business case analysis that provides fresh insights into business' contributions to peace and how business leaders in conflict zones pursue responsible strategies would be useful to both academic and practitioner communities. Given the diversity of violent contexts in the world, plus the attention that international companies have paid to them as opportunities for conducting business, original case work that yields new insights could be highly valuable.

4. *Does the analysis contain indigenous knowledge?* The interface between indigenous knowledge and ecological science is vital in the effort to preserve scarce natural capital in the world. Indigenous knowledge relates to "ecological knowledge held by place-based Indigenous peoples, accumulated intergenerationally within their specific cultural context and belief system (traditional ecological knowledge), and often supplemented by contemporary observations on local-to-regional scales (local knowledge)" (Ban, Frid, Reid, Edgar, Shaw & Siwallace, 2018, p. 1680). Indigenous knowledge matters because it provides a valuable perspective on the relationship between living and physical entities. It is more fine-grained and qualitative than much scientific knowledge, and it includes tradition and deeply held cultural norms concerning local environments (Ban et al., 2018). If a strategic business case analysis contained indigenous knowledge, actors in the various domains for impact will be more intrigued, interested, and ultimately more enlightened than in its absence.

5. *Does the analysis provide solutions in crisis management and coping with adversity?* Many different types of organisations are confronted by large-scale crises associated with grand challenges. Failure to cope can be catastrophic for organisations, leading to their demise and failure. Shocks may be economic in nature (e.g., negotiating global recessions), but also can relate to events such as natural disasters, health pandemics and manmade crises such as wars – grand challenges of the era. Correspondingly, the field of organisational resilience has grown as an academic area of focus. It is a multidiscipline field with scholars examining the phenomenon of how to cope with complex challenges at various levels of analysis from the individual level, through the organisational, to resilience in communities and wider economies (Williams & You, 2021). Much of this research has been case based; particularly in the context of accidents and disasters (Linnenluecke, 2017). Indeed, cases were originally a main methodological approach in resilience research. A strategic business case analysis that looks at resilience in relation to grand challenges can contribute to this field, academically as well as in the practitioner domain. While they may lack generalisability, cases can serve to provide a critical reflection on the usefulness of theory when extreme events occur; they are worth documenting in situations that are rare and uncommon (Bengtsson, 1999). Discovery within academia can be achieved when the analyst is proactive in engaging

with academics, as noted above. The onset of adversity can be both a catalyst and a focal point for conversations with the academic community. Discovery within the practitioner domain can also be amplified during times of crisis, particularly when the topic of a strategic business case analysis is aligned with – or even identical to – the unfolding crisis itself. The analysis can be used during conversations and direct involvement with organisations to signal knowledge and credibility on the part of the analyst with respect to their ability to help an organisation navigate through the crisis.

6. *Does the case provide useful knowledge on humanitarian issues?* Humanitarian crises are a specific form of crisis: large-scale, highly complex emergencies characterised by a mass loss of life, human upheaval and displacement, hunger, and other instances of tragedy (Väyrynen, 2022). Understanding how they come about and what can be done to prevent them occurring is vitally important, particularly when many governments around the world lack resources, and sometimes willingness, to help their own people. Academics have come under the spotlight in terms of how their research helps humanitarian efforts and in the usefulness of the knowledge they provide to practitioners in humanitarian aid. Besiou and Van Wassenhove (2020) argue that humanitarian organisations have had to change over time. They have needed to become more efficient and effective in the face of funding pressure following the onset of humanitarian crises. And as the frequency and diversity of humanitarian crises has increased, humanitarian organisations have had to become more flexible and adaptable. Academic publications on humanitarian response, however, despite being numerous in number, have been criticised as being not very well-matched to the on-the-ground problem solving and coping strategies that humanitarian organisations need as they respond to crises in real-time (Besiou & Van Wassenhove, 2020). Strategic business case analysis results can potentially be helpful and could help to bridge this divide. A strategic business case analysis is not an academic publication that has taken many years to progress from data collection to publication. It may yield results and insights that are more current. It may also be based on a humanitarian organisation or centred around a specific response to a humanitarian issue. The case analyst can translate the findings of the analysis into new and evolving humanitarian situations. Discovery and action can be brought about through the engagement of the analyst with one or more humanitarian organisations as crises unfold. Conversations and direct involvement – as shown in Figure 8.2 – could help to resolve the bridging problem between academic work and useful knowledge at times of humanitarian crisis.

7. *How easily can the analysis be combined with existing knowledge on UN SDGs?* Several scholars have emphasised the importance of knowledge integration in finding solutions to the UN SDGs. Sarkis and Ibrahim (2022) look at this from the perspective of production research, noting how the operations, supply chain, production, and manufacturing engineering (OSPM) field has faced an opportunity to integrate knowledge across different levels of analysis, across different theoretical traditions, and across social, economic, and environmental domains. Zeigermann (2021) examines scientific networks in different countries that have formed to address UN SDGs. Knowledge integration is at the heart of these networks. Zeigermann (2021) finds solution-oriented knowledge integration strategies to be very common in these networks, although in countries that

perform better in terms of SDG progress, assessment-oriented and learning-oriented strategies are identified. In this study, solution-oriented knowledge integration happens when practice-oriented innovations were shared across different types of stakeholders within a country, as well as with "external allies" (p. 169). This sharing happens through events and publications, often with a central convening institution within a country. Assessment-oriented approaches are more systematic and seek to undertake comprehensive scientific assessments. Learning-oriented approaches stress values and norms for learning amongst different stakeholders. Zimm, Sperling and Busch (2018) stress the need for integrated sustainable development pathways that incorporate several of the UN SDGs at the same time. The common denominator in this literature is the need for knowledge integration in networks to make progress against UN SDG targets. A strategic business case analysis that produces new insights – perhaps revelatory insights – in sustainable development would lend itself for dissemination in these different networks. The analyst will be able to create discovery and action based on their work if the results can be integrated with other work, across levels or with knowledge from different types of actors, or by attempting to contribute as one component in an integrated development pathway.

This is not an exhaustive list, but it does demonstrate the opportunity for discovery and action in relation to grand challenges. These questions can be posed to the analyst of a strategic business case analysis at the outset of the project, as well as after completion. They provide a flavour of the substantive features relating to grand challenges that could appeal to the different domains in Figure 8.1, increasing the chances of discovery and action. The use of cases in a revelatory mode (Seidel et al., 2013) is very interesting here. Revelatory cases are ones that expose a phenomenon that was previously unreported and therefore under-analysed, and in which there is an element of surprise (Bengtsson, 1999; Trigger et al., 2012). Seeking to develop revelatory insights from a strategic business case analysis in the context of grand challenges could enhance discovery and action by aligning with more than one of the questions posed above.

FORMER STUDENT VOICES

Reflection from Nick Waters MBA (airline pilot and lawyer):

I did not start the MBA with the intention of changing jobs or looking for an immediate promotion, my main motivations were personal – having said this, it has opened new avenues.

Outside my own employer, I have increased my network with both other MBA students and professionals, becoming involved in a range of projects from working with new start-ups to joint presentations with SMEs looking to grow into a particular area. One example is a software company developing a training product based on game theory, where I was able to identify parallels between software simulation and aviation simulation not just for training pilots, but as a general superior learning method. The thought processes enable you to think with a wider field of view.

I have also maintained a link to the academic world, being asked to present to existing MBA students not only at my previous business school, but two other universities. I became involved in an exercise to understand the need and outline a specification for a new Executive MBA course. As a mature student on my own MBA and having been out of the academic world for a while, benefits such as this were never on the original 'plan' but have come to be a rewarding and enjoyable experience – just by taking the journey, new doors always open.

Reflection from Katherine Neufield MBA (government analyst):

I certainly boosted my presence with respect to the department that was the subject of the case, being able to provide information on the spot. Nobody had slotted into this role before. People said to me: "You actually know about this". People are thinking about budgeting. They're thinking about timelines. They're thinking about model performance. They're not thinking about the staff. I was able use my new knowledge to make sure staff were well supported throughout and bring staff on board.

Another area I want to make a presence felt is at technology conferences. I became more confident to be able to give talks and presentations about change management and AI. I am also considering publishing a book. This would discuss the various stages of change management and AI, touching on a lot of areas: you've got the emotional component, the social component. I would like to make an impact in these critical areas.

KEY TAKEAWAYS

The following are key learning points from this chapter:

- While the researcher–practitioner gap has persisted for decades, a strategic business case analysis is an ideal way for researchers to exert a positive impact on a strategic issue
- Impact can be applied to the four domains for case knowledge: practitioners, the academic system, case writers, and students
- These four domains for case knowledge do overlap and how they overlap should be assessed when considering the external impact of a strategic business case analysis
- Two principal phases of impact are important: discovery (where a potential beneficiary organisation learns about the existence and potential usefulness of an analysis) and action (where the beneficiary organisation applies lessons from the analysis in practice)
- Delivering impact through discovery and action requires different activities, including ongoing conversations with beneficiary organisations, direct transmission of results, publication, use of social media, consultancy and direct involvement, and ongoing monitoring and learning

- The quest to resolve grand challenges can draw from a strategic business case analysis, especially when the work contains substantive features and insights that make it discoverable and useful in action: examples include content related to environmental sustainability and green transformation, coping in fragile states and with adversity, helping humanitarian organisations, and being able to be integrated with existing bodies of knowledge.

REFLECTIVE PRACTICE TASK

Review your strategic business case plan (if you are yet to start or are under way), or your completed work (if you have already finished). Reflect further on the following questions:

1. What?
    What domains of case knowledge do you think could benefit from your analysis?
2. So what?
    How do you think those domains would benefit?
3. Now what?
    Can you produce an action plan for externalising impact from your work, including a prioritisation of which domains you would like to target?

ADDITIONAL READINGS AND RESOURCES

Impactful action research

Lakiza, V., & Deschamps, I. (2019). How to develop an impactful action research program: Insights and lessons from a case study. *Technology Innovation Management Review, 9*(5), 34–43.

Conversation in action research

Feldman, A. (1999). The role of conversation in collaborative action research. *Educational Action Research, 7*(1), 125–147.

Tips for being a good consultant

www.consultingfact.com/blog/the-key-attributes-of-a-good-consultant/

Influential white papers

https://thatwhitepaperguy.com/most-influential-white-paper/

Grand challenges in global health

www.grandchallenges.org/about

NOTES

1   https://unfccc.int/process/bodies/supreme-bodies/conference-of-the-parties-cop, accessed 13 March 2023.

CHAPTER 9

Internalising impact of a strategic business case analysis

WHAT A STRATEGIC BUSINESS CASE ANALYSIS MEANS FOR YOU

The previous chapter examined ways to make an external impact through a strategic business case analysis. There is a valuable internal side too. This concerns what the experience will do for you personally, and how it will provide the basis for future career development and life fulfilment. By engaging in the project, you will develop new hard and soft skills. You will create new knowledge and insight, learning that will stay with you for many years. These internal aspects can help you develop your career in new directions, including in senior leadership, consultancy, or entrepreneurial roles. A strategic business case analysis can be one component in a broader array of self-development activities that provides success and fulfilment in life.

There are some clear links between a strategic business case analysis process conducted in a business education setting and the generic processes involved in all types of organisations in practice. Conducting a case analysis in an educational setting mirrors the process of strategic issue resolution in the real world. Firstly, there is the identification of a strategic issue. This happens in organisational reality all the time and is at the forefront of case work in an educational setting too. Secondly, there is the preparation stage prior to analysis. This involves breaking the issue down into key questions and putting the issue into context. Managers and their advisors do this continuously in the real world. Case analysts in an educational setting do too. Thirdly, there is the actual analytical task. Our advice in this book is to conduct this in a strategic business case project by taking a stance on the Case Analysis Spectrum (i.e., reductionist–hybrid–holistic). While managers may not be explicit about this in the real world, they will approach strategic issues somewhere along the spectrum, oftentimes without realising the stance they are taking. Finally, there is the action and impact creating aspect to case work. Change programmes and interventions in organisations happen all the time (Hodges, 2017). And case analysts may choose to pursue external impact following case work. So, at a generic level, the experiences of a case analyst on a strategic business case project will help prepare them for solving complex strategic issues in many other strategy situations in the future.

Conducting a strategic business case analysis should also help develop critical thinking and critical reflection skills. One of the central features of this type of project work is how it allows you to engage critically in real-world case data. Case analysts are encouraged to

DOI: 10.4324/9781003288916-12

think and reflect critically on both the evidence and the theory, and this ability to think and reflect critically will provide a basis for career development into more influential positions in business and society.

Critical thinking is the ability to objectively analyse a situation or issue and form a judgement. One main benefit of students researching, writing, and analysing their own cases is in bridging the gap between conceptual abstraction and practice (Ashamalla & Crocitto, 2001), this being essential for developing critical thinking skills. As Ashamalla and Crocitto (2001) note, student-written cases are rooted in realism, especially when the case organisation is one in which the student works or is personally familiar. Critical thinking skills can be developed when students are encouraged to apply "independent thought and judgement" (p. 526). You will have an opportunity to test out and develop your critical thinking skills in both organisational strategy in the real world, as well as in the realm of theory. By completing a strategic business case analysis, you would have improved your own ability to develop sound judgement in challenging situations.

Critical thinking skills matter to career advancement in personal development. Elder (2005) argues that critical thinking "should be the guiding force behind any and all professional development" (p. 39); it should be within the culture of any learning college. While the institution clearly has a role to play, it is the actual engagement of a management or executive student on a comprehensive strategic business case analysis that will allow them to develop and test their own critical thinking abilities outside of the education institution itself (i.e., outside of the class). Literature shows how case-based learning aids in the development of abilities to solve problems. This has been noted in diverse fields, including nursing (Thistlethwaite et al., 2012), teaching (Han, Eom & Shin, 2013), and consultancy (Williams, 2019). When students develop critical thinking skills through strategic business case analysis, they are better able to diagnose complex issues, identify and utilise analytical tools in an appropriate way, and form judgements on how strategic issues can be navigated. These skills will form the basis of personal and professional advancement.

Critical reflection is also to be encouraged as part of this process, especially reflection on assumptions. Critical reflection of assumptions is a specific form of reflection that is highly useful within a strategic business case analysis. It relates to critiques of "habits of the mind and related points of view" (Mezirow, 1998, p. 186) that we all have. A strategic business case analysis allows a management or executive student to challenge their own assumptions about how the organisational world works, how strategy comes about and how it can be made to work. Challenging these assumptions allows for the emergence of new opinions as ways of framing and resolving problems (Mezirow, 1998). The student – as case analyst – can test the limits of what they know, develop as an authority in an area of knowledge, and revise their interpretation of meanings that guide effective action (Mezirow, 1998). Upon completion, the same individual – as leader, consultant, or entrepreneur – will see the benefit of self-critique, of challenging assumptions that might have become outdated or irrelevant. Strategic business case analysis work involves the training and application of new knowledge, new ways of learning, and applying a "tacit judgment inasmuch as a decision is being made that an old way of thinking or behaving does not work in the specific [new] situation" (Mezirow, 1998, p. 191). This underpins dynamic learning, a capability that means you – as a strategist of the future – can make sense of how previous experience in a strategic business case analysis can be applied effectively in future situations.

There are also career progression implications for case analyses that have a global challenge component. In the last chapter we discussed ways in which the substance of strategic case analysis work can be discovered and made actionable by stakeholders involved with addressing grand challenges. This externalisation of impact can reinforce – and be reinforced by – internalisation of impact. In other words, by engaging with stakeholders on issues of grand challenge, you will develop new skills, knowledge, and networks. And by developing your skills, knowledge, and networks in areas of grand challenge, you will be able to make an impact with stakeholders. The role that a strategic business case analysis will play in this depends to a large extent on the substantive content of the project. For instance, you might reveal what a particular organisation is doing right and/or wrong in terms of environmental sustainability (Batle et al., 2018), green transformation and technology (Seidel et al., 2013), peace-building (Miklian & Schouten, 2014), indigenous knowledge (Ban et al., 2018), crisis management (Williams & You, 2021), humanitarianism (Besiou & Van Wassenhove, 2020), or any of the 17 UN SDGs and their 169 lower level targets. Indeed, you might reveal insights into knowledge pathways for addressing UN SDGs (Zimm et al., 2018).

When your case work contributes new knowledge in any of these areas, it is likely that this has been highly meaningful to you – in other words, that the project has had intrinsic interest. We noted in Chapter 2 that task enjoyment and intrinsic interest have a positive relationship on performance outcomes (Cerasoli et al., 2014; Leonard & Weitz, 1971); your work is more likely to be successful when it is meaningful to you. Of course, intrinsic interest does not necessarily relate to grand challenges. If it does, great! But your interest and motivation to research a complex case may relate to many other topic areas too (we used the examples of sport in Chapter 2). Two of the cases used in Part 2 of this book do not relate directly to UN SDGs (the Time Out Group and the Olympus cases). However, they were highly enjoyable to research, valuable to publish, and interesting to analyse.

If, when reflecting on a strategic business case analysis, you consider the exercise to have been intrinsically interesting and enjoyable, the likelihood that you will seek to reap further rewards from it will be higher. It would have been meaningful to you, allowing you to investigate a burning issue that you always wanted to investigate, and giving you an opportunity to grow as a management scholar. Will the journey stop there? People have a habit of continuing to do things they enjoy, continuing to learn about topics that they are interested in. Maehr (1975) examined this in his work on continuing motivation. This is defined as: "the tendency to return to and continue working on tasks away from the instructional context in which they were initially confronted" (p. 443). Maehr (1975) notes how continuing motivation outside of an educational context has similarities with persistence behaviour and intrinsic motivation. But he points out important differences. These include a need to complete tasks and the need to learn outside of the learning institution. He notes how continuing motivation is more than just persistence or is at least a "special case of persistence" (p. 446). Continuing motivation is a recurrent interest, outside of the classroom, and is seen as an education-related behaviour (p. 447).

There are clearly implications for the meaning of a strategic business case analysis for you at a personal level. These emanate from new skills and knowledge, including the ability to use critical thinking and critical reflection. They also include new networks and social connections, new communities, and stakeholders with whom you have become connected because of the project. You may have made a small – but important – contribution to understanding how we might solve grand challenges in this world, giving you a satisfaction that will endure. And the intrinsic interest and value that might be found (or validated) through the project may now spill over into continuing motivation to undertake more learning – possibly more case work – in your topic area.

Implications for the individual do not end here. From a professional and career advancement perspective, you may seek new ways to move into and grow within leadership roles, offer your services as a consultant and advisor, and perhaps consider entering or developing within the field of entrepreneurship (including setting up or running a social enterprise). These are not the only ways to advance one's career but are some of the main ways. They are also career paths that can be combined, e.g., becoming a leader in a consultancy on social enterprise. Let's consider these in turn.

LEADERSHIP

Conducting a strategic business case analysis can enhance your prospects in terms of becoming a leader and/or developing further as a leader if you are already in a leadership position. Leadership has various definitions and can be thought of in different ways. Many of us have influence in our organisations and communities without necessarily having hierarchical power. Many of us influence followers without having a job title to match. Winston and Patterson (2006) identified no less than 90 (ninety) variables that can make up the leadership construct. It is clearly a broad concept. The integrative definition they provide spans more than 600 words, incorporating how the leader applies their influence, the values they represent, how they enable their followers to act, and the role of trust-building. The opening sentence of their definition is useful:

> A leader is one or more people who selects, equips, trains, and influences one or more follower(s) who have diverse gifts, abilities, and skills and focuses the follower(s) to the organization's mission and objectives causing the follower(s) to willingly and enthusiastically expend spiritual, emotional, and physical energy in a concerted coordinated effort to achieve the organizational mission and objectives.
>
> (p. 7)

These core elements of supporting and influencing followers to achieve an organisation's mission are central to being a leader. The strategic business case analysis experience can help to strengthen these traits and abilities.

Let's consider the two scenarios of (1) becoming a leader and (2) developing as a leader:

1. *Becoming a leader*: One important aspect here is to recognise the difference between leading and managing. Nguyen and Hansen (2016) highlight this distinction, noting that leaders empower, they are focused on allowing others to 'do the right thing'. Managers, on the other hand, are concerned with control and 'doing things right'. They emphasise the importance of education and training to develop knowledge and understanding of these differences, including action-based training and case studies that can

help in deciding which mode (managing vs. leading) is needed in different situations (p. 12). Nguyen and Hansen (2016) highlight how it is important to switch between leading and managing modes, and the ability to do this is based on knowledge acquired through training: "leader–managers are made, not born" (p. 12). Strategic business case analysis work can help you to develop cognition of when management and leadership modes are appropriate within the context of a strategic and complex issue facing an organisation. Part of your critical reflection on completing your case project can be to determine which aspects of the recommendations you present are ones that require management, and which ones require leadership. You can identify your role in both processes as far as both discovery and action are concerned as you seek to externalise impact through your work. Another key aspect is to understand the transition process as you move from junior or middle ranking positions into senior leadership. Scholars note this is not an 'overnight' event, but rather a process that takes place over time (Denis, Langley & Pineault, 2000). In their study of new CEO integration in a large hospital, Denis, Langley and Pineault (2000) identify different processes occurring in different domains (in this case, an administrative domain versus a clinical domain). They also note different mechanisms used by a new leader and how these align with these different domains (a collaborative mode dominant in the clinical domain, and an affirmative mode in the administrative domain). Knowing when and how to apply these different approaches when moving into a new leadership position can be guided by career knowledge, of which a strategic business case analysis is one part. Case project work can provide evidence of different approaches used as new leaders assume positions and attempt to influence change in complex organisational settings. Case work can also provide substantive new knowledge for you on specific topic areas, as well as allow you to develop new collaborative skills. This will be useful as you decide how to both collaborate and affirm in different domains when taking up a position as a new leader. The completion of case work can signal leadership skillsets such that gatekeepers into senior leadership positions will be satisfied that you have the attributes to tackle complex organisational challenges as part of the new role. In this way, the strategic business case analysis, and the externalised impact you may seek from it, can give you a competitive advantage as you apply for and interview for senior leadership posts.

2. *Developing as a leader*: In many instances, students on management and executive programs are already in leadership positions. They may already have responsibility for large budgets and teams, and be able to provide empowerment to those around them to create followership advantages. Developing as a leader is often a reason for undertaking further executive study in business schools. In their work on "How to become a better leader", Toegel and Barsoux (2012) make some interesting observations. Effective leaders work hard to develop themselves, according to their article. The authors highlight how the "Big five" personality traits have been used to understand leaders as they are pushed to perform at higher levels of the career path. These are: (1) the need for stability: emotional stability can be good for handling stress; (2) extraversion: can be useful as leadership involves influence over other people; (3) openness: showing intellectual curiosity, being receptive to new ideas; (4) agreeableness: being compassionate and getting on with others; (5) conscientiousness: structuring and organising the work around us (Toegel & Barsoux, 2012). The authors argue how all of these can be

pitfalls as well as useful traits as individuals strive to develop as leaders under increasing levels of pressure and scrutiny. Conducting a strategic business case analysis gives you an opportunity to reflect on all these dimensions as they have arisen over the course of the project. Again, critical reflection has an important role to play in informing how the project can be meaningful to the self. Substantively, the case work can also reveal how leaders handle strategic issues and complex problems within the storyline of the case. The analysis provides an opportunity for you to scrutinise leadership responses to strategic issues and to gauge how any of the five dimensions highlighted by Toegel and Barsoux (2012) have had a role to play in producing effective outcomes.

This explicit emphasis on leadership reflection in your case work can help you develop as a leader in your own career path. Research on leadership improvement endorses this. Marcy and Mumford (2010) show how improving abilities in causal analysis changes the performance of leaders in complex environments. Effective leaders need to know "where and how to exert their influence to accomplish their objectives" (p. 2). Clearly, they cannot be in all places at once, especially as the organisation's size increases and the strategic issues become more complex. Critical reflection on the work done on a strategic business case analysis can help those in leadership positions improve as leaders through causal analysis. It does this by developing their mental models in complex situations and creating an opportunity to improve the quality of mental models before and after the analysis process. Reflecting on one's mental model concerning a given strategic issue before versus after the analysis is a form of self-training that can sharpen leadership skills of those who are already in leadership positions.

CONSULTANCY

Would you like to enter the consultancy industry, or progress within the industry if you are already a part of it? A strategic business case analysis can help. The nature of the case work, with its action orientation and emphasis on finding novel solutions to real-world strategic issues, will develop skills, knowledge, and networks for a successful consultancy career. There are several ways in which this can happen, including the development of your own human capital, nurturing of new social networks and social capital, and awareness of how organisational capital can be used to find useful solutions for client organisations.

1. *Human capital.* Many scholars have noted the importance of human capital in consultancy (Maister et al., 2021; Von Nordenflycht, 2010; Williams, 2019). Human capital relates to the knowledge and skills that you can apply to solve strategic issues for clients in the future. Human capital theorists stress the importance of training and education in developing human capital (Schultz, 1961), this clearly being centre stage in a strategic business case analysis project. A strategic business case analysis can develop your ability here in many ways, including how to frame and reframe strategic problems, how to understand the context(s) in which strategic problems are nestled, making decisions about what additional data needs to be collected to solve the problem, choosing the most appropriate analytical stance, and knowing how to deliver value to clients based

on close attention and listening skills. Linked to this is the reputational capital that can be strengthened through a strategic business case analysis, particularly if the results of the case work are taken further (see previous chapter), including into conferences, publications, and wider domains of influence. This process will build your reputation as an expert in your chosen space.

Human capital is a source of competitive advantage, not only for individuals, but also for the organisations in which they work. If you have plans to enter or grow within a consultancy organisation following your case work, your organisation will benefit from you becoming a more valuable asset. Consultants are seen as valuable when they possess unique knowledge and skills that client organisations do not have. Consequently, your employer will stand to gain from utilising your new insights when strengthening their relationships with existing clients or developing proposals for new clients. Ultimately, providing consultancy is an advice-giving activity. The value of the advice will be judged by the client organisation as it appraises the new insights provided and tries to implement any recommendations. It is therefore important for the advice to be well researched, accurate, based on evidence and logic, and feasible for implementation. Human capital on the part of the advice-giver underpins all these facets and they are all abilities that can be strengthened through strategic business case analysis work.

2. *Social capital.* This relates to the value that accrues due to social relations between people (Adler & Kwon, 2002). Consultants need to develop social capital with a range of stakeholders to be able to add value as advice-givers. This starts with the client base. The consultancy life cycle begins with pre-sales and efforts to sell consultancy work into client organisations (O'Mahoney & Markham, 2013). It is important for consultants to listen to their clients and gain a deep understanding of their issues; it is important to establish intimacy and trust (Maister et al., 2021). Consultancy involves socialisation with clients, and building up trustworthy relations, not just structural connections. Social capital also extends beyond the client interface. Within the consultancy organisation, individuals need to relate to each other, explore opportunities, and work together in search of solutions to propose and deliver to clients. There is an important internal side of social capital in consultancy that allows knowledge and learning to flow in the interests of the consultancy organisation (Williams & van Triest, 2021). And there are many other types of actors with whom consultants need to build strong relations. These include other consultants in networked arrangements (Sturdy & Wright, 2011), governments and regulators (Corcoran & McLean, 1998), and technological vendors and universities for those consultants working in the tech space as innovation intermediaries (Dalziel, 2010).

How can a strategic business case analysis help build your social capital and ability to create and exploit social capital? Firstly, it gives you an opportunity to identify stakeholders that you were not formerly connected with, and to gradually build new relationships with them. This can happen during the case work itself, for instance if you set about collecting additional primary data. And it is associated with the externalisation of impact that we discussed in the previous chapter. Pursuing new relations to create opportunities for discovery and action based on your case work will develop your social capital. New relations will prove to be useful to you as they give feedback on your work, allowing you to refine and improve your thinking and knowledge of a particular strategic issue and its solution. They will also be valuable as domains for applying and learning from your recommendations in practice. Secondly, you will be able to strengthen existing relationships that you previously had, including within an organisation that you were working in that was the subject of the case work. Strengthening relationships in this mode comes about as you show commitment to resolve the strategic issues faced by the organisation; you show that you care, and that you have undertaken some painstaking analysis to help the organisation. Your social capital with the strategic leaders of the organisation can benefit by facilitating discovery and action based on your case work. Thirdly, individuals and organisations within the domain for case knowledge (Figures 1.1 and 1.2, Chapter 1) that you might have known prior to your work or were introduced to as part of your work, will be a basis for developing social capital. It is not just about other practitioners (top left of Figure 1.2); the case writing community, supervisors and the academic community, and other students will also have potential interest in your project. You have the opportunity here to build new social capital with multiple stakeholders at the same time during the execution – and in the aftermath – of your case work.

3. *Organisational capital.* Organisational capital refers to practices and modes of control that support the functioning of the organisation (Acs & Fitzroy, 1989). This is an internal view of organisations, the practices, systems of control, and ways of organising that affect its ability to perform. Consultants have a key role to play in diagnosing the effectiveness of organisational capital in client organisations. Strategic issues arise not only because of external threats and dynamics in the industry or institutional environments, but also because of the ability of the organisation to cope with them. Consultants are often called in to help organisations understand what they are doing wrong and how they can organise and control their assets more effectively and efficiently, given strategic issues and threats. This includes the role of knowledge management systems and how knowledge is managed in complex organisations (Baker, Barker, Thorne & Dutnell, 1997). Williams (2019) notes how consultants themselves need to engage in reflective ability to perform, and that increasing use of virtualisation (online interactions with clients) in consultancy means new ways of working are encouraged. So, there are two important points here: (1) consultants needing to be able to analyse and encourage change in terms of organisational capital in clients, and (2) consultant organisations needing to understand and continuously reflect upon their own organisational capital in a competitive environment.

Strategic business case analysis can help on both counts. Firstly, there will be an organisation at the centre of the case work, a focal point for a defined strategic issue. There will be advantages and disadvantages with the organisational capital of the enterprise at the time of the decision point. There will be changes recommended by the case analyst in the organisational arrangements of the enterprise as it seeks to deal with its strategic issue. In other words, the strategic business case analysis is an ideal opportunity for you to play the role of consultant with a defined client, and to review organisational capital within the client with a view to developing recommendations for optimisation and renewed ways of working and controlling assets. Secondly, if you are already part of a consultancy organisation, or have become familiar with one that you are interested in joining, you will be able to assess the firm's ways of working and control. What is the culture like? What kinds of structures and practice areas exist for the coalescence of knowledge and expertise within the firm? What kinds of leadership styles are in use? Experience in appraising these features, and then diagnosing them in terms of fit with your own career objectives, are skills you can develop with case work. It could be that you chose to conduct your project within the consultancy industry; this would give you detailed knowledge of how a specific firm and the wider industry operates and how it is changing. In other cases, the generic skills that you have developed in diagnosing organisational capital can be applied to an existing consultancy firm; it can help you assess whether an existing consultancy firm is one that you want to join.

ENTREPRENEURSHIP

Perhaps you are interested in starting your own business and have some idea about the market you could focus on. Entrepreneurship is a large and complex field, and the world is splattered with failed entrepreneurial ventures. The likelihood is that you will fail, at least first time around. The conventional wisdom is that failure is good; it provides an abundance of knowledge that can be used in the next venture. This is often captured in the expression: "Fail fast and fail often" (Draper, 2017). As Draper (2017) notes, Thomas Edison, Henry Ford, Steve Jobs had many unsuccessful ventures before they found their most lucrative ones. Experts also put a spotlight on preparation, on working carefully to understand the value proposition, the market need and how your proposition can address that need, i.e., the fundamental business model (Osterwalder & Pigneur, 2010). Much research has been conducted on entrepreneurial orientation and what drives some people to become entrepreneurs and others to stay away from the risks. Individual level factors discussed in the literature include entrepreneurial self-efficacy (a belief that one has the capabilities to direct the course of action in life), alertness to opportunity (a perceptive trait), and fear of failure (this fear having a negative effect, i.e., stifling entrepreneurial risk-taking); these interacting with the institutional context in which the entrepreneur exists (Boudreaux, Nikolaev & Klein, 2019). A strategic business case analysis under your belt can help in your pursuit of becoming an independent entrepreneur. It can do this by helping to reduce the risks and sharpening your knowledge of the opportunity, how the opportunity can be pursued, and how you can remain agile as the entrepreneurial process unfolds.

1. *Knowledge of the opportunity*: Fuzziness and lack of definition of the opportunity at the outset is a common reason for entrepreneurial failure. Scholars have noted the difficulties entrepreneurs face in valuing an opportunity, coping with setbacks, and deciding whether to continue with an entrepreneurial path (Jenkins & McKelvie, 2016). According to Busenitz (1999), entrepreneurs face decisions differently compared to non-entrepreneurs, due to their biases and heuristics. They are predisposed towards risk in ways that managers in larger organisations are not; they think in different ways when confronted by an opportunity. Biases and heuristics play a role in allowing them to cope with highly uncertain situations where there is little time to conduct an extensive

data collection. Key heuristics include representativeness, a tendence to generalise from small samples, including personal experience. Another is overconfidence, having an optimistic attitude when data is scarce (Busenitz, 1999). A strategic business case analysis can help not only in providing knowledge about the existence of opportunities, but also in developing or challenging your biases and heuristics, such that your entrepreneurial alertness to an opportunity will become sharper. The case work can provide new knowledge – albeit situation specific and not representative – that acts to confirm what you already thought about a given opportunity. It can also help you reflect on your level of confidence such that you do not approach an opportunity in an overly optimistic way. In other words, by conducting a strategic business case analysis, your ability to make a 'go/no-go' decision about any opportunity you find in your case data will be sharpened. It could be that by conducting the case writing part of the project (in a situation where your institution does not assign the case to you), you have the chance to collect primary data from potential clients or users of a new product or service about their pain points and organisational needs. It could be that the analytical part of the case work triggers an 'a-ha' moment concerning a new commercial offering to address the strategic issue at the heart of the case. And it might also be the case that you reflect on your own biases and heuristics through the project to determine how your own risk appetite has changed.

2. *Developing the offering*: Scholars also note the problem of determining the feasibility of the solution for pursuing an opportunity (Jenkins & McKelvie, 2016). This has been referred to as entrepreneurial action in the literature; pursuit of an opportunity being debated between discovery theory (opportunities exist independent of entrepreneurs) and creation theory (opportunities are created by entrepreneurs) (Alvarez & Barney, 2007). The creation view supports the idea that entrepreneurs learn about what the opportunity really is during the process of pursuing it, i.e., with a specific solution or offering that a market will hopefully demand. As Alvarez and Barney (2007) note, there may be many iterative actions before an entrepreneur realises that they misinterpreted market signals. This underscores the importance of the process of offering development in an emergent and changing context, of multiple iterations and phases of testing different versions of offerings with users in a defined market space. A strategic business case analysis can help here too. The case project is a journey, running over many months. If you have an inkling that you might want to connect the project with a broader entrepreneurial mission, you can run a parallel exercise alongside the case work. This exercise could surface your assumptions about the nature of the opportunity and the nature of the offering needed to address that opportunity at different points along the journey: at the outset, as well as at various points in time. You could engage in some of the discovery and action techniques discussed in the previous chapter, including, importantly, conversations with various actors and direct involvement. This will allow you to test your assumptions about what a solution would need to look like to convince users to purchase it to solve their need. From a reputational standpoint, the existence of a strategic business case analysis that demonstrates your personal growth and evolved expertise in an area of specialism will be useful if the solution is a service-oriented one such as a consultancy or training offering. The case work can help you define and refine the content of your service offering as you learn more throughout the journey.

3. *Remaining agile throughout the entrepreneurial process*: As an entrepreneur moves from discovery or creation of an opportunity to servicing the market and seeking rents, the need for agility will become increasingly important. Agility can be seen in different ways, such as organisational agility (adjusting strategy and resource allocations within organisations) and intellectual agility (allowing staff to invest time to respond to challenges) (Dabić, Stojčić, Simić, Potocan, Slavković & Nedelko, 2021). As the entrepreneurial process unfolds, and you seek to build a business around a newly identified opportunity and offering, the ability to remain agile will be important. The environment will be competitive and hostile, and there will be other disruptors keen to stop you in your tracks. This requires individuals to "shift their modes of thinking, search for new information, and come up with novel solutions for present and prospective problems" (Dabić et al., 2021, p. 685). Entrepreneurial leaders must be able to detect environmental threats and changes and offer solutions. A strategic business case analysis can offer support in this more long-term requirement for entrepreneurial organisation. As an entrepreneurial leader, you will be able to recall the nuances of the strategic issue in your former case work, of the multiple dominant contexts and complexity, and the implications of various courses of action in your case. The case work can act as a template for deciding the key questions for analysis as employees detect issues and suggest change paths, for actual analysis using the Case Analysis Spectrum, and for implementation. Remaining agile will require analysis of inputs from various stakeholders, and your own entrepreneurial venture will become a case in its own right. The case work will also give you an appreciation of the need for change in complex and challenging environments, and how careful consideration of multiple paths of action can be negotiated through reductionist, hybrid, or holistic stances. Your case analysis can act as a reference point for many months and years following the launch of a new venture, albeit one reference point amongst many other sources of knowledge and guidance.

FORMER STUDENT VOICES

Reflection from Nick Waters MBA (airline pilot and lawyer):

Within my own organisation I have become more involved with business functions and some of the more complex operational functions. I know from feedback that I have been asked to assist in some areas and join project teams because of the perspective that I can 'think outside the box' and solve problems. This has brought me into greater contact with management levels. The tools and thought processes enhanced by the strategic case analysis have been an enabler in this regard.

Whilst my current career path (I changed from being a lawyer to an airline pilot) was not directly relevant to an MBA, I also felt it was a very useful and respected additional string to my bow – should I need it. If there is one thing the strategic case analysis taught me, it is how volatile my own industry can be, going from a period of explosive growth to catastrophic contraction in short timescales. It has also led to some unexpected and fulfilling additional work (like contributing to this book!)

Reflection from Katherine Neufield MBA (government analyst):

The strategic case analysis improved my change management knowledge and that was huge for me. Another big part was learning about the interaction between people and AI, and the emotional component that happens with people when they are working with AI. I was able to understand the connection between technology and the person. So, being able to better understand that and articulate that, especially in my department, was important. The case analysis was beneficial because I became better prepared to answer questions from management and staff. Many people don't have knowledge of AI, so they would come to me. I felt more confident, especially working within the AI space at a time of change.

Convincing people was important. If you can't convince people that this is a decent technology we could take on, and it's going to help us, then the technology is not going to be accepted. As a result of the strategic case analysis I can communicate and convince in an informed way. I became the go-to person with respect to change management with AI, an area that really hasn't been touched on much. Organizations that I worked with put the change management part at the very end, right before they put it into production. I started pushing towards having a more influential role in change management and AI.

KEY TAKEAWAYS

The following are key learning points from this chapter:

- A strategic business case analysis simulates the process of strategic issue resolution in real-world organisations
- The project work helps develop skills in critical thinking and critical reflection
- Detailed analytical case work can be highly meaningful to the individual when the individual has intrinsic interest, leading to continuing motivation outside of the educational setting
- In terms of leadership, case work can help an individual move into a leadership position, or become a better leader, through critical reflection
- A strategic business case analysis can help an individual move into – or progress within – consultancy, by developing the individual's human, social, and organisational capital as they relate to consultancy assignments
- Case work can also form the basis of entrepreneurship and new venture creation as it provides detailed substance on knowledge of opportunity, insights into the offering that needs to be developed for a beneficiary, as well as skills in agility and flexible thinking.

REFLECTIVE PRACTICE TASK

Review your strategic business case plan (if you are yet to start or are under way), or your completed work (if you have already finished). Reflect further on the following questions:

1. What?

    What career directions are you considering following the competition of your case work?

2. So what?

    How will the pursuit of each of those options provide fulfilment for you?

3. Now what?

    Can you critically reflect on your strategic business case analysis (planned or completed) and make explicit connections between it and your career options?

ADDITIONAL READINGS AND RESOURCES

Leadership

Benjamin, B., & O'Reilly, C. (2011). Becoming a leader: Early career challenges faced by MBA graduates. *Academy of Management Learning & Education, 10(3)*, 452–472.

Consultancy

Sturdy, A., Handley, K., Clark, T., & Fincham, R. (2010). *Management consultancy: Boundaries and knowledge in action*. Oxford Unversity Press.

Entrepreneurship

Lerner, J., & Malmendier, U. (2013). With a little help from my (random) friends: Success and failure in post-business school entrepreneurship. *The Review of Financial Studies, 26(10)*, 2411–2452.

CHAPTER 10

Summary

Business cases are very rich stories of organisational life. They tell the ups and downs of organisations in different sectors, countries, and stages of development. They show how leaders have succeeded and failed, and how the environments in which they operate provide both opportunities for economic and social development, as well as presenting challenges and obstacles that make organisational life very tricky. To navigate through this, organisations need to deal with strategic issues continually. This comes with a high degree of complexity. There is often high ambiguity and uncertainty, and different stakeholders with different views and interests in the case organisation may have completely different views on how to proceed.

Strategic business case analysis is an ideal way to learn and develop skills in an educational setting that can be used when leading organisations through strategic issues. Management and executive students often lack capabilities in case writing and analysis, and they must often work under considerable time pressure to deliver their case work. This causes stress and anxiety, and can cause conflicts between family life, work life, and study time.

The approach taken in this book recognises these issues and aims to give management and executive students contemplating a strategic business case analysis an opportunity to reflect on how they can maximise the experience for the benefit not only of their own careers, but also the world around. By putting careful thought into the preparation stage, by being clear about the options for how to analyse a complex case strategically, and by reflecting on options to externalise and internalise impact in the aftermath of the project, the process is more likely to be meaningful and intrinsically motivating for the student. This will have a positive spill-over effect on others, including family, friends, and work colleagues, as the student undertakes the project.

There are different perspectives on case analysis, going beyond the student, and including that of the practitioner(s) at the heart of the strategic issue being addressed. They also include the views of the case writing community, as well as the academic institutions that provide experiences for students to conduct strategic business case analysis projects. It is important to be aware of these different perspectives because they each have different views of – and interests in – case knowledge, what it is, and what it means in business education. Moreover, they are all domains in which impact can be exercised through conducting case analysis work.

Preparing for a strategic business case analysis project should be done carefully and deliberately. What we suggest in this book is an explicit process for preparation involving

DOI: 10.4324/9781003288916-13

dedicating time and thought to several steps. This starts with case choice (as this sets the whole agenda for the work), having the student develop their own case selection criteria depending on what matters for them, and deciding on whether grand challenges are important to include in the work. It proceeds to an explicit exercise in placing the case in a strategic context. This involves understanding the nature of context and how multiple and overlapping contexts may influence the strategic issue in the case. This is a kind of 'pre-analysis', a useful exercise before the main analysis, that will help build the analytical platform. It then moves on to deciding on the questions to analyse. This step also should not be rushed. There are different types of questions, each with a say on how the analysis will then unfold. And there are such things as 'good' and 'bad' questions. There is literature on this that can guide the student on what constitutes a good question. Questions may be nested in a question tree to aid the direction forward into the analysis proper.

Analysing a business case strategically should flow naturally from this preparation phase. In this book we offer a way to approach analysis based on the concept of a Case Analysis Spectrum. On the one end of the spectrum the analyst can take a reductionist stance, breaking the work down into discrete components, all defined differently and with different purposes. The results of each sub-analysis must be recombined when answering the primary question. At the other end of the spectrum, one takes a holistic stance. Here, we treat the case as an integrated whole and use systems techniques that embrace complexity and a non-linear process for analysis. We also introduce an 'in-between' stance in this book that we call hybridism. This combines elements of both reductionism and holism, normally moving from one to the other as the analysis process unfolds or using methods from the different stances in a mixed-method approach. Here, we seek to combine the best of both worlds, combining the macro and the micro, the simple and the complex. The examples provided in Chapter 7 illustrate analysis using each of these stances in turn. The case analyst should not only prepare carefully for the analysis but should also put some serious thought into which stance to adopt, and the reasons for adopting that stance, before jumping into any specific technique and writing up results.

Maximising impact from a strategic business case analysis requires the student – as case analyst – to consider how to create benefit outside of satisfying the academic requirements of the higher education institution hosting the course. There is a life beyond the academic institution, and the possibility exists that the work conducted can make a real difference. We divide this into two parts: external and internal. On the external side, we discussed how case work can be fed back into the different domains for case knowledge, including the practitioner domain. This involves allowing potential beneficiaries first to discover the existence and potential usefulness of the case analysis, and second, allowing the conditions for action to then follow. Beneficiary organisations will need to combine case analysis insights with many other types of knowledge from many other sources as they create concrete plans for change to address the strategic issue. Different mechanisms for discovery and action are possible, including conversations, direct transmission, publication, social media, and consultancy/direct involvement. For impact to be maximised it is important for the case analyst to continually monitor and learn from these dissemination and engagement mechanisms. On the internal side, a strategic business case analysis can be highly meaningful to management and executive students as they graduate and go forward in the world. Critically reflecting on the process and the insights gained is useful here, as well as identifying ways in which the case work underpins career progression in leadership, consultancy and/or entrepreneurial terms. It is here that we find the construct of intrinsic interest and the choice that the student – as case analyst – now has with respect to continuing to work in this or similar topic areas in the months and years ahead.

The deliberate process described in this book allows a lot of flexibility and is not set in stone. It stresses consideration, planning, and reflection at critical junctures, before, during, and following the project. But it is also flexible and does not aim to give precise timings for case activity – there is no one-size-fits-all solution to strategic issues. It is a pragmatic approach that aims to optimise the chances of completing an excellent piece of work that is highly interesting for the student, tightly link to their career needs, and that has a positive influence on debates and interventions used in the reality of strategy. It can also allow the student to feed back into teaching and research of the topic of strategy in the academic system. This broader perspective of strategic business case analysis asks the student to co-create case knowledge alongside other stakeholders with an interest in the same case knowledge, while making sure their work is well structured and designed for impact. While deviations to the process described here are certainly possible, there will be little pushback against the core principles expressed here – that work as important as this on a capstone management or executive module needs to be treated as an investment in individual, economic, and social development in the same way one would with any large-scale investment of money, time, and effort.

References

Abedin, B., Kordnaeij, A., Fard, H. D., & Hoseini, S. H. K. (2015). Investigating what determines strategic issues in organizations: A qualitative study. *Mediterranean Journal of Social Sciences, 6*(5), 553.

Acs, Z. J., & Fitzroy, F. R. (1989). Inside the firm and organizational capital: A review article. *International Journal of Industrial Organization, 7*(2), 309–314.

Adler, P. S., & Kwon, S. W. (2002). Social capital: Prospects for a new concept. *Academy of Management Review, 27*(1), 17–40.

Agee, J. (2009). Developing qualitative research questions: A reflective process. *International Journal of Qualitative Studies in Education, 22*(4), 431–447.

Al-Kuwari, M. M., Al-Fagih, L., & Koç, M. (2021). Asking the right questions for sustainable development goals: Performance assessment approaches for the Qatar education system. *Sustainability, 13*(7), 3883.

Allen, T. D., McManus, S. E., & Russell, J. E. (1999). Newcomer socialization and stress: Formal peer relationships as a source of support. *Journal of Vocational Behavior, 54*(3), 453–470.

Alvarez, S. A., & Barney, J. B. (2007). Discovery and creation: Alternative theories of entrepreneurial action. *Strategic Entrepreneurship Journal, 1*(1–2), 11–26.

Amit, R., & Zott, C. (2001). Value creation in e-business. *Strategic Management Journal, 22*(6–7), 493–520.

Andersen, H. (2001). The history of reductionism versus holistic approaches to scientific research. *Endeavour, 25*(4), 153–156.

Andersen, L. B., Bjørnholt, B., Bro, L. L., & Holm-Petersen, C. (2018). Achieving high quality through transformational leadership: A qualitative multilevel analysis of transformational leadership and perceived professional quality. *Public Personnel Management, 47*(1), 51–72.

Anderson, L. W., & Krathwohl, D. R. (2001). *A taxonomy for learning, teaching, and assessing: A revision of Bloom's taxonomy of educational objectives.* Longman.

Andrews, B., & Wilding, J. M. (2004). The relation of depression and anxiety to life-stress and achievement in students. *British Journal of Psychology, 95*(4), 509–521.

Ansoff, H. I. (1980). Strategic issue management. *Strategic Management Journal, 1*(2), 131–148.

Arvidsson, S., & Dumay, J. (2022). Corporate ESG reporting quantity, quality and performance: Where to now for environmental policy and practice?. *Business Strategy and the Environment, 31*(3), 1091–1110.

Ashamalla, M. H., & Crocitto, M. M. (2001). Student-generated cases as a transformation tool. *Journal of Management Education, 25*(5), 516–530.

Augier, M., & March, J. (2011). *The roots, rituals, and rhetorics of change: North American business schools after the Second World War.* Stanford University Press.

Autio, E., Kenney, M., Mustar, P., Siegel, D., & Wright, M. (2014). Entrepreneurial innovation: The importance of context. *Research Policy, 43*(7), 1097–1108.

Ayres, L., Kavanaugh, K., & Knafl, K. A. (2003). Within-case and across-case approaches to qualitative data analysis. *Qualitative Health Research, 13*(6), 871–883.

Baker, M., Barker, M., Thorne, J., & Dutnell, M. (1997). Leveraging human capital. *Journal of Knowledge Management, 1*(1), 63–74.

Ban, N. C., Frid, A., Reid, M., Edgar, B., Shaw, D., & Siwallace, P. (2018). Incorporate Indigenous perspectives for impactful research and effective management. *Nature Ecology & Evolution, 2*(11), 1680–1683.

Bartlett, C. A., & Ghoshal, S. (1991). Global strategic management: impact on the new frontiers of strategy research. *Strategic Management Journal, 12* (Summer Special Issue: Global Strategy), 5–16.

Basile, G., & Caputo, F. (2017). Theories and challenges for systems thinking in practice. *Journal of Organisational Transformation & Social Change, 14*(1), 1–3.

Batle, J., Orfila-Sintes, F., & Moon, C. J. (2018). Environmental management best practices: Towards social innovation. *International Journal of Hospitality Management, 69*, 14–20.

Bengtsson, P. (1999). Multiple case studies – not just more data points. Term paper in graduate course in Research Methodology. Publisher Unknown, 1–9.

Benjamin, B. (2006). The case study: storytelling in the industrial age and beyond. *On the Horizon, 14*(4), 159–164.

Bennett, A., & Elman, C. (2006). Complex causal relations and case study methods: The example of path dependence. *Political Analysis, 14*(3), 250–267.

Berends, H., & Antonacopoulou, E. (2014). Time and organizational learning: A review and agenda for future research. *International Journal of Management Reviews, 16*(4), 437–453.

Besiou, M., & Van Wassenhove, L. N. (2020). Humanitarian operations: A world of opportunity for relevant and impactful research. *Manufacturing & Service Operations Management, 22*(1), 135–145.

Birkinshaw, J. (1997). Entrepreneurship in multinational corporations: The characteristics of subsidiary initiatives. *Strategic Management Journal, 18*(3), 207–229.

Birkinshaw, J. & Hood, N. (1998). Multinational subsidiary evolution: capability and charter change in foreign-owned subsidiary companies. *Academy of Management Review, 23*, 773–795.

Bloom, B. S. (1956). *Taxonomy of educational objectives.* London: Longman Green

Bonini, S. M., Mendonca, L. T., & Oppenheim, J. M. (2006). When social issues become strategic. *McKinsey Quarterly, 2*, 20.

Boubakri, N., Cosset, J. C., & Guedhami, O. (2009). From state to private ownership: Issues from strategic industries. *Journal of Banking & Finance, 33*(2), 367–379.

Boudreaux, C. J., Nikolaev, B. N., & Klein, P. (2019). Socio-cognitive traits and entrepreneurship: The moderating role of economic institutions. *Journal of Business Venturing, 34*(1), 178–196.

Bourgeois, L. J., & Brodwin, D. R. (1984). Strategic implementation: Five approaches to an elusive phenomenon. *Strategic Management Journal, 5*(3), 241–264.

Bradford, M., Richtermeyer, S. B., & Roberts, D. F. (2007). System diagramming techniques: An analysis of methods used in accounting education and practice. *Journal of Information Systems, 21*(1), 173–212.

Brown, A., Rich, M., & Holtham, C. (2014). Student engagement and learning: Case study of a new module for business undergraduates at Cass business school. *Journal of Management Development, 33*(6), 603–619.

Busenitz, L. W. (1999). Entrepreneurial risk and strategic decision making: It's a matter of perspective. *The Journal of Applied Behavioral Science, 35*(3), 325–340.

Camillus, J. C., & Datta, D. K. (1991). Managing strategic issues in a turbulent environment. *Long Range Planning, 24*(2), 67–74.

Caputo, F. (2021). Towards a holistic view of corporate social responsibility. The antecedent role of information asymmetry and cognitive distance. *Kybernetes, 50*(3), 639–655.

Carlson, D. S., Derr, C., & Wadsworth, L. L. (2003). The effects of internal career orientation on multiple dimensions of work–family conflict. *Journal of Family and Economic Issues, 24*(1), 99–116.

Carpenter, M. A., & Westphal, J. D. (2001). The strategic context of external network ties: Examining the impact of director appointments on board involvement in strategic decision making. *Academy of Management Journal, 44*(4), 639–660.

Carton, G., & Mouricou, P. (2017). Is management research relevant? A systematic analysis of the rigor-relevance debate in top-tier journals (1994–2013). *M@n@gement, 20*(2), 166–203.

Cerasoli, C. P., Nicklin, J. M., & Ford, M. T. (2014). Intrinsic motivation and extrinsic incentives jointly predict performance: A 40-year meta-analysis. *Psychological Bulletin, 140*(4), 980.

Chai, S., & Kim, M. (2012). A socio-technical approach to knowledge contribution behavior: An empirical investigation of social networking sites users. *International Journal of Information Management, 32*(2), 118–126.

Chang, H. (2015). Reductionism and the relation between chemistry and physics. In T. Arabatzis, J. Renn, and A. Simões (Eds.), *Relocating the history of science* (pp. 193–209). Springer.

Chao, R.O. & Terry, C. (2012). *Arcadia Medical Center: Emergency Department Crowding (A)*. Darden (UVAOM1468).

Clarke, V., Braun, V., & Hayfield, N. (2015). Thematic analysis. *Qualitative Psychology: A Practical Guide to Research Methods, 222*(2015), 248.

Corcoran, J., & McLean, F. (1998). The selection of management consultants: How are governments dealing with this difficult decision? An exploratory study. *International Journal of Public Sector Management, 11*(1), 37–54.

Cunliffe, A. L., & Scaratti, G. (2017). Embedding impact in engaged research: Developing socially useful knowledge through dialogical sensemaking. *British Journal of Management, 28*(1), 29–44.

Dabić, M., Stojčić, N., Simić, M., Potocan, V., Slavković, M., & Nedelko, Z. (2021). Intellectual agility and innovation in micro and small businesses: The mediating role of entrepreneurial leadership. *Journal of Business Research, 123*, 683–695.

Dalziel, M. (2010, June). Why do innovation intermediaries exist? In DRUID Summer Conference, Imperial College London Business School (Vol. 2010, p. 24).

Davids, B., Aspler, C., & McIvor, B. (2002). General Electric's action learning change initiatives: Work-Out™ and the change acceleration process. In Y. Boshyk (Ed.), *Action learning worldwide* (pp. 76–89). Palgrave Macmillan.

Dean-Coffey, J. (2013). Graphic recording. *New Directions for Evaluation, 2013*(140), 47–67.

Debela, M. C., & Muhye, H. K. (2017). Water supply and demand scenario of Dilla Town, Southern Ethiopia. *International Journal of Water Resources and Environmental Engineering, 9*(12), 270–276.

Denis, J. L., Langley, A., & Cazale, L. (1996). Leadership and strategic change under ambiguity. *Organization Studies, 17*(4), 673–699.

Denis, J. L., Langley, A., & Pineault, M. (2000). Becoming a leader in a complex organization. *Journal of Management Studies, 37*(8), 1063–1100.

Dieleman, M., & Boddewyn, J. J. (2012). Using organization structure to buffer political ties in emerging markets: A case study. *Organization Studies, 33*(1), 71–95.

Dominici, G. (2012). Why does systems thinking matter? *Business Systems Review, 1*(1), 1–2.

Dongping, F. (2007). Towards complex holism. *Systems Research and Behavioral Science: The Official Journal of the International Federation for Systems Research, 24*(4), 417–430.

Draper, N. (2017). Fail fast: The value of studying unsuccessful technology companies. *Media Industries Journal, 4*(1). https://doi.org/10.3998/mij.15031809.0004.101

Dubey, U., Kothari, D. P., & Awari, G. K. (2016). Quantitative techniques in business, management and finance: A case-study approach. Chapman & Hall/CRC.

Dunning, J. H. (2000). The eclectic paradigm as an envelope for economic and business theories of MNE activity. *International Business Review, 9*(2), 163–190.

Dutton, J. E., & Duncan, R. B. (1987). The creation of momentum for change through the process of strategic issue diagnosis. *Strategic Management Journal, 8*(3), 279–295.

Dwyer, C. (2011). Socio-technical systems theory and environmental sustainability. In Proceedings of SIG-Green Workshop. Sprouts: Working Papers on Information Systems, 11(3). https://aisel.aisnet.org/sprouts_all/431

Eden, L., & Miller, S. R. (2004). Distance matters: Liability of foreignness, institutional distance and ownership strategy. In M. A. Hitt and J. L. C. Cheng (Eds.), *Theories of the multinational enterprise: Diversity, complexity and relevance* (vol. 16, pp. 187–221). Emerald Group Publishing.

Edwards, M., Benn, S., & Starik, M. (2017). Business cases for sustainability-integrated management education. In J. A. Arevalo and S. F. Mitchell (Eds.), *Handbook of sustainability in management education* (pp. 45–66). Edward Elgar.

Eisenhardt, K. M., & Martin, J. A. (2000). Dynamic capabilities: What are they?. *Strategic Management Journal, 21*(10–11), 1105–1121.

Elder, L. (2005). Critical thinking as the key to the learning college: A professional development model. *New Directions for Community Colleges, 2005*(130), 39–48.

Eldh, A. C., Årestedt, L., & Berterö, C. (2020). Quotations in qualitative studies: Reflections on constituents, custom, and purpose. *International Journal of Qualitative Methods, 19*, 1–6.

Erskine, J. A., & Cruji, C. (1999). *Campbell Management Consulting.* Ivey Publishing (9A99D003).

Falkenberg, L., & Woiceshyn, J. (2008). Enhancing business ethics: Using cases to teach moral reasoning. *Journal of Business Ethics, 79*(3), 213–217.

Field, A. P., & Gillett, R. (2010). How to do a meta-analysis. *British Journal of Mathematical and Statistical Psychology, 63*(3), 665–694.

Fisher, G., Stevenson, R., Neubert, E., Burnell, D., & Kuratko, D. F. (2020). Entrepreneurial hustle: Navigating uncertainty and enrolling venture stakeholders through urgent and unorthodox action. *Journal of Management Studies, 57*(5), 1002–1036.

Fraenkel, J. R. (1966). Ask the right questions!. *The Clearing House: A Journal of Educational Strategies, Issues and Ideas, 40*(7), 397–400.

Gasparatos, A., El-Haram, M., & Horner, M. (2008). A critical review of reductionist approaches for assessing the progress towards sustainability. *Environmental Impact Assessment Review, 28*(4–5), 286–311.

George, G., Howard-Grenville, J., Joshi, A., & Tihanyi, L. (2016). Understanding and tackling societal grand challenges through management research. *Academy of Management Journal, 59*(6), 1880–1895.

Gill, T. G. (2016). Viva the fundamental revolution! Confessions of a Case Writer. *Constructivist Foundations, 11*(3), 478–481.

Gioia, D. A., & Chittipeddi, K. (1991). Sensemaking and sensegiving in strategic change initiation. *Strategic Management Journal, 12*(6), 433–448.

Gioia, D. A., Corley, K. G., & Hamilton, A. L. (2013). Seeking qualitative rigor in inductive research: Notes on the Gioia methodology. *Organizational Research Methods, 16*(1), 15–31.

Giurco, D., & Cooper, C. (2012). Mining and sustainability: Asking the right questions. *Minerals Engineering, 29*, 3–12.

Goodman, M. (1997). Systems thinking: What, why, when, where, and how. *The Systems Thinker, 8*(2), 6–7.

Graetz, F. (2002). Strategic thinking versus strategic planning: Towards understanding the complementarities. *Management Decision, 40*(5), 456–462.

Grewatsch, S., Kennedy, S., & Bansal, P. (2021). Tackling wicked problems in strategic management with systems thinking. *Strategic Organization*. https://doi.org/10.1177/14761270211038635

Grodal, S., & O'Mahony, S. (2017). How does a grand challenge become displaced? Explaining the duality of field mobilization. *Academy of Management Journal, 60*(5), 1801–1827.

Hacklin, F., & Wallnöfer, M. (2012). The business model in the practice of strategic decision making: Insights from a case study. *Management Decision, 50*(2), 166–188.

Hair Jr, J. F., Matthews, L. M., Matthews, R. L., & Sarstedt, M. (2017). PLS-SEM or CB-SEM: Updated guidelines on which method to use. *International Journal of Multivariate Data Analysis, 1*(2), 107–123.

Hamann, R., Makaula, L., Ziervogel, G., Shearing, C., & Zhang, A. (2020). Strategic responses to grand challenges: Why and how corporations build community resilience. *Journal of Business Ethics, 161*(4), 835–853.

Han, I., Eom, M., & Shin, W. S. (2013). Multimedia case-based learning to enhance pre-service teachers' knowledge integration for teaching with technologies. *Teaching and Teacher Education, 34*, 122–129.

Hatcher, M., & Tofts, C. (2004). *Reductionism isn't functional*. Hewlett-Packard Technical Reports.

Haynes, R. B. (2006). Forming research questions. *Journal of Clinical Epidemiology, 59*(9), 881–886.

Henderson, S., & Segal, E. H. (2013). Visualizing qualitative data in evaluation research. *New Directions for Evaluation, 2013*(139), 53–71.

Heng, H. H. (2008). The conflict between complex systems and reductionism. *Jama, 300*(13), 1580–1581.

Heracleous, L. (2022). Helping at NASA: Guidelines for using process consultation to develop impactful research. *Information and Organization, 32*(1), 100388.

Hicks, J., & Lehmberg, D. (2012). *Collision course: Selling European high performance motorcycles in Japan*. Ivey Publishing (9B12M025_P).

Hiekkanen, K., Helenius, M., Korhonen, J. J., & Patricio, E. (2013). Aligning alignment with strategic context: A literature review. In *Digital Enterprise Design and Management 2013: Proceedings of the First International Conference on Digital Enterprise Design and Management DED&M 2013* (pp. 81–98). Springer Berlin Heidelberg.

Hirt, E. R., Melton, R. J., McDonald, H. E., & Harackiewicz, J. M. (1996). Processing goals, task interest, and the mood–performance relationship: A mediational analysis. *Journal of Personality and Social Psychology, 71*(2), 245–261.

Hodges, J. (2017). *Consultancy, organizational development and change: A practical guide to delivering value*. Kogan Page.

Hunt, S. D. (2021). The nature and origins of impactful research in marketing. *Journal of Global Scholars of Marketing Science, 31*(2), 130–141.

Jackson, K. F. (2013). Participatory diagramming in social work research: Utilizing visual timelines to interpret the complexities of the lived multiracial experience. *Qualitative Social Work, 12*(4), 414–432.

Jackson, M. C. (1991). The origins and nature of critical systems thinking. *Systems Practice, 4*(2), 131–149.

Jackson, M. C. (2019). *Critical systems thinking and the management of complexity*. John Wiley & Sons.

Jenkins, A., & McKelvie, A. (2016). What is entrepreneurial failure? Implications for future research. *International Small Business Journal, 34*(2), 176–188.

Jennings, D. (1997). Researching and writing strategic management cases: A systems view. *Management Decision, 35*(2), 100–105.

Johnson, C. (1982). *MITI and the Japanese miracle: the growth of industrial policy, 1925–1975*. Stanford University Press.

Judge, W. Q., & Douglas, T. J. (1998). Performance implications of incorporating natural environmental issues into the strategic planning process: An empirical assessment. *Journal of Management Studies, 35*(2), 241–262.

Kaiser, M. I. (2011). The limits of reductionism in the life sciences. *History and Philosophy of the Life Sciences, 33*(4), 453–476.

Kakabadse, A. P. (2007). Being responsible: Boards are reexamining the bottom line. *Leadership in Action: A Publication of the Center for Creative Leadership and Jossey-Bass, 27*(1), 3–6.

Kane, G. C., Palmer, D., Phillips, A. N., Kiron, D., & Buckley, N. (2015). Strategy, not technology, drives digital transformation. *MIT Sloan Management Review, 14*(1–25).

Katsos, J. E., & Fort, T. L. (2016). Leadership in the promotion of peace: Interviews with the 2015 Business for Peace honorees. *Business Horizons, 59*(5), 463–470.

Kitchenham, B., Brereton, O. P., Budgen, D., Turner, M., Bailey, J., & Linkman, S. (2009). Systematic literature reviews in software engineering: A systematic literature review. *Information and Software Technology, 51*(1), 7–15.

Kitchin, R. M. (1994). Cognitive maps: What are they and why study them?. *Journal of Environmental Psychology, 14*(1), 1–19.

Kloss, R. J. (1988). Toward asking the right questions: The beautiful, the pretty, and the big messy ones. *The Clearing House, 61*(6), 245–248.

Köhler, H. J., Nickel, U., Niere, J., & Zündorf, A. (2000, June). Integrating UML diagrams for production control systems. In *Proceedings of the 22nd International Conference on Software Engineering.* ACM Press: New York (pp. 241–251).

Korman, A. K. (1968). Task success, task popularity, and self-esteem as influences on task liking. *Journal of Applied Psychology, 52*(6, Pt.1), 484–490.

Kotchen, M., & Moon, J. J. (2012). Corporate social responsibility for irresponsibility. *The BE Journal of Economic Analysis & Policy, 12*(1), 1–23.

Kraus, S., Breier, M., & Dasí-Rodríguez, S. (2020). The art of crafting a systematic literature review in entrepreneurship research. *International Entrepreneurship and Management Journal, 16*(3), 1023–1042.

Kuhlmann, S., & Rip, A. (2014). *The challenge of addressing grand challenges.* Conference of Rectors and Presidents of European Universities of Technology, Gothenburg, Sweden, 19–20 September 2014.

Lai, E. R. (2011). Critical thinking: A literature review. *Pearson's Research Reports, 6*(1), 40–41.

Langley, A. (1999). Strategies for theorizing from process data. *Academy of Management Review, 24*(4), 691–710.

Lapointe, L., & Rivard, S. (2005). A multilevel model of resistance to information technology implementation. *MIS Quarterly, 29*(3), 461–491.

Lei, D., Hitt, M. A., & Bettis, R. (1996). Dynamic core competences through meta-learning and strategic context. *Journal of Management, 22*(4), 549–569.

Leenders, M. R., Mauffette-Leenders, L. A., & Erskine, J. A. (2001). *Writing cases.* Ivey Publishing.

Leonard, A. (1996). Team syntegrity: A new methodology for group work. *European Management Journal, 14*(4), 407–413.

Leonard, S., & Weitz, J. (1971). Task enjoyment and task perseverance in relation to task success and self-esteem. *Journal of Applied Psychology, 55*(5), 414.

Liedtka, J. M. (1998). Linking strategic thinking with strategic planning. *Strategy & Leadership, 26*(4), 30.

Linnenluecke, M. K. (2017). Resilience in business and management research: A review of influential publications and a research agenda. *International Journal of Management Reviews, 19*(1), 4–30.

Lundberg, C. C., Rainsford, P., Shay, J. P., & Young, C. A. (2001). Case writing reconsidered. *Journal of Management Education, 25*(4), 450–463.

Maehr, M. L. (1976). Continuing motivation: An analysis of a seldom considered educational outcome. *Review of Educational Research, 46*(3), 443–462.

Mahmoudi, S., Jafari, E., Nasrabadi, H. A., & Liaghatdar, M. J. (2012). Holistic education: An approach for 21st century. *International Education Studies, 5*(2), 178–186.

Maister, D. H., Galford, R., & Green, C. (2021). *The trusted advisor*. Free Press.

Malhotra, A., Melville, N. P., & Watson, R. T. (2013). Spurring impactful research on information systems for environmental sustainability. *MIS Quarterly, 37*(4), 1265–1274.

Malhotra, M. K., Steele, D. C., & Grover, V. (1994). Important strategic and tactical manufacturing issues in the 1990s. *Decision Sciences, 25*(2), 189–214.

Marcy, R. T., & Mumford, M. D. (2010). Leader cognition: Improving leader performance through causal analysis. *The Leadership Quarterly, 21*(1), 1–19.

Mason, R. O., & Mitroff, I. I. (1981). *Challenging strategic planning assumptions: Theory, cases, and techniques*. John Wiley & Sons.

McDade, S. A. (1995). Case study pedagogy to advance critical thinking. *Teaching of Psychology, 22*(1), 9–10.

McMillan, E., Stanga, N., & Van Sell, S. (2018). Holism: A concept analysis. *International Journal of Nursing and Clinical Practices, 5*(4), 282–288.

Mezirow, J. (1998). On critical reflection. *Adult Education Quarterly, 48*(3), 185–198.

Miklian, J., & Schouten, P. (2014). Business for peace: The new paradigm of international peacebuilding and development. Available at SSRN 2538113.

Murphy, J. J. (1989). Identifying strategic issues. *Long Range Planning, 22*(2), 101–105.

Nakamoto, S. (2008). Bitcoin: A peer-to-peer electronic cash system. *Decentralized Business Review*, 21260.

Nathan, P. (2013). Academic writing in the business school: The genre of the business case report. *Journal of English for Academic Purposes, 12*(1), 57–68.

Nguyen, N., & Hansen, J. Ø. (2016). Becoming a leader–manager: A matter of training and education. *Development and Learning in Organizations: An International Journal, 30*(6), 10–12.

Nonaka, I., & Takeuchi, H. (1995). *The knowledge creating company: How Japanese companies create the dynamics of innovation*. Oxford University Press.

O'Mahoney, J., & Markham, C. (2013). *Management consultancy*. Oxford University Press.

Osterwalder, A., & Pigneur, Y. (2010). *Business model generation: A handbook for visionaries, game changers, and challengers* (Vol. 1). John Wiley & Sons.

Özesmi, U., & Özesmi, S. L. (2004). Ecological models based on people's knowledge: A multi-step fuzzy cognitive mapping approach. *Ecological Modelling, 176*(1–2), 43–64.

Pangarkar, N. (2008). Internationalization and performance of small- and medium-sized enterprises. *Journal of World Business, 43*(4), 475–485.

Paredes, M. R., Barrutia, J. M., & Echebarria, C. (2014). Resources for value co-creation in e-commerce: a review. *Electronic Commerce Research, 14*, 111–136.

Pedersen, C. S. (2018). The UN sustainable development goals (SDGs) are a great gift to business!. *Procedia Cirp, 69*, 21–24.

Ponte, B., Costas, J., Puche, J., De la Fuente, D., & Pino, R. (2016). Holism versus reductionism in supply chain management: An economic analysis. *Decision Support Systems, 86*, 83–94.

Puca, R. M., & Schmalt, H. D. (1999). Task enjoyment: A mediator between achievement motives and performance. *Motivation and Emotion, 23*(1), 15–29.

Purssell, E., & McCrae, N. (2020). *How to perform a systematic literature review: A guide for healthcare researchers, practitioners and students*. Springer Nature.

Reid, I., & Smyth-Renshaw, J. (2012). Exploring the fundamentals of root cause analysis: Are we asking the right questions in defining the problem?. *Quality and Reliability Engineering International, 28*(5), 535–545.

Richardson, R. C. (1979). Functionalism and reductionism. *Philosophy of Science, 46*(4), 533–558.

Rosenberg, S., & Mosca, J. (2011). Breaking down the barriers to organizational change. *International Journal of Management & Information Systems, 15*(3), 139–146.

Runfola, A., Perna, A., Baraldi, E., & Gregori, G. L. (2017). The use of qualitative case studies in top business and management journals: A quantitative analysis of recent patterns. *European Management Journal, 35*(1), 116–127.

Sarkis, J., & Ibrahim, S. (2022). Building knowledge beyond our experience: integrating sustainable development goals into IJPR's research future. *International Journal of Production Research, 60*(24), 7301–7318.

Saunders, M., Lewis, P. H., & Thornhill, A. D. (2019). *Research methods for business students* (8th ed.). Pearson Education.

Schaupp, D. L., & Lane, M. S. (1992). Teaching business ethics: Bringing reality to the classroom. *Journal of Business Ethics, 11*(3), 225–229.

Scheibe, K. P., & Blackhurst, J. (2018). Supply chain disruption propagation: a systemic risk and normal accident theory perspective. *International Journal of Production Research, 56*(1–2), 43–59.

Schein, E. H. (1969). *Process consultation: Its role in organization development.* Addison-Wesley.

Schultz, T. W. (1961). Investment in human capital. *The American Economic Review, 51*(1), 1–17.

Seawright, J., & Gerring, J. (2008). Case selection techniques in case study research: A menu of qualitative and quantitative options. *Political Research Quarterly, 61*(2), 294–308.

Seidel, S., Recker, J., & Vom Brocke, J. (2013). Sensemaking and sustainable practicing: Functional affordances of information systems in green transformations. *MIS Quarterly, 37*(4), 1275–1299.

Senge, P. M., & Scharmer, C. O. (2008). Community action research: Learning as a community of practitioners, consultants and researchers. In P. Reason and H. Bradbury (Eds.), *Handbook of action research* (pp. 195–206). Sage.

Sharma, G., & Bansal, P. (2020). Cocreating rigorous and relevant knowledge. *Academy of Management Journal, 63*(2), 386–410.

Shrivastava, P. (1987). Rigor and practical usefulness of research in strategic management. *Strategic Management Journal, 8*(1), 77–92.

Shukla, N., Keast, J. E., & Ceglarek, D. (2017). Role activity diagram-based discrete event simulation model for healthcare service delivery processes. *International Journal of Systems Science: Operations & Logistics, 4*(1), 68–83.

Slingerland, E. (2008). Good and bad reductionism: Acknowledging the power of culture. *Style, 42*(2–3), 266–271.

Slone, D. J. (2009). Visualizing qualitative information. *The Qualitative Report, 14*(3), 489.

Smith, J. (2011). *Applying sentiment analysis to the Bible.* www.openbible.info/blog/2011/10/applying-sentiment-analysis-to-the-bible/ accessed 1January 2023.

Smith, S. D. (1991). Reductionism in legal thought. *Columbia Law Review, 91*, 68.

Smuts, J. C. (1926). *Holism and evolution.* Macmillan.

Snyder, L. G., & Snyder, M. J. (2008). Teaching critical thinking and problem solving skills. *The Journal of Research in Business Education, 50*(2), 90.

Strutzenberger, A., & Ambos, T.C. (2014). Unravelling the subsidiary initiative process: A multilevel approach. *International Journal of Management Reviews, 16*, 314–339.

Sturdy, A., & Wright, C. (2011). The active client: The boundary-spanning roles of internal consultants as gatekeepers, brokers and partners of their external counterparts. *Management Learning, 42*(5), 485–503.

Tabrizi, B., Lam, E., Girard, K., & Irvin, V. (2019). Digital transformation is not about technology. *Harvard Business Review, 13*(March), 1–6.

Tecon, R., Mitri, S., Ciccarese, D., Or, D., van der Meer, J. R., & Johnson, D. R. (2019). Bridging the holistic-reductionist divide in microbial ecology. *MSystems, 4*(1), e00265–18.

Teece, D. J., Pisano, G., & Shuen, A. (1997). Dynamic capabilities and strategic management. *Strategic Management Journal, 18*(7), 509–533.

Tellis, G. J. (2017). Interesting and impactful research: on phenomena, theory, and writing. *Journal of the Academy of Marketing Science, 45,* 1–6.

Tenenhaus, M., Vinzi, V. E., Chatelin, Y. M., & Lauro, C. (2005). PLS path modeling. *Computational Statistics & Data Analysis, 48*(1), 159–205.

Thistlethwaite, J. E., Davies, D., Ekeocha, S., Kidd, J. M., MacDougall, C., Matthews, P., ... & Clay, D. (2012). The effectiveness of case-based learning in health professional education. A BEME systematic review: BEME Guide No. 23. *Medical Teacher, 34*(6), e421–e444.

Thomas, K. W., & Tymon Jr, W. G. (1982). Necessary properties of relevant research: Lessons from recent criticisms of the organizational sciences. *Academy of Management Review, 7*(3), 345–352.

Toegel, G., & Barsoux, J. L. (2012). How to become a better leader. *MIT Sloan Management Review, 53*(3), 51–60.

Trigger, D., Forsey, M., & Meurk, C. (2012). Revelatory moments in fieldwork. *Qualitative Research, 12*(5), 513–527.

Trist, E. L. (1981). *The evolution of socio-technical systems* (Vol. 2). Toronto: Ontario Quality of Working Life Centre.

Ulph, A., & Ulph, D. (2007). Climate change—environmental and technology policies in a strategic context. *Environmental and Resource Economics, 37*(1), 159–180.

Validi, S., Bhattacharya, A., & Byrne, P. J. (2014). A case analysis of a sustainable food supply chain distribution system—A multi-objective approach. *International Journal of Production Economics, 152,* 71–87.

Väyrynen, R. (2022). Complex Humanitarian Emergencies: Concepts and Issues. In: *Raimo Väyrynen: A pioneer in international relations, scholarship and policy-making*. Pioneers in Arts, Humanities, Science, Engineering, Practice, vol. 28. Springer.

Vermeulen, F. (2005). On rigor and relevance: Fostering dialectic progress in management research. *Academy of Management Journal, 48*(6), 978–982.

Verschuren, P. J. (2001). Holism versus reductionism in modern social science research. *Quality and Quantity, 35*(4), 389–405.

Verschuren, P. (2003). Case study as a research strategy: Some ambiguities and opportunities. *International Journal of Social Research Methodology, 6*(2), 121–139.

Von Bertalanffy, L. (1950). The theory of open systems in physics and biology. *Science, 111*(2872), 23–29.

Von Nordenflycht, A. (2010). What is a professional service firm? Toward a theory and taxonomy of knowledge-intensive firms. *Academy of Management Review, 35*(1), 155–174.

Vukšić, V. B., Ivančić, L., & Vugec, D. S. (2018). A preliminary literature review of digital transformation case studies. *International Journal of Computer and Information Engineering, 12*(9), 737–742.

Wang, C. L., & Ahmed, P. K. (2007). Dynamic capabilities: A review and research agenda. *International Journal of Management Reviews, 9*(1), 31–51.

Wassermann, S. (1992). *Asking the right question: The essence of teaching*. Fastback 343.

Waters, L. K., & Roach, D. (1972). Self-esteem as a moderator of the relationship between task-success and task-liking. *Psychological Reports, 31*(1), 69–70.

Welter, F., Gartner, W. B., & Wright, M. (2016). The context of contextualizing contexts. In F. Welter and W. Gartner (Eds.), *A research agenda for entrepreneurship and context* (pp. 1–15). Edward Elgar.

Wickert, C., Post, C., Doh, J. P., Prescott, J. E., & Prencipe, A. (2021). Management research that makes a difference: Broadening the meaning of impact. *Journal of Management Studies*, *58*(2), 297–320.

Wiles, R., Crow, G., & Pain, H. (2011). Innovation in qualitative research methods: A narrative review. *Qualitative Research*, *11*(5), 587–604.

Williams, C. (2019). *Management consultancy for innovation*. Routledge.

Williams, C., & Durst, S. (2019). Knowledge at risk during information system offshore outsourcing: exploring the transition phase, *Journal of Business Research*, *103*, 460–471.

Williams, C., Hailemariam, A. T., & Allard, G. (2022). Exploring entrepreneurial innovation in Ethiopia. *Research Policy*, *51*(10), 104599.

Williams, C., & Lee, S. H. (2011). Entrepreneurial contexts and knowledge coordination within the multinational corporation. *Journal of World Business*, *46*(2), 253–264.

Williams, C., & Steriu, R. (2022). MNE market entry and social investment in battle-weary countries: Evidence from Heineken. *Journal of World Business*, *57*(4), 101342.

Williams, C., & van Triest, S. (2021). Innovativeness in the Professional Services Industry: A Practice Level Analysis. *European Management Review*, *18*(3), 263–276.

Williams, C., & You, J. J. (2021). *Organizing for resilience: Leading and managing risk in a disruptive world*. Routledge.

Williams, C., You, J. J., & Joshua, K. (2020). Small-business resilience in a remote tourist destination: exploring close relationship capabilities on the island of St Helena. *Journal of Sustainable Tourism*, *28*(7), 937–955.

Wimsatt, W. C. (2006). Reductionism and its heuristics: Making methodological reductionism honest. *Synthese*, *151*(3), 445–475.

Winston, B. E., & Patterson, K. (2006). An integrative definition of leadership. *International Journal of Leadership Studies*, *1*(2), 6–66.

Wood, T., & Caldas, M. P. (2001). Reductionism and complex thinking during ERP implementations. *Business Process Management Journal*, *7*(5), 387–393.

Workman Jr, J. P. (1993). Marketing's limited role in new product development in one computer systems firm. *Journal of Marketing Research*, *30*(4), 405–421.

Xiao, Y., & Watson, M. (2019). Guidance on conducting a systematic literature review. *Journal of Planning Education and Research*, *39*(1), 93–112.

Yin, R. K. (2011). *Applications of case study research*. Sage.

You, J.J. (2022). A "sensitising" perspective on understanding students' learning experiences in case studies. *The International Journal of Management Education*, *20*(2), 100615.

You, J.J. & Williams, C. (2023). Organizational resilience and inter-organizational relationships: An exploration of Chinese business-service firms. *European Management Review*. http://doi.org/10.1111/emre.12558.

Zeigermann, U. (2021). Scientific knowledge integration and the implementation of the SDGs: Comparing strategies of sustainability networks. *Politics and Governance*, *9*(1), 164–175.

Zimm, C., Sperling, F., & Busch, S. (2018). Identifying sustainability and knowledge gaps in socio-economic pathways vis-à-vis the Sustainable Development Goals. *Economies*, *6*(2), 20.

Index

Page numbers in *italics* refer to figures and exhibits. Page numbers in **bold** refer to tables.